SO WE
READ
ON

Also by Maureen Corrigan

Leave Me Alone, I'm Reading

SO WE READ ON

HOW *THE GREAT GATSBY* CAME TO BE AND WHY IT ENDURES

MAUREEN CORRIGAN

LITTLE, BROWN AND COMPANY
New York Boston London

Little, Brown and Company
Hachette Book Group
237 Park Avenue, New York, NY 10017
littlebrown.com

First Edition: September 2014

Little, Brown and Company is a division of Hachette Book Group, Inc. The Little, Brown name and logo are trademarks of Hachette Book Group, Inc.

The publisher is not responsible for websites (or their content) that are not owned by the publisher.

The Hachette Speakers Bureau provides a wide range of authors for speaking events. To find out more, go to hachettespeakersbureau.com or call (866) 376-6591.

Excerpts from *A Life in Letters* by Matthew J. Bruccoli, editor, reprinted with the permission of Scribner Publishing Group. Copyright © 1994 by The Trustees under agreement dated July 3, 1975, created by Frances Scott Fitzgerald Smith. All rights reserved.

Excerpts from *The Letters of F. Scott Fitzgerald* by Andrew Turnbull reprinted with the permission of Scribner Publishing Group. Copyright © 1963 by Frances Scott Fitzgerald Lanahan. Copyright renewed © 1991. All rights reserved.

Excerpts from F. Scott Fitzgerald's ledger, notebooks, selected letters, manuscript of "The Swimmers," handwritten notes in his personal copy of Andre Malraux's *Man's Hope*, Zelda Fitzgerald's letters, and *Scottie* by Eleanor Lanahan reprinted with the permission of Harold Ober and Associates Incorporated. Some photographs reprinted courtesy of Harold Ober and Associates Incorporated.

Library of Congress Cataloging-in-Publication Data

Corrigan, Maureen, author.
So We Read On : How The Great Gatsby Came to Be and Why It Endures / Maureen Corrigan. — First edition.
pages cm
Includes bibliographical references and index.
ISBN 978-0-316-23007-0 (hardback)
1. Fitzgerald, F. Scott (Francis Scott), 1896-1940. Great Gatsby.   I. Title.
PS3511.I9G83196 2014
813'.52—dc23   2014018062

10 9 8 7 6 5 4 3 2 1

RRD-C

Printed in the United States of America

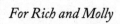

For Rich and Molly

Contents

SO WE READ ON

Introduction

Forget *great*. *The Great Gatsby* is the *greatest*—even if you didn't think so when you had to read it in high school. I didn't think so back then either. As a high-school senior, I couldn't "identify" with the bland Nick or enigmatic Gatsby; nor could I connect with golden girl Daisy, who acted too much like the mean girls in the cafeteria, flaunting their shining hair and their knowingness. I thought *The Great Gatsby* was a boring novel about rich people.

Flash forward almost forty years. It's shortly after midnight on what is now officially Thanksgiving Day 2010. I'm fifty-five years old, an English professor at an elite university, an NPR book critic. This cultural capital is without value right now: I'm standing on a long line with my husband, Rich, in the Greyhound Bus Terminal on Forty-Second Street in New York City, waiting to board a bus that will get us back to Washington, DC, where we live, at around five a.m.—just enough time for us to take a short nap and then pick up the pre-ordered "Traditional Turkey Feast for Six" for the oddly assorted Pilgrims (our mothers, both in their nineties; our twelve-year-old daughter; a good friend; and two dogs) set to gather at our house later that day. We'd taken Greyhound up from Washington sixteen hours earlier. Ordinarily, with this tight a schedule, we would have availed ourselves of the middle-class option of Amtrak or one of those newer deluxe buses, but Greyhound was the only thing moving that still had seats left for a round trip to and from New York on the Two Worst Travel Days of the Year. Why the urgency? We did it for love. We'd lucked into two tickets for the sold-out run of *Gatz* at Joseph Papp's Public Theater. *Gatz* was the sensation of the 2010 theater season in New York—a marathon seven-hour production in which *The Great Gatsby*, in its entirety, was read aloud and simultaneously acted by the Elevator Repair Service theater company. We had to see it; after all, it was *The Great Gatsby*.

If anyone had told me when I was in high school that I would one day be making such a nutty pilgrimage just to *hear The Great Gatsby* read aloud for hours and hours, I would have thought that was as likely as, say, an African American president being elected in my lifetime. Even more jaw-dropping would I have found the revelation that the adult me would voluntarily reread *Gatsby* upwards of fifty times, teach it to generations of college kids, and travel around the country enthusing about it to gatherings of curious readers. What happened to me, a former high-school apostate (idiot), is exactly what happened throughout America, broadly speaking, in the 1940s and '50s; like me, those midcentury critics and readers gave *Gatsby* a second chance and were knocked out.

Gatsby's magic emanates not only from its powerhouse poetic style—in which ordinary American language becomes unearthly—but from the authority with which it nails who we want to be as Americans. Not who we are; who we *want to be*. It's that wanting that runs through every page of *Gatsby*, making it our Greatest American Novel. But it's also our easiest Great American Novel to underrate: too short; too tempting to misread as just a love story gone wrong; too mired in the Roaring Twenties and all that jazz. Compared to its two closest contenders, *Gatsby* seems confined. *Moby-Dick* takes place on the ocean; *Gatsby* offers a swimming pool. *Huckleberry Finn* "light[s] out for the territory"; *Gatsby* restlessly commutes the few miles of new roadway back and forth between East and West Egg and Manhattan. Being short gives *Gatsby* one clear advantage over the big boys: it's more likely to be assigned as required reading. In fact, *Gatsby* is the one American novel that most educated Americans have read. The bad news is that we read it in high school or even (shudder) junior high, when we're much too young, too defensive emotionally, too ignorant about the life-deforming powers of regret. When we make our first chain-gang shuffle into *Gatsby*, we spend so much time preparing for standard test prompts on the eyes of Dr. T. J. Eckleburg and the color of Gatsby's car and—above all—the symbol of the green light at the end of Daisy's dock that the larger point of the novel gets lost. It's not the green light, stupid; it's Gatsby's *reaching* for it that's the crucial all-American symbol of the novel. Because it's been a mainstay for over half a century on high-school reading lists across the land, *The Great Gatsby* is the one Great American Novel we think we've read but probably haven't—at least, not enough.

Given the worldwide familiarity with, if nothing else, its title, the novel seems too much with us even before we've read it for the first time. The name Gatsby lends a touch of class to restaurants, condo developments, computer games, custom-tailoring stores (those beautiful shirts!), beauty salons, Kate

Spade clutch purses (made to look like hardcover editions of the book), and hot tubs (really in poor taste when you consider the role of the swimming pool in the novel). The baby-name website Nameberry.com reports that Gatsby is gaining traction as both a boy's and a girl's name and that it has "a lot of energy and that great pedigree." Riffs on Fitzgerald's title are legion. An overweight rock musician is dubbed "the Great Gutsby." A California vineyard runs a wine-tasting-and-book-discussion series called the Grape Gatsby. A friend sends around a Facebook cat joke featuring the Great Catsby. The variations accrue like hairballs, encasing the actual novel within puns and all manner of consumer dreck. Then there are the higher cultural spin-offs: the five movies (the latest is Baz Luhrmann's 3-D effort, which premiered as I was writing this book); a ballet; an opera; the radio and stage plays, including the aforementioned hybrid of staged reading and play, *Gatz*. Countless modern novels have helped themselves to *The Great Gatsby* as a template for their own stories: Ross Macdonald's *Black Money*, Caitlin Macy's *The Fundamentals of Play*, Joseph O'Neill's *Netherland*, and Tom Carson's *Daisy Buchanan's Daughter*, to name a few. Enough already: *Gatsby* is overexposed, mined out. But excavate your old paperback copy of *The Great Gatsby* and read it again. For many of us who've done just that, the novel has become, in Fitzgerald's own iridescent words, "something commensurate to [man's] capacity to wonder."[1]

First, though, you have to wise up a little, get older, become more vulnerable to both the sadness of everyday life and its loveliness. Nick, our narrator, certainly has to wise up. It takes him two years before he can tell Gatsby's story in any coherent way, and still you know that, like the Ancient Mariner in Coleridge's poem, Nick will spend his life thinking about Gatsby and the implications of the events that took place during the summer of 1922. Nick *rereads* Gatsby's story as he tells it to us, and, in doing so, he shows us how crucial it is to listen closely, go back and pay more attention to the details, look at passages again and again. I see all the time what happens to people who have the experience of rereading *Gatsby* after being away from the novel for even a year or two. "It becomes a better novel," my hip grad-student teaching assistant—a budding gender and sexuality theorist—coolly assured our freshman literature class last semester. "It's the Sistine Chapel of American literature in a hundred and eighty pages!" declared a brilliant history major who likes to stop by during my office hours to talk about literature. Those students—and scores of others—didn't start out thinking *Gatsby* was great; they grew into the novel, more alert to its layers and layers of meaning.

Over the past few years, I've barnstormed libraries and bookstores and civic halls around America to give lectures on *Gatsby* for the Big Read program sponsored by the National Endowment for the Arts. Part literary idealism, part showbiz razzmatazz, the Big Read is a program straight out of the New Deal: a federally funded attempt to jump-start the nationwide reading (or rereading) of canonical American novels like *To Kill a Mockingbird, Fahrenheit 451, Huckleberry Finn, Their Eyes Were Watching God,* and, of course, *The Great Gatsby.* In most of the towns and cities I visited, the weeks preceding my talk were filled with spirit-raising events like Roaring Twenties balls and screenings of the drowsy 1974 Robert Redford/Mia Farrow film of the novel. The Bluebonnet regional branch of the East Baton Rouge Parish Library even sponsored a blue tarp/duct tape fashion show in which local teenagers researched books on flapper fashions and constructed and modeled 1920s outfits made out of, well, blue tarp and duct tape. (The event combined an homage to *Gatsby* with a nod to the devastation of Hurricane Katrina, when blue tarp and duct tape were everywhere.) I missed out on that celebration, but I did get to play Peoria, where a local resident exhumed an ancestor's colorful flapper dresses with their matching wrap coats and displayed them at my Big Read lecture at the local Italian restaurant.

Extraneous nonsense abounded during these lectures and so did Tom Buchanan–type remarks. A new wrinkle in *Gatsby* discussions over the past decade or so is the obsession about the last page of chapter 2, where Nick tells us about leaving the drunken party in Myrtle Wilson's apartment and then finding himself woozily standing beside the bed of her neighbor the photographer Mr. McKee. Across America, that passage now activates gaydar detectors and puts readers on red alert. Fashionable cultural criticism and high-spirited looniness aside, the one true comment about *Gatsby* that I heard over and over again on these Big Read pilgrimages was "It's a lot better than I remembered it." Amen, brothers and sisters. It sure is.

Despite the legitimate arguments against the idea of anointing any book the Great American Novel, if there is such an animal, then *The Great Gatsby* is it. When I served as one of three jurors for the Pulitzer Prize in Fiction in 2012, *Gatsby* was our North Star. We were always on the lookout for a novel that managed to pull off the near impossible trick that *Gatsby* executed; that is, to say something big about America *and* be beautifully written. How did *Gatsby* come to soar so high and why does it stay aloft, fighting off critics and changing tastes in fiction? Why did *The Great Gatsby* come to be the American novel that shows up on curricula in high schools across the country? And why is *Gatsby* the American novel that deserves to be read at least twice in one's life, if not, say, every five years?

This book considers those questions as a way of trying to grasp the enduring power of *Gatsby*. My dream as an English professor would be to someday teach a seminar solely on the novel. We'd approach *Gatsby* the way some James Joyce fans approach *Finnegans Wake:* once a week, we'd meet to furrow our collective brow over a few pages of the novel. So far, my university hasn't jumped at the idea of funding such a course. (In the economics of reading and teaching, a book is worth more if it weighs more: a jumbo classic like *Paradise Lost,* for instance, justifies the expense of a semester-long seminar.) But what does size matter if every line, every page of the work in question, is just about perfect? That's what I think about *Gatsby;* it's the only undisputed masterpiece that F. Scott Fitzgerald, who died at the age of forty-four, lived to write, and it's as perfect as a novel can be. Not one narrative misstep. (Although Fitzgerald, famously, did goof up on a few words: talking about the *retinas* of Dr. T. J. Eckleburg when he probably meant *irises;* describing Gatsby and Nick riding from Great Neck into Astoria to drive onto the Queensboro Bridge when, in reality, as his friend Ring Lardner corrected him, that side of the bridge stands in Long Island City.)

I say that *The Great Gatsby* is just about perfect despite the fact that it goes against every expectation of what a Great American Novel should be. As the eminent literary scholar Morris Dickstein has observed, the novel "violates the first commandment of all writing programs—show, don't tell." Sure enough, almost every page of the book is about telling; nothing happens in the present of *Gatsby* except remembering. Anytime you try to explain to someone who hasn't read it what *The Great Gatsby* is "about," the book fades into just another novel about love gone wrong. ("Well, it's about a man who's been obsessed with a woman for many years and she's married…") Flailing around, you fall back on the truth: that maybe it's not so much the plot of *Gatsby* that makes it great but the way it's told, that incredible language again.

Here's another strike against *Gatsby:* judging from its plot and retrospective narration, it seems like it could have been written by a European, maybe one of those gloomy existentialists. Parts of it are almost as bleak as Sartre's *Nausea*, written a decade later. Like a classic film noir—which it resembles in plot (three violent deaths!) and technique (the first-person voice-over of Nick's narration, which fills most of the book)— *Gatsby* has a fated feel to it. All exit doors are locked before the story begins: the tragedies that transpire in the story have already happened; the end is preordained. Jay Gatsby himself fits the profile of the standard noir patsy when he acts like the past is under his control. (Classic film noir is populated with doomed dreamers: Robert Mitchum's heroic sap in the suggestively titled *Out of the Past,* and the gorgeous young Burt Lancaster—smitten by the even-more-gorgeous young Ava Gardner—in *The Killers* who just lies in his crummy bed in the framing shots of that great noir, resigned to the bitter knowledge that the past, like Frankenstein's monster, has a life of its own and it's going to seek out and destroy him.) In its ultimate pessimism about breaking free of the past, *Gatsby* shares the same glum worldview as these noirs and the stories that inspired them—hard-boiled detective novels that were, like *Gatsby*, a literary invention of the 1920s. To any reader familiar with the hard-boiled and, later, noir traditions, Gatsby's most famous tagline in the novel spells curtains: "Can't repeat the past?...Why of course you can!"[2]

Only the delusional think that they can extend the remembered bliss of the past into the present, that the ones they love will remain faithful and forever golden, that the future is theirs to determine. Given what happens to its main character, *Gatsby* hardly qualifies as an upbeat read. Then again, taken together, many of the candidates for our Great American Novels—*Moby-Dick, Invisible Man, The Scarlet Letter, Huckleberry Finn, To Kill a Mockingbird, Beloved*—constitute a general chorus of restlessness and disappointment, to put it mildly. These books fly directly into the sunny face of that vaunted American optimism; in many ways, they are all *un*-American. Maybe *Gatsby's* ending desolation comes as more of a shock because the first movements of the novel (after Nick's retrospective introduction) are awash with the bubbly optimism of the Roaring Twenties. But the party ends and the lights go out. In *Gatsby* World, as opposed to Disney World, America is exhausted before it ever got going. It's all over, Nick decrees on the very last page of the novel.

But he does so in the most beautiful sentences ever written about America. Gatsby's fall from grace may be grim, but the language of the novel is buoyant; Fitzgerald's plot may suggest that the American Dream is a mirage, but his words make that dream irresistible. *Gatsby* has it both ways. Far from being an easy read sized just right for quick digesting by our nation's high-school students, *The Great Gatsby* is an elegant trickster of a novel, spinning out all sorts of inspired and contradictory poetic patter about American identity and possibilities.

I want to reread *Gatsby* in the pages of this book and try to figure out how this strange, skinny masterpiece came to be and what it means. I also want to talk about how *Gatsby* was read and reread by Fitzgerald himself, who wrote untold drafts of the manuscript. When *The Great Gatsby* was published in 1925, the critics took their turns reading—and misreading—it; eventually, so did the movies. By the time Fitzgerald died, in 1940, his greatest novel had pretty much disappeared. In fact, during the years he was living in Hollywood, Fitzgerald would try to buy it as a gift for friends, but when he went into bookstores and asked for *The Great Gatsby*, he'd be greeted by blank looks. (Some of those booksellers thought that F. Scott Fitzgerald was dead and were shocked to find out that the customer requesting *Gatsby* was the man himself.) Flash forward to May of 2013 as *Gatsby* frenzy reached a peak thanks to the glitzy Baz Luhrmann film. The paperback sales of the novel crested at number two in overall book sales in the United States. In an ordinary year, approximately 500,000 copies of the novel are sold (including 185,000 copies of *Gatsby* in e-book format), but that figure more than tripled in 2013. Worldwide, an estimated twenty-five million copies of *Gatsby* have been sold, and the novel has been translated into forty-two languages.[3]

How did this resurrection happen, and why? Just what's so great about *Gatsby*? To answer those questions, I get up from my desk and go on the road. I visit Fitzgerald treasure troves at Princeton University and the University of South Carolina; I find paper traces of Scott and Zelda Fitzgerald filed away in the New York City Municipal Archives. I talk to *Gatsby* experts and civilian readers in Bowling Green, Kentucky; Perry, Iowa; Boston; Washington, DC; and the aforementioned Peoria. By land and by sea, I tour the places where *The Great Gatsby* is set as well as some of the sites important to F. Scott Fitzgerald. And, in my own small way, I try to revisit, if not repeat, the past by going back to my old high school—which still stands, in the *Gatsby* locale of Astoria, Queens—and sitting in on classes where students are discussing the novel for the first time. That trip ends up making me rethink my bedrock assumption that high school is too young for most of us to start reading *Gatsby*. Through it all, I talk about F. Scott Fitzgerald's life, an undertaking I have mixed feelings about. I love Fitzgerald and I've grown to love him even more in the course of researching this book. He had an open, generous heart and a deep sense of responsibility to those he loved. He stuck with Zelda throughout the long years of her mental illness, paying the steep bills for the best private care. And, contrary to the conventional wisdom that famous writers make lousy dads, Fitzgerald was a loving, if overly strict, father. Indeed, for long stretches during the 1930s, when Zelda was hospitalized in sanitariums, Scott was essentially a single parent to their only child, daughter Scottie. But Fitzgerald also had his demons: they were called gin, beer, and champagne. (Later in his short life, a fourth demon appeared, called pills.) By all accounts, alcohol made Fitzgerald a different, much nastier person. Hemingway did an excellent hatchet job on Fitzgerald as a bad drunk in *A Moveable Feast*, but there are also plenty of other depressing descriptions in memoirs by Sheilah Graham, Budd Schulberg, and Lost Generation hanger-on Morley Callaghan.

It's painful to see Fitzgerald at his worst and also to see what his shining marriage to Zelda was reduced to by the end. Don C. Skemer, the curator of manuscripts at Princeton and the keeper of the extraordinary Fitzgerald Papers there, told me that when the library staff began to catalog the postcards and letters a hospitalized Zelda sent to Scott during the late 1930s, the librarians found that those missives commonly began with the words *Thank you for the check.*

Fitzgerald may not have had the happiest of lives, but he was lucky in his friends and admirers. He had the best of editors and agents in Maxwell Perkins and Harold Ober, respectively. His last secretary, Frances Kroll Ring, who was a girl of twenty when she first started working for him in 1939 in Hollywood, is, as of this writing, still alive and a self-effacing champion of Fitzgerald's humanity and genius. And his daughter, Scottie, grew up to be a devoted steward of her father's work. Their names will come up frequently in this book, along with those of Fitzgerald scholars like the late Matthew J. Bruccoli, a professorial tough guy who devoted much of his life to studying and collecting Fitzgerald's work.

"There's nothing but bones to pick over," Skemer told me by way of consolation on the afternoon I had to regretfully wrap up my research trip to the F. Scott Fitzgerald Papers at Princeton. He meant that Fitzgerald's life has been mined more deeply than that of almost any other American author. Adding to the paper pileup, Fitzgerald also chronicled his own life exhaustively, through his ledger, his notebooks, his letters, and his short stories and novels. So much material by and about him has already been published, and the manuscript of *The Great Gatsby*, as well as Fitzgerald's ledger and some of his other works, now float in digitized form on the Internet for all to see, courtesy of the Fitzgerald collections at Princeton and the University of South Carolina. I'm not trying to add to the scholarly or biographical pile here. This is, above all, a personal excursion into the novel I love more than any other. Many, many other people also love *The Great Gatsby*, and my book is intended for those who want to reread *Gatsby* along with me, as well as for those few who haven't read it but are curious. I invoke literary and historical criticism when I think it's useful; however, this book attempts to emulate the open embrace of those midcentury public intellectuals, critics like H. L. Mencken, Alfred Kazin, Lionel Trilling, Mary McCarthy, and Fitzgerald's old friend Edmund Wilson. Those critics wrote for a wide audience of educated nonspecialists, the same kind of audience I assume I'm speaking to every week in my book reviews for *Fresh Air* on NPR.

"Are you tired of it yet?" my husband and close friends would ask me every so often during the time I was writing this book and, of course, rereading *The Great Gatsby*. I can still honestly answer "No." I don't know how he did it, but Fitzgerald wrote a novel that shows me new things every time I read it. That, for me, is the working definition of a great book: one that's inexhaustible. As I've reread *Gatsby* in more recent years, its toughness has really come to the fore—a toughness of attitude that clashes with the lyricism of its language. Here are a few of the subjects *Gatsby* is tough about, subjects that I'll be exploring throughout this book:

Social class. Class remains our national awkward topic, usually mumbled over in academic diversity workshops; indeed, most people don't know how to talk about class without automatically coupling it to race. That's because we Americans are loath to recognize that the sky's-the-limit potential we take as our birthright comes at a price far beyond what many Americans—of any race—can pay.

The Great Gatsby is America's greatest novel about class. In fact, it's the only one of its canonical peers (*Moby-Dick, Huckleberry Finn, To Kill a Mockingbird, Invisible Man, Beloved*) that foregrounds class instead of race. Yet, in our high-school readings of *Gatsby*, if the subject of class is acknowledged at all, it's mentioned as an obstacle that's been overcome. Consider the Ben Franklin–like rise of Jay Gatsby himself. (See where hard work, single-mindedness, and bootlegging can get you in this country?) But if the novel were indeed the wistful endorsement of the American Dream that Gatsby's pathetically proud father and so many readers are encouraged to think it is, it would end happily, with Gatsby alive in his mansion and Daisy at his side, tinkling away with that voice "full of money." (Baz Luhrmann, by the way, bafflingly omitted this crucial line from his 2013 film, part of a larger project, I think, to defang the novel's class criticism.) Class is the invisible net that snags Gatsby, ultimately pulling him down, down, down into the chilly depths of his leaf-strewn swimming pool. In the novel's climactic confrontation scene at the Plaza Hotel, Tom Buchanan sneeringly dismisses Gatsby as "Mr. Nobody from Nowhere."[4] For folks like Tom who are to the manner born, the reinvented James Gatz is always going to be too nouveau riche to pass as old money and be welcomed to the inner circles of high society. Some critics have delved further into the subject of passing by musing over Gatsby's hard-to-place original last name and the references to his "golden" skin. Who knows what ethnic and racial strains taint the mysterious Mr. Gatsby's blood? No wonder, given the anxious cultural politics of the novel, Gatsby is cosmically denied a happy ending with Daisy, the embodiment of Southern "white girlhood."[5]

Because American society was on the move after World War I (a jitteriness that's depicted in this novel in which nobody ever sits still), every chapter of *The Great Gatsby* contains scenes where characters quickly size one another up and decide where they fit, socially. The very first words out of Nick Carraway's mouth present his own class credentials for our inspection:

"In my younger and more vulnerable years my father gave me some advice that I've been turning over in my mind ever since.

"'Whenever you feel like criticizing anyone,' he told me, 'just remember that all the people in this world haven't had the advantages that you've had.'"[6]

That little speech should clue us in on how much breeding is going to count in this novel—as well as on just how slippery the meaning of *The Great Gatsby* is going to be. Indeed, the thick ambiguity of *Gatsby*'s language is one of the reasons why, despite its scant number of pages, it reads like a much longer story. Are we supposed to think Nick is a prig for introducing his pedigree to us? Are we supposed to give him points for being aware of his own class privileges and acknowledging his social empathy? Whatever impression Nick wants to make, the novel has opened by trumpeting its obsessive subject: class. We might as well be in the turn-of-the-century New York City of Edith Wharton.

So what gives? This is America in the Roaring Twenties, after all, when, as Fitzgerald later recalled in "My Lost City," the old order had been overthrown: Taking over from Great

Britain, America was now "the greatest nation" and New York its premier city.[7] But perhaps because it was written in the midst of the 1920s, without the softening glaze of nostalgia, *Gatsby* is more clear-eyed than some of Fitzgerald's later writing. The novel warns that not all of the conventional social rules and divisions have been ground under the Cuban heels of those bouncing flappers' shoes. Then, as now, class consciousness and snobbery discreetly retreat underground when explicit discrimination is out of fashion. Nick may be broad-minded enough to sit down to lunch at Gatsby's invitation with the likes of a Meyer Wolfshiem, but the novel also condones Nick's anti-Semitic shudder at Wolfshiem—a shudder that's "excused" by Wolfshiem's stagy Yiddish accent (he keeps talking about his business "gonnegtion" with Gatsby) and by the bizarre fashion accessory Fitzgerald decks Wolfshiem out in. Remember? My students, much to my bafflement, almost never do: Wolfshiem has cuff links made out of human molars. Like Shylock, Wolfshiem is a moneylender who'll presumably yank out debtors' gold-filled teeth if they're late with their payments. As much as the New York novels written by Henry James and Wharton, *The Great Gatsby* is closely attuned to the social nuances of characters' accents and clothing and birthplaces and last names.

Last names…Over the decades I've taught *Gatsby*, I've sometimes pointed out to students that my own last name is included in that screwball, pages-long list of all the people who went to Gatsby's house parties. Though you might expect the snider species of student would sometimes beat me to it, none ever do, because *nobody but the most crazed Fitzgerald fan ever reads that list all the way through*. But there my name is, near the beginning of chapter 4, in the middle of the list's fourth paragraph:

Also from New York were the Chromes and the Back-hyssons and the Dennickers and Russel Betty and **the Corrigans** [emphasis mine] and the Kellehers and the Dewars and the Scullys and S. W. Belcher and the Smirkes and the young Quinns, divorced now, and Henry L. Palmetto, who killed himself by jumping in front of a subway train in Times Square.

Clearly Fitzgerald put together a list of names he found comical and immigrant-sounding: Jewish, Russian, Italian, and Irish. Self-conscious about his own wobbly social position, he was always hypersensitive about class. (Fitzgerald grew up mostly in Minnesota, the offspring of well-to-do "lace-curtain Irish" merchants on his mother's side and landed patriots without the money to match their pedigree on his father's.) When I spotted my own last name in that list (probably the second or third time I read *Gatsby;* first time round, I'm sure I skipped over that mammoth list of names too), I felt a start, as though the novel had looked through my intellectual pretensions and found me out: *At best, a West Egger,* the novel sniffed, *more likely, a valley of ashes dweller.*

The frisson of "being read" by *Gatsby*—something everyone who falls under the novel's spell experiences—was intensified for me by the fact that I grew up in Sunnyside, Queens, quite near the "valley of ashes," in Corona. In the 1960s, when going for a drive was still a recreational activity, my mother, father, and I would pile into our Rambler Classic almost every weekend and drive out to Long Island—often on Northern Boulevard through Great Neck and Manhasset, the very same West Egg and East Egg of the novel. After a day spent at Oak Beach or Teddy Roosevelt's house Sagamore Hill or some other shimmering North Shore spot, we'd pile again into the Rambler for the return trip to Sunnyside, where we belonged. As the greenery of Gold Coast Long Island gave way to the dingy beige apartment buildings and car dealerships of Queens, my mood would sink. The weekend was over, school was looming, and we would be cooped up in our small, dark apartment. Like Joyce's Leopold Bloom unconsciously reenacting the wanderings of Ulysses as he walked through Dublin on June 16, my parents and I unknowingly replayed Gatsby's rise and fall, back and forth, for years, until those weekend pilgrimages ended when I broke away to begin my own shaky class climb through college and up into the Ivy League (not Fitzgerald's Princeton, but Ben Franklin's University of Pennsylvania). Sometimes, as we were driving through East Egg and environs, my father, a refrigeration mechanic and proud shop steward of his Steamfitters' local, would point to a gated mansion and rumble, "I wonder how many people that guy had to step on to get that house." The deep poignancy of *The Great Gatsby*'s unsentimental reading of class in America is that Gatsby himself is one of the bastards who steps on other people to get his fortune, yet, at the same time, he's also stuck in the car with the likes of the Corrigans—always on the outside looking in. The rich *are* different from you and me: they know where they belong.

The Great Gatsby exposes another hard fact of life in the modern age: God no longer exists. *Gatsby* belongs to that elite company of theologically skeptical to contemptuous masterpieces written after World War I. At the end of *The Sun Also Rises* (1926), when Jake Barnes says, "Isn't it pretty to think so," he's doing more than deflating Lady Brett's fantasies of romance; he's also demolishing the Victorian worldview of "God's in His heaven All's right with the world." Jake's response to the possibility of a benevolent, all-seeing Deity is rueful; *Gatsby*'s response is ruthless. The valley of ashes, where Myrtle and George Wilson live over their gas station, offers not only a drive-by tour of the American Dream hopelessly detoured but also a vision—consciously indebted to T. S. Eliot's *Waste Land* (1922)—of what a landscape abandoned by God looks like. Turns out, it looks an awful lot like a World War I battlefield. Here's Nick describing the terrain, as well as the twentieth century's new idol—advertising:

> Above the gray land and the spasms of bleak dust which drift endlessly over it, you perceive, after a moment, the eyes of Doctor T. J. Eckleburg. The eyes of Doctor T. J. Eckleburg are blue and gigantic—their retinas are one yard high. They look out of no face, but, instead, from a pair of enormous yellow spectacles which pass over a nonexistent nose. Evidently, some wild wag of an oculist set them there to fatten his practice in the borough of Queens, and then sank down himself into eternal blindness, or forgot them and moved away. But his eyes, dimmed a little by many paintless days under sun and rain, brood on over the solemn dumping ground.[8]

The solemn dumping ground. Like other novels of its shell-shocked generation, *Gatsby* asks what kind of God would allow the apocalypse of World War I to happen and answers its own question by drawing our attention to that billboard of the blind Deity. The second time we're presented with the image of Dr. Eckleburg is during the climax of the novel, when the grief-stricken new widower, George Wilson, stays up all night rambling on to poor Michaelis, the owner of a nearby coffee shop, about his last argument with the unfaithful Myrtle. Wilson warned her:

"God knows what you've been doing, everything you've been doing. You may fool me, but you can't fool God!"

Michaelis then sees "with a shock that [Wilson] was looking at the eyes of Doctor T. J. Eckleburg, which had just emerged, pale and enormous, from the dissolving night.

"'God sees everything,' repeated Wilson.

"'That's an advertisement,' Michaelis assured him."[9]

The idea of God reduced to a faded advertisement; by the time he wrote *The Great Gatsby*, Fitzgerald had left his teenage fantasies of becoming a Catholic priest far behind.

Despite the fact that it's known as a great love story, the novel is as withering about romantic love as it is about theology. *Gatsby* is a novel about idol worship, about the flat-out submission of the self to another. Readers love that swooning aspect of *Gatsby* so much that we often ignore the fact that the object of Gatsby's quest turns out to be as fake as the Maltese falcon in Dashiell Hammett's hard-boiled classic of 1930. Our last glimpse of Daisy in the novel is damning. It's the dead of night and Daisy is sitting up at her kitchen table with Tom, "conspiring" over a meal of beer and cold chicken. Gatsby patrols the grounds outside the house since he's naively anxious that Tom will be furious at Daisy for killing Myrtle and for admitting that she loved Gatsby. Not to worry. Myrtle and Gatsby have already been discarded by these wealthy survivors, who're as cold as that fried chicken they're getting ready to gnaw. Nick says that Gatsby remained outside, a faithful knight keeping a sacred "vigil." But that's not where the chapter ends. There's one more sentence, in which we're told that Gatsby spent the night before his own death, "standing there in the moonlight—watching over nothing."[10] Daisy is ultimately "nothing," a holy grail made out of papier-mâché.

The Great Gatsby is one of the first modern novels to look squarely at the void, yet it stops short of taking a flying leap. Blame the lingering influences of Fitzgerald's lapsed Catholicism and the romantic bent of his sensibilities. Fitzgerald's favorite poet, after all, was John Keats. In the end, Fitzgerald always wants to want, even if nothing out there quite measures up. It's Fitzgerald's thin-but-durable urge to affirm that finally makes *Gatsby* worthy of being our Great American Novel. Its soaring conclusion tells us that, even though Gatsby dies and the small and corrupt survive, his longing was nonetheless magnificent. The last movement of the novel also makes clear that the earthbound desire that doomed Gatsby (all that Herculean effort for a pretty rich girl he met a lifetime ago!) is but an expression of a yearning for something greater that can never quite be grasped or even named. That's why Nick Carraway, like generations of the book's readers, is so haunted by Gatsby: Gatsby reached out, strained the farthest, ran the fastest, trying to grasp something while everyone else in the novel was anesthetized by liquor or greedy self-regard. There's no talk of "living in the moment" or Oprah-esque gratitude journals for Jay Gatsby; even before he meets Daisy, Gatsby the poor boy comes of age scribbling self-improvement lists like Ben Franklin, another antsy American social climber.

Guided by the Franklin reference and all those elegant elbow jabbings in the last paragraphs of the book about "Dutch explorers" and the "fresh, green breast of the new world," we readers come to understand that, in Fitzgerald's view, longing is our national inheritance as Americans—or at least it is for those few Americans who, like Gatsby, are brave enough or rash enough to claim it. Gatsby's glorious gesture of stretching out his hands to that distant green light affirms the best in what used to be called, quaintly, our "national character." That Thanksgiving Eve at the Public Theater, the audience—fatigued by seven-plus hours of the performance but nonetheless rapt—murmured, as one, the final line of the novel: "So we beat on, boats against the current, borne back ceaselessly into the past."[11] Nobody in the theater that night—nobody who's ever read *Gatsby*—completely understands that line, and yet we all sense it says something true about this country and the doomed beauty of *trying*.

That last line, like the novel as a whole, has it both ways: it's wiser to recognize the inevitability of limitations; it's magnificent to risk all to surmount them. The structure of *Gatsby* stokes the ambivalence about its ultimate message: *Gatsby* plays on an endless loop. Nick begins by recalling events of the momentous summer of 1922. He retells the story of Gatsby and then ends with the benediction—or curse—of the enigmatic last line of the novel that pulls us "back ceaselessly into the past." And so we start the rumination about Gatsby and the meaning of his life all over again. It's like an earworm, that last line: once you get it into your head, it burrows deep. By 1975, when the remains of Scott and Zelda Fitzgerald were moved at Scottie's request and reinterred in the Fitzgerald family plot in Old St. Mary's Church in Rockville, Maryland, those words had come to be recognized as Fitzgerald's definitive statement on Gatsby and on America. Scott and Zelda lie together beneath a slab that quotes the line.

We don't have any site in this country akin to Westminster Abbey—a sacred last resting place for our great writers and poets. Even so, Old St. Mary's Cemetery is an especially unimpressive location for one of America's greatest authors to be buried, given that it's inches away from Rockville Pike, a busy major highway. Fitzgerald couldn't roll over in his grave; he'd be hit by speeding commuters. Old St. Mary's Church, at least, has some historical significance: it was a stop on the Underground Railroad. But a newer church was eventually crammed in next to the tiny original structure. The modern church is a white eyesore that looks like a space pod. I visit Fitzgerald's grave pretty frequently because it's a few blocks away from the car dealership where I take my wheezing Mazda for service. That's the kind of suburban wasteland that surrounds Fitzgerald's final resting place: not the valley of ashes, but not East Egg either. I've visited in winter, when I've had to brush snow off the gravestone to read those last words of *The Great Gatsby;* I've walked over in the heat and humidity of summer, when the grass in the churchyard is brown and the air feels solid. I've never seen other people at the grave, but always there are tributes: flowers, coins, and miniature liquor bottles. This book, too, is a kind of tribute, though Fitzgerald, surely, would rather have had the booze.

1

Water, Water, Everywhere

There were many low points in F. Scott Fitzgerald's life, but 1936 has to have been his rock-bottom year. Fitzgerald was staying at the Grove Park Inn in Asheville, North Carolina, close to Highland Hospital, a sanitarium where Zelda was being treated for schizophrenia. Fitzgerald himself was recovering from one of his recurrent flare-ups of tuberculosis and valiantly trying to stay on the wagon. The previous year, in an effort to dry out, he had gone so far as to seclude himself in a "dollar hotel"[1] in Hendersonville, North Carolina, for a few weeks, where he lived on potted meat and crackers and washed his shirts out in the bathroom sink. Fitzgerald recalled that "it was funny coming into the hotel and the very deferential clerk not knowing that I was not only thousands, nay tens of thousands in debt, but had less than 40 cents cash in the world and probably a $13. deficit at my bank."[2]

For almost all of Fitzgerald's adult life, debt, like TB, had been a chronic condition. Ever since *This Side of Paradise* made him the sage of what he'd dubbed the Jazz Age in 1920,

Fitzgerald had borrowed against his projected earnings as a writer to support the lavish style of living—servants, blowout parties, European travel, rented mansions—that he and Zelda had adopted. But by 1936, Fitzgerald was sunk in debt so deep that a veritable grand staircase built out of bestsellers would have been required to help him climb up onto firm ground again…and those bestsellers weren't appearing. The only things that were appearing were bills. Fourteen-year-old Scottie was enrolled in a tony girls' school in Connecticut; Zelda had been a resident for long stretches at private mental institutions in the United States and Europe ever since her first breakdown, in the fall of 1929 in France, when she was not yet thirty years old.

Fitzgerald's confidence in his ability to write his way up and out of his financial messes had collapsed during the Great Depression, when literary tastes turned away from stories of giddy extravagance and toward socially conscious "proletarian fiction." *Tender Is the Night* came out in 1934 to gentle applause and sold even fewer copies than *The Great Gatsby*, whose second printing had been gathering dust in the Scribner's warehouse ever since it was published in 1925. His short stories, which had always been Fitzgerald's bread and butter, were now being rejected by the very same magazines—the *Saturday Evening Post, McCall's, Collier's*—that had made him one of the highest paid American writers of the 1920s. Ill and deeply depressed, Fitzgerald diagnosed himself as being in a state of "emotional bankruptcy."[3]

Those were just some of the by-now-familiar miseries of Fitzgerald's life in 1936—a "nightmare" year that, as he would later tell his old Princeton friend John Biggs, had "a long build up to it.… After about six good punches you can be knocked down by carefully blown beans and that was what was happening."[4] Some of those punches were self-inflicted. While he'd been holed up in that crummy hotel in Hendersonville in 1935, Fitzgerald had written three essays that surgically probed his own despair. *Esquire* magazine bought the essays, later collected and released as *The Crack-Up*, at the bargain price of two hundred and fifty dollars apiece and began publishing them in February 1936. If Fitzgerald was generally dismissed as a Jazz Age literary relic in the Dirty Thirties, he was way too far ahead of his time with these confessional essays. Nowadays, the *Crack-Up* trilogy is venerated for its self-flagellating brilliance, but when the essays first appeared, they were greeted with regret by Fitzgerald's great friend and editor Maxwell Perkins—he referred to them as the "cracked-plate" essays—and with scorn by chest-thumping peers like John Dos Passos and Ernest Hemingway.[5]

Hemingway in particular was appalled by such a public display of weakness from the writer who had once been his more famous contemporary. A great believer in toughing out depression with ridicule, Hemingway responded to a glum letter he'd received from Fitzgerald in 1935 by playfully suggesting that he, Hemingway, could arrange to have Fitzgerald murdered in Cuba so that Scottie and Zelda could collect the life insurance. On a roll, Hemingway further proposed scattering the dead Fitzgerald's innards around significant landmarks of his life, donating "your liver...to the Princeton Museum, your heart to the Plaza Hotel...[and] if we can still find your balls I will take them via the Ile de France to Paris...and have them cast into the sea off Eden Roc."[6] Hemingway must have really gotten a kick out of that last image because he concluded this nasty letter with an even nastier poem he'd made up in the punning modernist style of T. S. Eliot and James Joyce. The poem is entitled "Lines to Be Read at the Casting of Scott Fitzgerald's Balls into the Sea from Eden Roc (Antibes Alpes Maritimes)." Its last line imagines Fitzgerald's manhood flung into the waves, "no ripple make as sinking sanking sonking sunk."

As in so many of these exchanges after the first bloom of the friendship had faded, Hemingway comes off sounding like a bullying Tom Buchanan to Fitzgerald's vulnerable Gatsby.

Then, as if the worst year of Fitzgerald's life cried out for a symbolic moment to encapsulate his sense of being *all washed up*, summer came round and tempted Fitzgerald to go swimming. Every biography of Scott and Zelda presents a slightly different version of this story, but I prefer the one that Fitzgerald's first biographer, Arthur Mizener, tells because it includes Zelda.[7] One hot day in July, Scott drove over to Highland Hospital and checked Zelda out for a day trip to a local pool. The Fitzgeralds had always liked sloshing about. So many of the famous photographs of the couple and anecdotes about their lives involve water: pools and fountains; oceans and bathtubs. When Nancy Milford wrote her bestselling biography *Zelda* in 1970, she interviewed former classmates of Zelda's who still remembered her as a beautiful teenager in Montgomery, Alabama, in 1916, scandalizing onlookers at a pool with her one-piece flesh-colored bathing suit that gave the illusion she was swimming in the buff.[8] During their Roaring Twenties heyday in New York, Scott and Zelda were notorious for their impromptu leaps into fountains at Union Square and in front of the Plaza Hotel. There are even stories about Scott and Zelda, together and individually, making an "impression" at parties in the 1920s by taking off their clothes and disappearing into their host's bathtub. These devil-may-care displays had grown more disturbing by 1926. That summer, Scott and Zelda were vacationing on the Riviera in the company of Gerald and Sara Murphy, the wealthy couple who served as hosts to so many artists and writers of the period (and who partly inspired the characters of Nicole and Dick Diver in *Tender Is the Night*). One evening, Zelda decided she wanted to climb diving rocks high above the sea. She stripped to her slip and turned to Scott, asking if he cared for a swim. He accepted her dare. The two dived from successively higher and higher rocks until they both finished the last dive at thirty feet. When Sara Murphy chided Zelda for her reckless behavior (the Fitzgeralds' daughter, Scottie, would have been just four at the time), Zelda responded in her soft Southern accent: "But Sayra—didn't you know, we don't believe in conservation."[9]

On that summer's day in 1936 at the pool in Asheville, the now middle-aged and ailing Fitzgeralds must have been walking examples of the physical and mental consequences of not believing in "conservation." Happily, though, Scott was feeling good that day. Maybe his unexpected sense of well-being made him flash back to that night on the Riviera a decade ago when he and Zelda had played Russian roulette with the rocks below and won. In any event, he got careless: Diving from a fifteen-foot board ("which would have seemed modest in the old days," Fitzgerald lamented afterward to a friend[10]), he became over-confident and started "to show off for Zelda."[11] He fractured his shoulder in midair, and his arm was so badly damaged it dangled a couple of inches out of the socket.

"No ripple make as sinking sanking sonking sunk."

The great theme running throughout all of Fitzgerald's writing—and his life—is the nobility of the effort to keep one's head above water despite the almost inevitable certainty of drowning. While the name of the hero in Fitzgerald's last completed novel has always struck me as comic-book silly, *Dick Diver* bluntly spells out what Fitzgerald's work is all about. His best characters dive into life with abandon and then must fight to stay afloat. By the end of their stories, they're almost always going under, if not altogether sunk, weighted down by money worries, overwhelming desire, the burden of their pasts.

The upward arc of the dive is all about aspiration, and it's glorious: think of Gatsby flinging himself into a frenzy of

A snapshot of an anonymous diver from Fitzgerald's personal photo album of his first trip to the Riviera. (MATTHEW J. & ARLYN BRUCCOLI COLLECTION OF F. SCOTT FITZGERALD, UNIVERSITY OF SOUTH CAROLINA LIBRARIES)

parties and home redecoration in order to win back Daisy. Like the high-flying Gatsby, Fitzgerald himself started out by aiming for "the silver pepper of the stars."[12] Indeed, Fitzgerald recorded in his notebooks that his very first word as a baby was *up*. But what goes up must come down. It's a literal downer to read through any of the thirty-some-odd biographies of F. Scott Fitzgerald. There were so many evenings when I'd come home from my office at Georgetown or from the Library of Congress after finishing yet another account of Fitzgerald's rise and fall and be good for nothing but walking the dog in the gloaming and then going to bed. Retracing Fitzgerald's doomed life story over and over again reminded me of shuffling around the Stations of the Cross during Lent, back when I was a student in Catholic school—something Fitzgerald would have done, too, in his Catholic boyhood. Both pilgrimages end with a triumphant resurrection, but there's a hell of a lot of misery to wade through first. Here are just a few selected stops on the Fitzgerald journey. Station 1: Disappointing sales and mixed reviews of *Gatsby*: "F. Scott Fitzgerald's Latest a Dud" crows the headline in the *New York World* on April 12, 1925. Station 2: Following her initial hospitalization in Paris, Zelda enters Prangins, a Swiss mental clinic, in the summer of 1930, after bizarre behavior culminating in a suicide attempt becomes impossible to ignore. The Fitzgeralds' marriage falls apart as Zelda spends the rest of her life in and out of mental institutions. In 1938, Fitzgerald writes to one of Zelda's doctors: "I cannot live in the ghost town Zelda has become."[13] Skipping now to Station 4: Treasured friendship with Hemingway disintegrates. (One major irritant was the fact that Gertrude Stein had opined to both Hemingway and Fitzgerald that Fitzgerald was the better writer, the one with "the brightest flame.") And now to Station 7: After nine years of work, in 1934, Fitzgerald finally finishes *Tender Is the Night.* Reception and sales in the depths of the Great Depression were respectable, but Fitzgerald regarded it as a "stillbirth."[14] Station 11: Weeks after the diving accident, at four o'clock in the morning, Fitzgerald, still in a plaster cast, trips on his way to the bathroom and makes an agonizing crawl to the hotel-room phone to call for rescue. A bad cold and arthritis set in. Mean-spirited "birthday interview" with Fitzgerald appears on front page of the *New York Post* on September 25, 1936. The headline of the article by Michel Mok reads: "The Other Side of Paradise: F. Scott Fitzgerald, 40, Engulfed in Despair." Shortly thereafter, Fitzgerald attempts suicide. When he regains his spirits, Fitzgerald begins referring to Mok as "Michael Muck." Station 13: Move to Hollywood, where Fitzgerald is treated dismissively by MGM as a Mr. Fix-It man on a number of scripts, including *Gone with the Wind.* Station 14: Fitzgerald dies on December 21, 1940. His promising Hollywood novel, which he planned to call *The Love of the Last Tycoon,* remains unfinished at his death. Fitzgerald's funeral mirrors Gatsby's: both services are held in the rain and are sparsely attended. In her unpublished memoir, Scottie Fitzgerald recalled that the Protestant minister who buried her father said, "The only reason I agreed to give the service, was to get the body in the ground. He was a no-good, drunken bum, and the world was well-rid of him."[15]

Throughout the 1930s, Fitzgerald would be hospitalized several times for alcoholism. (During his worst binges, he would consume a quart of gin and twelve bottles of beer a day.)[16] One can understand why he wanted to drown his sorrows in liquor. But even during his long, long free fall, Fitzgerald never stopped trying to reclaim the success that had been his as a young man of twenty-three, when *This Side of Paradise* came out. "Can't repeat the past?" asks Gatsby in his signature line, "Why of course you can!" In the foolhardy attempt to once more strain upward, a prematurely aged Fitzgerald fractured his shoulder; a few short years later, he'd be dead. The official cause was a heart attack. Factors contributing to Fitzgerald's frailty—he was a mere forty-four years old—were a lifetime awash in liquor and his recurrent TB, which had plagued Fitzgerald as early as his Princeton years. TB can fill a sufferer's lungs with fluid, so maybe it's not too morbidly fanciful to say that even when Fitzgerald was at the height of his Roaring Twenties success, he always carried the threat of drowning within his own body.

Sink or swim. It's the founding dare of America, this meritocracy where everyone—theoretically, at least—is free to jump in and test the waters. The fear is, however, that if you don't make it, you'll vanish beneath the waves. So much of American literature is saturated with images of drowning, dissolving, being absorbed by the vastness of the landscape or crowds: it's our national literary nightmare. Need I do more to start off the soggy Great Books parlor game than mention *Moby-Dick*? We spend so much time on our initial high-school forays into *Gatsby* focusing on those look-at-me! symbols of the green light and the eyes of Dr. T. J. Eckleburg (tailor-made for AP English exam questions) that we overlook the most pervasive symbol of all: water. Permit me, then, to begin this voyage out into *Gatsby* by retrieving some of the crucial messages about going under that inform Fitzgerald's anxious masterpiece.

Almost every page of the novel references water; even the briefest summary of its plot is soaked to the bone: James Gatz is born again as Jay Gatsby through a watery rite of passage on Dan Cody's yacht; he drowns (symbolically) in his pool when his dreams spring a leak and he can no longer float. Page for compact page, *The Great Gatsby* may be our dampest exemplar of the Great American Novel. Fitzgerald didn't just stick his toes in the water here; in this, his most perfect meditation on the American Dream and its deadly undertow, he dives in and goes for broke.

People who don't really know much about Fitzgerald's work think, as so many of his proletarian critics in the 1930s did, that all he wrote about were the beautiful people buoyed up on bootlegged champagne bubbles. (When *Tender Is the Night* came out, Philip Rahv reviewed it for the *Daily Worker* and, invoking the novel's Riviera setting, famously took Fitzgerald to task for his attraction to the rich: "Dear Mr. Fitzgerald, You can't hide from a hurricane under a beach umbrella."[17]) People think that Fitzgerald loves the rich, the good swimmers in this extended metaphor. How ironic that *The Great Gatsby* has been casually thought of by generations of readers (and moviegoers) as a celebration of Jazz Age wretched excess. Think, if you will, of the product tie-ins to the recent Baz Luhrmann film of *Gatsby*. Advertisements for the Tiffany and Brooks Brothers Gatsby collections touted a vintage pearl and diamond headpiece for $200, a straw boater for $198, and, of course, the famous pink suit—yours for a cool $1,000. Fitzgerald himself bears some blame for the cultural fascination with the bling in the novel. He and Zelda reveled in conspicuous consumption. When Fitzgerald describes *Gatsby* Land, he does so with an avid connoisseur's eye, so its sumptuous details lodge in our brains: the chauffeur tricked out in a uniform of "robin's egg blue," the buffet tables groaning with "salads of harlequin designs and pastry pigs," the bedrooms "swathed in rose and lavender silk," and, most of all, the shirts—"shirts of sheer linen and thick silk and fine flannel...shirts with stripes and scrolls and plaids in coral and apple green and lavender and faint orange with monograms of Indian blue."[18]

But don't whip out the credit cards just yet. Simultaneous with all this delight in extravagance, there's also a vigorous resentment of the upper class in Fitzgerald. Remember, this is the guy who famously said, "The test of a first-rate intelligence is the ability to hold two opposed ideas in the mind at the same time, and still retain the ability to function."[19] Fitzgerald may not have been overtly political in his life or writing the way that contemporaries like Hemingway and Dos Passos were (Fitzgerald quietly voted for Roosevelt), but his class politics were personal and intense. At key moments in his writing Fitzgerald betrays the scorn of the poor relation, the self-made man, railing against (and envying) those trust-fund babies who take their privilege for granted. In his 1931 essay "Echoes of the Jazz Age," Fitzgerald anticipates the rhetoric of Occupy Wall Street when he talks about the "upper tenth": "It [the Jazz Age] was borrowed time anyhow—the whole upper tenth of a nation living with the insouciance of grand dukes and the casualness of chorus girls."[20]

One place you can hear Fitzgerald's ideas about class and America's meritocratic promise expressed with uncharacteristic directness is in his letters to his daughter. Beginning in adolescence, Scottie was sent to exclusive East Coast boarding schools and eventually to Vassar. At times, Fitzgerald worried that she was in danger of turning into an entitled layabout. His "Tiger Dad" letters to Scottie, most of them written in the late thirties when Fitzgerald was working in Hollywood, constitute a series of epistolary kicks in the butt on the virtues of hard work and "keep[ing] your scholastic head above water."[21] In one letter, Fitzgerald worries that Scottie may be "accepting the standards of the cosmopolitan rich" and warns that "if I come up and find you gone Park Avenue, you will have to explain me away as a Georgia cracker or a Chicago killer."[22] Preparing Scottie for her first year at Vassar, Fitzgerald, surprisingly, writes: "You will notice that there is a strongly organized left-wing movement there.... I do *not* want you to set yourself against this movement. I am known as a left-wing sympathizer and would be proud if you were."[23] In an undated fragment that comes from the same period, Fitzgerald recommends Marx: "Sometime when you feel very brave and defiant and haven't been invited to one particular college function, read the terrible chapter in *Das Kapital* on 'The Working Day,' and see if you are ever quite the same."[24] And then there's this letter, written six months before he died, in which Fitzgerald puts himself forward as exhibit A of a great talent damaged by sloth and self-doubt. It's addressed to Scottina, one of the many nicknames Fitzgerald gave to his daughter: "What little I've accomplished has been by the most laborious and uphill work, and I wish now I'd *never* relaxed or looked back—but said at the end of *The Great Gatsby:* 'I've found my line—from now on this comes first. This is my immediate duty—without this I am nothing.'"[25]

Even allowing for the fact that these letters are written by a middle-aged and often depressed Fitzgerald, they don't sound like the thoughts of a man who uncritically worships wealth and luxury consumer goods. Yet the most famous anecdote about Fitzgerald—the one that even people who've never read him know—ridicules what's alleged to be his wide-eyed reverence for the rich. The fact that, as so many scholars have pointed out, the anecdote is false doesn't make a dent in its malicious authority. Hemingway and Fitzgerald are talking one day in Paris, and Fitzgerald breathlessly declares: "The rich are different than you and me." Hemingway, comeback at the ready, growls, "Yeah, they have more money." It might be pretty to think so, but that's not the way that conversation actually happened. Hemingway and the critic Mary Colum had a conversation in the 1920s during which Hemingway uttered "the rich are different" line and Colum gave him the witty comeback. Later, Hemingway made Scott the butt of the joke in "The Snows of Kilimanjaro" and in his beautiful-but-corrupt memoir of Paris in the 1920s, *A Moveable Feast.* Here's Fitzgerald, through the unnamed narrator of his 1926 story "The Rich Boy," giving quite another spin to those lines that Hemingway later distorted:

"Let me tell you about the very rich. They are different from you and me.... They think, deep in their hearts, that they are better than we are...because we had to discover the compensations and refuges of life for ourselves. Even when they enter deep into our world or sink below us, they still think that they are better than we are. They are different."[26]

Sure, Fitzgerald writes about the rich and enjoyed living large, but he's clear-eyed about the limits of money. He knows how near impossible it is to swim the marathon distance between West Egg and East Egg. "Americans should be born with fins," he wrote in his bluntly titled story of 1929 "The Swimmers." "Perhaps they were," he continues, "perhaps money was a kind of fin."[27] But Fitzgerald also knows that money isn't enough to keep a striver afloat; breeding counts too. Even in one of the lushest, most romantic moments of the novel—the reunion of Daisy and Gatsby in chapter 5—Fitzgerald wedges in an ominous comment about class differences. Gatsby is showing Daisy around his mansion and calls in Klipspringer, the freeloading houseguest, to provide background music on the piano. What song does Klipspringer bang out after he finishes a rendition of "The Love Nest"? The 1920 foxtrot "Ain't We Got Fun," with its lines that declare "The rich get richer and the poor get—children."

Look again at those words about the rich spoken by Fitzgerald's narrator in "The Rich Boy": *Even when they enter deep into our world or sink below us, they still think that they are better than we are. They are different.* That's a statement about class, not money; it's a statement about an internalized sense of privilege born out of wealth and out of what Fitzgerald called in a 1933 letter to his friend and fellow novelist John O'Hara "breeding." Fitzgerald is one of our most sensitive literary chroniclers of class. He obsesses on the subject throughout most of his short stories and novels but nowhere more exquisitely and painfully than in *Gatsby*.

In focusing on class, Fitzgerald was following the old saw of "write what you know." He came from people who were never quite certain where they stood, economically and socially. As a child, he saw firsthand what it was like for his family to almost go under. Of all our great writers, especially in the modern age, he has the most finely tuned antennae for the facial expressions, accents, manners, clothes, and posture that separate those to the manner born from those who desperately wanna be. Remember the comical way in which Nick, upon first seeing Jordan Baker, describes the way she holds her head? "She was...completely motionless and with her chin raised a little as if she were balancing something on it which was quite likely to fall."[28] That's the posture of a girl who's so snootily self-assured, she doesn't even bother to lower her head to nod at her hostess's cousin. No wonder Nick falls (a little) for her.

That quick moment in *Gatsby* reveals one of Fitzgerald's big insights about the rich: he knows that what makes them different is that they don't need to try as hard as other people do. They float as if by birthright. Floating images cluster like jellyfish throughout *Gatsby*. They first surface in that aforementioned opening scene, where Nick enters the Buchanan mansion and glimpses Daisy and Jordan: "The only completely stationary object in the room was an enormous couch on which two young women were buoyed up as though upon an anchored balloon. They were both in white, and their dresses were rippling and fluttering as if they had just been blown back in after a short flight around the house."[29] People generally remember that passage, even if it's been many years since they read *Gatsby* in high school, because its language and images are so gorgeous. Daisy and Jordan loll about in such languid fashion, they're virtually weightless. Tom, admittedly, is filled with passionate intensity about the invading hordes of darker-skinned immigrants pouring into America; otherwise, he's idle. Early in the novel—before he rouses himself to obstruct Gatsby's campaign for Daisy—Tom is little more than a wealthy former college football player gone to seed; he plays at life, the same way our entitled narrator, Nick, dabbles at learning the investment business.

It's clear from that very first scene that Gatsby doesn't belong with this crowd, that he's never going to win Daisy precisely because he must try too hard to do so. That's another reason why the novel begins with Nick presenting his class credentials for our inspection: we implicitly understand, as the story unfolds, that though Gatsby has plenty of money, he lacks breeding as well as cultural capital. The fact that he fills up a library with finely bound volumes (though, tellingly, their pages are uncut and, thus, unread) underscores that Gatsby feels his lack of education. Gatsby possesses merely what Meyer Wolfshiem calls "gonnegtions." Briefly summarized, Fitzgerald's waterlogged masterpiece about the realities of class in America is the story of a poor boy, "Mr. Nobody from Nowhere," who, by his wits, contrives to get pulled up out of the waves of Lake Superior by a rich man, Dan Cody, who's aimlessly sailing around the world on his yacht. Cody transforms young Gatz into a successful sailor (blue coat, six pairs of white duck trousers, and a yachting cap). But Gatz—by now metamorphosed into Gatsby—makes the fatal mistake of succumbing to a siren.

Though the film versions of *The Great Gatsby* would tell us otherwise, Daisy is never described in the novel as a total knockout. Instead, the thing that lures men close is her voice, a voice "full of money."[30] Gatsby tries hard to win her and what she represents. The first time we see him in the novel, he's standing in the dark, stretching out his arms to Daisy's green light across Long Island Sound. She's in East Egg, he's in West Egg, and they're separated by the Sound. That odd geographical formation of "the pair of enormous eggs"[31] claims so much attention that, understandably, the fact that a body of water separates the eggs is barely noticed by most readers on their first forays into the novel. Fitzgerald, however, devotes more space in the novel to describing Manhasset Bay and Long Island Sound than he does the eggs.

In the pivotal reunion scene between Gatsby and Daisy, Gatsby's death by drowning is already foretold. Recall that it rained almost all day. When the unsuspecting Daisy arrives for tea at Nick's cottage, Gatsby, who's been waiting anxiously for her, flees. Then there's a knock at the door. Nick opens it to find that "Gatsby, pale as death, with his hands plunged like weights in his coat pockets, was standing in a puddle of water glaring tragically into my eyes."[32] In *Gatz* and in the 2013 Baz Luhrmann film of *Gatsby*, this scene gets a lot of laughs from the audience—particularly in the latter, given that screen idol Leonardo DiCaprio was the guy standing at that door, dripping wet. Fitzgerald, however, isn't playing this moment strictly for comedy.

The last time we see Gatsby, he's literally dead in the water. Gatsby may have been killed by George Wilson's bullets, but he's a dead man the minute he falls for Daisy the siren. Gatsby "run[s] faster, stretch[es] out [his] arms farther," until, propelled by all that yearning, he leans too far out toward Daisy's dock, falls into the Sound, and drowns. Gatsby's pool, with its "little ripples that were hardly the shadows of waves,"[33] is the Long Island Sound in miniature.

Skeptics out there may think that the claim about Gatsby's

pool symbolically standing in for the Long Island Sound is, to use twenties slang, "all wet." I'll top it. This novel's obsession with water and drowning imagery seeps into its very punctuation. I've already quoted part of the penultimate paragraph of *Gatsby*, but here's the entire famous passage:

"Gatsby believed in the green light, the orgastic future that year by year recedes before us. It eluded us then, but that's no matter—tomorrow we will run faster, stretch out our arms farther.... And one fine morning——"[34]

Some critics have been struck by that extra-extra-long dash at the end of the final sentence fragment, "And one fine morning——" A few have even suggested that that supersize dash is a visual representation of the end of Gatsby's own dock, near where we first see him at the close of chapter 1, stretching out his arms to Daisy's dock across the Sound. If, to invoke Fitzgerald's own language, we "run faster, stretch out our arms farther," then, inevitably, there will come a day, like the day Gatsby died in his pool, when we reach the end of the dock, fall off, and drown. If you buy that reading, as I do, then that dash-as-dock punctuation that Fitzgerald implanted near the very end of *Gatsby* may just be one of the first graphic novel moments in American literature.

Whether all our frantic effort is noble or wasted—whether, in short, meritocracy really exists in America—is one of *The Great Gatsby*'s central questions. That's the reason the novel so incessantly splashes about in water and drowning imagery: to consider the question of just how far a nobody in America can swim before he sinks. No wonder, then, that in the recent years of our own Great Recession, when mortgages are underwater and people are drowning in credit card debt, Gatsby has been cited frequently by cultural commentators. As Fitzgerald himself was thrashing about in the depths of his own personal depression in 1936 (when, as he chillingly put it in that interview with Michel Mok, "it's always 3:00 in the morning, day after day"[35]), he too must have wondered about whether, as a writer, he was still afloat above the masses or going, going, gone.

There's one character in *The Great Gatsby* who bobs between the high-class world of the wealthy (the floaters) and the lower-class one of the strivers—including that "poor son-of-a-bitch" who drowns. I'm talking, of course, about our narrator, Nick Carraway. Nick is such a likable guy that it's easy to forget that he's one of Them. But Nick is, after all, Daisy's cousin; he's got breeding and bucks. Despite the fact that he's crashing for the summer in a cottage in "less fashionable"[36] West Egg, virtually in the shadow of Gatsby's garish mansion, Nick is an American aristocrat interning on Wall Street. In the light of the romance that dominates *Gatsby*'s plot and the enigma that is our title character, Nick's opening riff on his pedigree (which reads as though he's trying to impress the co-op board of an exclusive New York City apartment building) would mark him as a shallow snob, except for the fact that, as his last name signals to readers, he's been *carried away* by Gatsby. Unlike Daisy and company, Nick possesses emotional depth and the secret soul of a poet. We need a character like Nick in *The Great Gatsby*, someone who's an insider but who's alienated and sensitive enough to appreciate—indeed, love—a noble striver like Gatsby. We also need Nick in this novel for practical reasons: he's our survivor. The only reason we readers are treated to Gatsby's story in the first place is that Nick dodges not only the wreck that kills poor Myrtle Wilson, but the two other violent deaths that follow, which effectively end the party that was the summer of 1922. I do mean *wreck* in the maritime sense too. Nick follows in the wet footsteps of *Moby-Dick*'s Ishmael as well as those of the unnamed narrator of *The Rime of the Ancient Mariner*, Samuel Taylor Coleridge's poem about a shipwreck that Fitzgerald particularly liked. Nick, our Jazz Age Ishmael, survives to tell the tale—or, rather, write it, since he makes reference to "these pages" in the prologue to the novel. To do that, he's got to make it back to dry land. Dry land is the solid ground of the Midwest, the place where F. Scott Fitzgerald was born and first began to absorb his ideas about class and the rise and fall in status that America might just make possible.

Francis Scott Key Fitzgerald: It's quite a name. In fact, it's a name that suggests the baby's parents, Mollie McQuillan and Edward Fitzgerald, were not averse to "putting on airs." Shortly after he was born in St. Paul, Minnesota, on September 24, 1896, Fitzgerald was christened with that triple-decker moniker that bespeaks Early American connections. Well, sort of. Fitzgerald was indeed related to Francis Scott Key of "Star-Spangled Banner" fame, but the link was distant: they were second cousins three times removed. Fitzgerald's father, Edward, traced his family roots back to seventeenth-century Maryland. During the Civil War, the Fitzgeralds were sympathetic to the Confederacy. Another, even closer relative (who wasn't claimed so ostentatiously) was Mary Surratt, who was hanged for conspiracy in the assassination of Abraham Lincoln. The Fitzgeralds, therefore, had "breeding,"[37] unlike the McQuillans (Fitzgerald's mother's family), who had merely lots of cash. Fitzgerald's "black Irish" maternal grandfather was the quintessential self-made man, an immigrant who, by the mid-nineteenth century, had risen to become a grocery mogul in St. Paul. Mollie McQuillan, Fitzgerald's mother, grew up in a Victorian mansion, was educated at a convent school, and traveled to Europe three times. At the near over-ripe age of twenty-nine, she met and married the charming thirty-seven-year-old Edward Fitzgerald. Soon after, the Irish Catholic princess, Mollie, would find that she had gotten herself hitched to more of a show horse than a sure thing.

Edward was president of a wicker furniture factory in St. Paul; in 1898 it went out of business and he took a job as a wholesale grocery salesman with Procter & Gamble in Buffalo, New York. Three years later, he was transferred to Syracuse, then again back to Buffalo. The family, which by 1901 included Scott's sister Annabel, lived in apartment hotels and rented flats, anticipating a nomadic pattern that Fitzgerald would follow throughout his adult life.[38] Then, in 1908, his father lost his salesman's job at Procter & Gamble. Edward Fitzgerald was fifty-five, and, as his son recalled in the depths of his own dark night of the soul almost thirty years later, his father "came home that evening, an old man, a completely broken man. He had lost his essential drive, his immaculateness of purpose. He was a failure the rest of his days."[39] The day his father lost his job, eleven-year-old Scott overheard his mother talking about the frightening news on the telephone. When his mother hung up, Scott nobly gave her back the quarter she had just given him to go swimming, because he was sure the family was about to founder.

What happened next was a move into the sort of neighborhood

and situation designed to produce—in the kind of sensitive boy Fitzgerald was—a permanent feeling of never quite measuring up. (In that 1933 letter to John O'Hara, where he reflected on his family background, Fitzgerald diagnosed his lifelong problem as "a two-cylinder inferiority complex.") The Fitzgeralds moved back to St. Paul, to the Summit Avenue section of the city where Mollie's family owned property. There, Edward was given a job by his brother-in-law, and for the next decade or so, the Fitzgerald family rented apartments and houses in what was then one of the swankiest residential sections of any city in the world. Summit Avenue, at the time Fitzgerald lived there, has been likened to the Fifth Avenue of the Gilded Age. Among the mansions were the University Club, designed by some of the same architects responsible for New York's Grand Central Station, and the majestic residence of railroad tycoon James J. Hill, who would serve as an inspiration for *Gatsby*'s Dan Cody.

Thanks to Mollie's inheritance from her tycoon father, the Fitzgeralds had the money to rent in the Summit section; thanks to their Catholicism and Edward Fitzgerald's iffy income, they never belonged there in an assured way. When Fitzgerald pilgrims tour Summit Avenue, they can visit two sites associated with the author: his birthplace, at 481 Laurel Avenue, and the row house at 599 Summit Avenue where his parents were living in 1919, the year Fitzgerald moved back home after his engagement with Zelda was broken. The Summit Avenue house is the place where Fitzgerald sealed himself into the top floor throughout the summer of 1919 and doggedly rewrote his draft of *This Side of Paradise* into a publishable book. Mildly interesting as those sites may be, there is no Fitzgerald

House in the way that there is an Emily Dickinson House and a Herman Melville House and a Mark Twain House. Fitzgerald, like his parents, never owned a home. He was a renter all his life.

The sense of being on the outside looking in, of wanting wealth and status and at the same time loathing the easeful rich who take their advantages for granted: these are bedrock elements in Fitzgerald's fiction and their source can be traced to Summit Avenue. If childhood landscapes engrave themselves on our developing psyches, then Summit Avenue imprinted on Fitzgerald an inner geography of yearning, riven with contempt.

I love that odd moment early in *Gatsby* where Nick, stuck at that interminable, drunken party in the far Upper West Side love nest shared by Tom Buchanan and Myrtle Wilson, mentally splits into two people: the reluctant insider and the excluded observer:

"I wanted to get out and walk eastward toward the park through the soft twilight but each time I tried to go I became entangled in some wild strident argument which pulled me back.... Yet high over the city our line of yellow windows must have contributed their share of human secrecy to the casual watcher in the darkening streets, and I was him too, looking up and wondering. I was within and without, simultaneously enchanted and repelled by the inexhaustible variety of life."[40]

This is W.E.B. DuBois's famous "double consciousness" dramatized through the scrim of class, not race. Alone among Fitzgerald's novels, *The Great Gatsby* dramatizes that deeply felt social and psychic split in its very structure. Nick, our narrator, is a watcher, largely shut out of the main events of the story featuring his "high-bouncing" hero Gatsby. But the class situation is even more complicated because Fitzgerald's "insider," Gatsby, can't comfortably settle into the world he's attained. In terms of social class, Nick is much more of a natural-born insider than the man whose life he's observing. The constant anxious calibration of insider-outsider status that runs throughout the conversations and descriptive passages in *Gatsby* constituted Fitzgerald's everyday reality: he always felt one step down from his wealthier childhood playmates on Summit Avenue, his Princeton classmates, and, later, his fellow writers and artists, many of whom he idolized. He might well have appreciated the black humor surrounding his "first" funeral, where his body was denied interment in the Fitzgerald family plot by the Catholic Church. A final snub.

These rejections — subtle and overt; imagined and real — ate away at Fitzgerald's self-confidence. It's striking, too, how many times in his life Fitzgerald displayed over-the-top hero worship of his artistic idols. He flung himself at the feet of Edith Wharton, when he met her for the first time in Scribner's New York offices, and Isadora Duncan, when he met her in a restaurant on the Riviera. (Wharton was taken aback; Duncan lapped the adulation up.) At a dinner in Paris, Sylvia Beach, the owner of the legendary bookstore Shakespeare & Company, introduced Fitzgerald to James Joyce, and Fitzgerald knelt in front of his idol and feverishly declared that he would show his admiration for Joyce's genius by jumping out of a nearby window. Joyce stopped him and afterward commented, in puzzlement: "That young man must be mad—I'm afraid he'll do himself some injury."[41] (The copy of *The Great Gatsby* that Fitzgerald presented to Beach as a token of his thanks for that evening is housed in Princeton's Firestone Library; the inside cover is decorated with a charming drawing in ink by Fitzgerald of that odd dinner party, with Fitzgerald on his knees before Joyce.) The stories about Fitzgerald abasing himself before his disloyal friend Hemingway are especially cringe-making. Toward the end of his life, Fitzgerald definitively threw in the towel on the struggle with his rival when he wrote in his last notebook: "I talk with the authority of failure, Ernest with the authority of success. We could never sit across the same table again."[42]

When I think of these and a dozen more examples of Fitzgerald's self-deprecating behavior, Frank O'Hara's wonderful poem about his screen idol Lana Turner falling on a New York City sidewalk comes to mind. The last line of "Poem (Lana Turner Has Collapsed!)" reads: "oh Lana Turner we love you get up." Fitzgerald always prostrated himself before those he revered or thought were his betters. The feeling of being at home in his own skin, of being enough—in terms of class or talent—was a utopian state that Fitzgerald never attained.

Bullies—from the ones in Fitzgerald's childhood years to Hemingway—naturally took advantage of Scott's tendency to defer. His angelic good looks couldn't have helped. Judging by the many photographs that exist, Scott Fitzgerald was the kind of boy—more pretty than handsome—that mothers coo over and that other kids immediately label *victim*. His hair was golden, his eyes were light (different accounts describe them as green, blue, or gray), and his frame delicate. He liked clothes a lot and cared too much about his appearance; biographer Matthew J. Bruccoli says that "at seven he carried a cane when he went with his father to have their shoes shined on Sunday mornings."[43] Fitzgerald also had a passion for football, but he lacked the build for it. Though he made some friends on Summit Avenue, Fitzgerald didn't have an easy social passage through childhood and adolescence. For Fitzgerald's sixth birthday, back in Buffalo, his mother threw him a birthday party and invited a crowd of children. Fitzgerald waited for his guests all afternoon. None of them showed up. At the St. Paul Academy, a private school that Fitzgerald entered at age twelve, he rubbed his classmates the wrong way by nervously bragging about himself. The school magazine, *Now and Then*, ran an article in which Fitzgerald was described as the know-it-all who freely dispensed wisdom about "How to Run the School"; the article snidely asked if there were not someone who would "poison Scotty or find some means to shut his mouth."[44]

You want to telepathically and retroactively tell young F. Scott Fitzgerald to calm down, act cooler. But that was never his style. Like the young James Gatz who made Benjamin Franklin–type self-improvement lists on the flyleaf of his copy of *Hopalong Cassidy*, Fitzgerald was a zealous list-maker from the time he was a boy until his death.[45] He made daunting self-improvement lists for himself and for his kid sister, Annabel. He wrote a stern letter to her in 1915 in which he enumerated her good and bad physical points: "A girl should always be careful about such things as…long drawers showing under stocking, bad breath, messy eyebrows (with such splendid eyebrows as yours you should brush them or wet them and train them every morning and night"[46]). He put together exhaustive reading lists for Scottie, for Sheilah Graham (who wrote an entire book, *College of One*, about his Henry Higgins–like tutorials of her), and even for his private-duty nurse Dorothy Richardson, whom he hired after that diving accident in 1936 while he was once again trying to stop drinking. Such relentless striving would get Fitzgerald where he wanted to be, but it didn't endear him to his schoolmates.

As he would later do at Princeton, Fitzgerald threw himself into the kinds of groups that have always been refuges for social outsiders (these days we might say *nerds*): the debate club and the drama club. So enthusiastic was Fitzgerald's participation that his grades tanked. Fitzgerald's wealthy aunt Annabel agreed to foot the bill for a more rigorous Catholic boarding school, and in 1911 Fitzgerald was packed off to the Newman Academy in Hackensack, New Jersey. Newman's students were "drawn from the Roman Catholic families of wealth in all parts of the United States."[47] There, too, Fitzgerald promptly alienated himself from the other boys by trying too hard, by being boastful, by his determined-but-poor athletic performances, and, worst of all, by not hiding his desire to be acknowledged as special. He was the most unpopular boy at the school, disliked by both students and faculty. In his ledger, Fitzgerald bitterly summarized the school year 1911–1912 as "a year of real unhappiness."[48]

Isolating as it sounds, Fitzgerald, as most of us do, muddled through. He was particularly helped by his burgeoning ability to achieve notice through his stories printed in the school newspaper and by the saving interventions of Father Sigourney Fay, a thirty-seven-year-old priest who would later serve as headmaster of Newman. These days, any mention of a priest taking special interest in a lonely young boy—especially a pretty one—sets off alarms, but nothing sinister has ever surfaced about their relationship. Portly Father Fay seems to have been one of those worldly priests that one finds in Evelyn Waugh novels: he was attracted to art, good conversation, and creature comforts. The two traveled together to Washington, DC, and the resort town of Deale, Maryland, where Fay's family had a house. Father Fay fostered his young friend's literary bent, introducing him to important writers like Henry Adams and the Irish novelist Shane Leslie. (Fitzgerald had a lifelong admiration for the Father Brown mysteries by G. K. Chesterton, perhaps another literary legacy of Father Fay.) Fitzgerald acknowledged the kindness of his priestly mentor when he dedicated *This Side of Paradise* to Fay (who died in 1919, a year before it was published). It's likely that Fitzgerald was also thinking of his priestly mentor and friend when he gave Daisy *Fay* as her last name.

Fay also exerted a spiritual influence over Fitzgerald, stoking the adolescent's flames of Catholic piety. By the time he entered Princeton, Fitzgerald was no longer a practicing Catholic, but, as many of us Catholic-school veterans are wont to say, "They get you early and they get you good." Fitzgerald's Catholicism seems to diffuse throughout his work like incense; occasionally, it coalesces into something more solid. In 1922, Fitzgerald wrote to his editor Max Perkins to say that he was working on a novel with Catholic themes. This is a fragment known to Fitzgerald scholars as the ur-*Gatsby*. All that remains of this ur-*Gatsby* is the moody short story "Absolution," which describes an encounter between a young boy (possibly a childhood version of James Gatz) and a Catholic priest on the verge of a nervous breakdown. Since *Gatsby* is a novel about worship, it makes sense that its origins would lie in Fitzgerald's own religious background. Or, to put it another way, *Gatsby* started life baptized Catholic.

While at Newman, Fitzgerald escaped to Broadway whenever he could, wrote plays during the summer for a local St. Paul amateur group, and published short stories in the school newspaper. Despite all this extracurricular literary activity, Fitzgerald's graduation-year report card from Newman records that the man who would become one of America's greatest writers received mediocre grades for his final two semesters of English: a C and a B. (A couple of decades later, Fitzgerald wrote an essay called "How I Would Grade My Knowledge at 40." The highest mark he gave himself—a B+— was in "Literature and the attendant arts" and "History and biography." Among the other subjects listed, "Military Tactics & Strategy" rated a D+ and "Marxian Economics" a D.)[49] Years later, when Scottie was in a slump in high school, Fitzgerald lectured her via letter: "I *still* believe you are swimming, protozoa-like in the submerged third of your class."[50] At the end of his own high-school career, Fitzgerald himself was just another protozoa.

Entering Princeton in the fall of 1913 (tuition paid thanks to the timely death of Grandmother McQuillan that summer), Scott must have felt as though he were forever handcuffed to the same soul-deadening social treadmill at school. Football was the ticket to distinction at Princeton, so Fitzgerald gamely reported for freshman practice. At five foot seven and 138 pounds, he was a washout; some accounts say that he was cut from the squad on the first day. To add to his frosh humiliation, Scott went on to garner an alarming number of votes as "the prettiest" member of his class at Princeton.

But his social stock rose in other ways. Fitzgerald wrote musicals for the Triangle Club and stories for the *Princeton Tiger* (the humor magazine). As a sophomore, he became a member of the Cottage Club, one of the most prestigious eating clubs on campus. In 1938, looking back in a by-then-characteristic self-pitying mood, Fitzgerald recalled: "That was always my experience—a poor boy in a rich town; a poor boy in a rich boy's school; a poor boy in a rich man's club at Princeton...I have never been able to forgive the rich for being rich, and it has colored my entire life and works."[51] At the time, things didn't seem altogether bleak: he made lasting friendships with the poet John Peale Bishop and with Edmund Wilson, both then upperclassmen, who would help form Fitzgerald's reading tastes and, in Wilson's case, proclaim Fitzgerald's literary greatness during and after his lifetime. It was to Wilson that Fitzgerald wrote the vulnerable letter in college that included this question: "I want to be one of the greatest writers who ever lived, don't you?"[52]

By the time he returned home for the Christmas holidays in his sophomore year, Fitzgerald was every inch the Midwestern boy who'd conquered Princeton, and he was besieged with invitations to Christmas dances. It was at one of those dances that he met sixteen-year-old Ginevra King, who was visiting from Connecticut. Fitzgerald fell hard.

It's always easy to diagnose (and feel superior to) other people's neurotic patterns when it comes to relationships. In the three major romances of his life, Fitzgerald was drawn to the same type like a lemming to the sea. The girl—and she would always be "the girl" in his romantic imagination—was young, pretty, daring, very popular, and unavailable. Just as ordinary girls barely appear in his fiction, Fitzgerald himself never seemed to pay much attention to the waitresses and receptionists and secretaries by whom he was surrounded in the streets and offices of New York and Hollywood. Unlike his creator, Nick Carraway briefly goes slumming in *The Great Gatsby:* Nick tells us that while he was working on Wall Street during that fateful summer of 1922, he "even had a short affair with a girl who lived in Jersey City and worked in the accounting department." So faintly does this affair register, however, that when the anonymous girl takes a vacation in July, Nick says, "I let it blow away."[53] The kind of alpha girls Fitzgerald idolized were not likely to let themselves be blown off.

Sheilah Graham, Fitzgerald's last love during his Hollywood years, was a Bright Young Thing engaged to the Marquess of Donegal when Fitzgerald first saw her at a party in the notorious Garden of Allah villas on Sunset Boulevard. Graham surely must have fascinated Fitzgerald because, like Gatsby, she had created a somebody out of a nobody: she had begun life in England as Lily Shiel, a poor Jewish girl who grew up largely in an orphanage in London's East End. By the time Fitzgerald spotted her, she had been married once and was on her way to becoming a feared Hollywood gossip columnist. Zelda Sayre was the live-wire belle of Montgomery, Alabama, when she and Fitzgerald met, in 1918; Zelda kept many beaux on the string even after she and Fitzgerald became engaged, but the man who presented the greatest impediment to their union was Zelda's father, the imperious Judge Sayre, who refused to give his daughter's hand in marriage to Scott until he could prove himself capable of supporting her in the grand style to which she was accustomed. But before Zelda and

Sheilah, there was Ginevra King. At that holiday party in 1914, the eighteen-year-old Scott Fitzgerald met his first out-of-reach, glittering girl to love, worship, and, in this case, lose. The Ernest F. Hollings Special Collections Library at the University of South Carolina has one of Ginevra's dance cards. It's tiny, meant to be worn around her wrist in a booklet or decorative case. Ginevra's prospective dance partners wrote their names on the card, and one of them was a Princeton student who signed himself *Scot Fitz* on the fifth line with an *X* next to his name. An *X* is also written on line six; presumably, Scot Fitz booked a double whirl around the dance floor with Ginevra. So it began.

Because she's the one who got away, Ginevra—even more than Zelda—is the love who lodged like an irritant in Fitzgerald's imagination, producing the literary pearl that is Daisy Buchanan. Wistfully reflecting, decades later, on their romance, Fitzgerald referred to Ginevra as: "my first girl 18–20 whom I've used over and over and never forgotten."[54]

Ginevra was petite and dark. (Again, those distorting movie versions of *The Great Gatsby* have imposed Zelda's blond radiance on Daisy, but in the novel, she, like Ginevra, is what the beauty magazines used to call a "brown-ette.") All accounts describe her as beautiful and very rich; we're talking serious "Diamond as Big as the Ritz"–type money. Ginevra's father was a Chicago stockbroker, and the family owned a mansion in that city that appears, in photographs, to be the size of a department store. There was also a sprawling country retreat in Lake Forest. Ginevra was used to a life of tennis and polo ponies, private-school intrigues and country-club flirtations. She was one of a clique of Chicago debutantes who became famous in their day for (obnoxiously) referring to themselves as "the Big Four," because of their uncontested beauty and social desirability. Fitzgerald may have internally identified with the wannabes, but he always dated the queen bees.

Given that Ginevra floated in another galaxy far removed from Fitzgerald's own—geographically and economically—their two-year romance was mostly conducted via intense letters. Fitzgerald's to Ginevra were destroyed, at his request, when the relationship ended, but Ginevra's letters and a diary of hers written mostly during their time together came to light in 2003. In her early letters and diary entries, she sounds endearingly like a teenage girl in the throes of a huge crush: "Am absolutely gone on Scott!" Ginevra's ardor, though, inevitably waned; after all, Scott was only one of her many beaux. "She ended by throwing me over with the most supreme boredom and indifference,"[55] he reminisced in a letter to Scottie. Decades after the two parted, Fitzgerald agreed to meet the visiting and now divorced Ginevra for an afternoon in Santa Barbara, California. On and off the wagon throughout his Hollywood years, Fitzgerald was memorably "off" that day and drank too much in order to fortify himself for their reunion. When Ginevra asked him if she had inspired any of the women in his fiction, Fitzgerald responded, "Which bitch do you think you are?"[56]

Fitzgerald should have forthrightly told her, *Many of them.* Daisy is the most significant literary incarnation of Ginevra, but almost all of the elusive socialite teases in his other novels and short stories bear strong resemblances to her. There's Isabelle Borge of *This Side of Paradise* and Judy Jones of the 1922 short story "Winter Dreams," which Fitzgerald described to his editor Max Perkins in a letter of June 1924 as "a sort of first draft of the Gatsby idea."[57] Also in the mix is Paula Legendre, the "dark serious beauty" of "The Rich Boy," written in 1924 while Fitzgerald was working on *Gatsby*. Of course, even more than the resemblances to Ginevra, these works have in common their resemblances to Fitzgerald's anguished feelings about her. In his wound-licking but lyrical 1936 essay "Afternoon of an Author," Fitzgerald said that the distinctive emotional tone of his fiction was "taking things hard—from Genevra to Joe Mank—: That stamp that goes into my books so that people can read it blind like brail.... Whether it's something that happened twenty years ago or only yesterday, I must start out with an emotion—one that's close to me and that I can understand."[58] Fitzgerald was a notoriously lousy speller, hence the misspelling of the name of the girl whose allure stayed with him all his life. In a letter of advice to a young family friend aspiring to be a writer, Fitzgerald recalled: "In *This Side of Paradise* I wrote about a love affair that was still bleeding as fresh as the skin wound on a haemophile."[59] The date of that letter was 1938, yet the language in which Fitzgerald captures his heartbreak over Ginevra is raw.

In addition to serving as a model for Daisy, Ginevra provided Fitzgerald with three other crucial *Gatsby* ingredients: first, an introduction to her friend Edith Cummings, another one of the Big Four and a celebrated golfer known as "the Fairway Flapper." Cummings, who in 1922 became the first female athlete to grace the cover of *Time* magazine, inspired the character of *Gatsby*'s androgynous sportswoman Jordan Baker. Ginevra also may have nudged Fitzgerald closer to his plot for *Gatsby* when she sent him an awkward short story that she had written at his urging about the reunion of two lovers (named Scott and Ginevra) whose relationship has been disrupted by the girl's marriage.[60] Finally, Ginevra gave Scott the "gift" of class humiliation. The oft-repeated story goes that during an unhappy visit Scott paid to Ginevra's Lake Forest vacation villa in the summer of 1916, her father pontificated, in a loud voice meant to be overheard: "Poor boys shouldn't think of marrying rich girls."[61] Fitzgerald might have been happier, but literature would have suffered had he heeded this boor's advice.

Princeton, also, was to become a prize that remained out of reach for Fitzgerald. Preoccupied with his social success and with writing and acting for the prestigious Triangle Club, he had racked up incompletes in Latin and chemistry; in the fall of 1915, he flunked his makeup exams in those subjects. At the end of the fall term, weakened from either an attack of malaria or an exacerbation of his tuberculosis, Fitzgerald voluntarily withdrew from Princeton. Ten months earlier, in February 1915, Fitzgerald had written in his ledger: "If I couldn't be perfect I wouldn't be anything."[62] That declaration—so earnest, so young—must have come back to haunt him many times in his life.

He gamely returned in the fall of 1916, but the chances of his making up all the missing course work were as good as, twenty years later, the chances of his quickly making good on all the debts he owed. To rub salt into his wounded ego, he was now ineligible for an honor he had assumed to be his: the presidency of the Triangle Club. Fitzgerald must have felt as though he were separated from the rest of his world-conquering classmates by a pane of glass.

Fitzgerald seems so lost at this point in his life. One gets the strong sense that, even though his parents were not without some capital, they couldn't provide much guidance to Fitzgerald in his flailing efforts to make something of himself. Indeed, the older Fitzgeralds hardly make an appearance in his recorded life after he enters Princeton. Extraordinary for a writer who— like almost every other writer—mined his personal life for material to be transfigured into fiction, Fitzgerald wrote comparatively little about his parents. There was an essay on his mother after her death in 1936 and a moving piece called "The Death of My Father" that was posthumously published in 1951 in the *Princeton University Library Chronicle*. Some references to both parents pop up in letters and interviews, but in his published fiction, only the figure of Gatsby's father seems to owe something to the real-life original—and even there, the debt is impressionistic rather than direct. Henry C. Gatz of Minnesota is described as "old" and "helpless" and "dismayed"[63] when he turns up at Gatsby's mansion for the funeral, alerted, impersonally, by the coverage of his son's death in the Chicago newspapers. After the initial shock passes, however, Gatsby's father is mostly distinguished by his uncomprehending pride in his son "Jimmy's" accomplishments. Waving the youthful self-improvement list under Nick's nose, Mr. Gatz exclaims: "Jimmy was bound to get ahead....Do you notice what he's got about improving his mind? He was always great for that. He told me I et like a hog once and I beat him for it."[64]

By all accounts, Edward Fitzgerald was a reticent Southern gentleman whose table manners, we might assume, were beyond reproach, but the aching emotion that's captured so vividly in those few pages where Mr. Gatz belatedly visits is one of parental bewilderment at a child who's gone far beyond the known world of the parent. Surely, Edward and Mollie Fitzgerald must have felt left in the dust by their high-flying son, the Ivy League boy who became a famous author and was on easy terms with other writers and movie stars; the big spender who rented homes on the Riviera and estates in Delaware. The schism was between generations—the Victorian Age versus the Jazz Age—and between classes. Fitzgerald not only had more money than his parents (at times) but also acquired the intellectual chops and cosmopolitanism that even Summit Avenue couldn't supply. With the exception of that one scene in *The Great Gatsby,* there were not many backward glances, not much avowed guilt. Like Gatsby, F. Scott Fitzgerald, to some extent, sprang from a "Platonic conception of himself,"[65] but the upward arc was bumpy.

By the time he withdrew from Princeton, Fitzgerald had been slapped down a number of times and in a number of ways. He acutely understood what it felt like to yearn for approval and be denied. The hunger and humiliation would be channeled into *Gatsby.* It's not a big scene nor, apparently, a memorable one. (Most of my students and other folks whom I've lectured to about *Gatsby* over the years need to have their memories jogged about its existence.) But in terms of nailing the silent and brutal ways insiders communicate exclusion to outsiders, it's a masterful passage. The scene takes place in chapter 6, right after Gatsby has finally achieved his reunion with Daisy at Nick's cottage and right after we've heard, via flashback, about how Dan Cody fished the young James Gatz out of the waters of Lake Superior. Nick begins by telling us that he hasn't seen Gatsby for several weeks; he (Nick) has occupied himself with brushing up on bonds and "trotting around with

Jordan," and Gatsby is presumably busy with Daisy. But one Sunday afternoon, Nick wanders over to Gatsby's mansion, and a few minutes after he arrives, Tom Buchanan and two friends (a man named Sloane and an unnamed "pretty woman") arrive on horseback. They seem to be propelled by Sunday boredom and the faint desire to sniff around a local curiosity; otherwise, there's no reason given for their visit. Here's Gatsby's vigorous greeting followed by a strange aside by Nick:

"'I'm delighted to see you,' said Gatsby standing on his porch. 'I'm delighted that you dropped in.'

"As though they cared!"[66]

Nick hardly ever interrupts the flow of a remembered scene this way, but here he can't restrain himself. It's as though Nick, in replaying the scene, wants to do what he wishes he had done at the time: armor Gatsby against the cruelty to come by preemptively insulting these uninvited guests. Sadly, since Nick can only relay past events, not change them, the scene continues to unfold. Gatsby, always so eager to please his guests, scurries around offering refreshment (it's turned down) and energetically asking questions (he receives curt replies). Finally, the "pretty woman" warms up after two highballs and invites Gatsby to her mansion for dinner. This invite—a signal, perhaps, that he's being admitted into this haughty equestrians' circle—sends Gatsby into a tizzy. As socially insecure people tend to do, he responds by apologizing.

"I haven't got a horse," Gatsby says. "I used to ride in the army but I've never bought a horse. I'll have to follow you in my car. Excuse me for just a minute."[67]

And then, when Gatsby goes inside to gather his things (you can imagine him dashing into a nearby bathroom and running a wet comb through his hair; rifling through the closet to find something smart), the men mock Gatsby for not "getting it" that the woman's invitation is insincere. Mr. Sloane and his lady friend and Tom mount their horses, and Sloane directs Nick, "Tell him we couldn't wait, will you?" It's evident that Nick and Sloane, as members of the same social club, understand the unspoken insult that's being inflicted on Gatsby. Nick tells us that he shook hands with Tom (his cousin-in-law, after all), but that "the rest of us exchanged a cool nod." Meanwhile, the one person who is most decidedly not "cool" in this scene arrives to find he's been left flat. The trio disappeared down the drive "just as Gatsby with hat and light overcoat in hand came out the front door."

Do you feel the rejection? That horrible sixth birthday party, the mean boys at the St. Paul Academy, the other mean boys at Newman ("the best Catholic families"), Ginevra King's father, Princeton's football team, Princeton's dean's office, and all the other slights of Fitzgerald's young life are all swirled into that scene. It's even, in a prescient way, the Baltimore Archdiocese deciding that Fitzgerald isn't fit to nestle in the Catholic cemetery alongside his ancestors. Gatsby is trying so hard and he's just brushed off by those "careless people" who don't need to bother to try at all.

In danger of being kicked out of Princeton for good, in October 1917, Fitzgerald enlisted and received his commission as a second lieutenant. Always particular about his appearance, he took the train from Princeton to New York City to have his uniforms made at Brooks Brothers. A picture of Fitzgerald in that uniform is now posted on a creepy Tumblr site called My Daguerreotype Boyfriend whose motto is Where Early

Photography Meets Extreme Hotness. Women (mostly, I assume) go on this site to post black-and-white photos of long-dead hunks. The woman ("Wendy") who posted Fitzgerald's photo in uniform wrote underneath it: "Anyhow, he's adorable if you ask me."

That "Anyhow" refers to a short summary of Fitzgerald's military record, also posted by Wendy, which notes that Fitzgerald was never sent overseas during World War I. This lack of combat experience troubled Fitzgerald the rest of his life. On his first trip to France, Fitzgerald bought a collection of some one hundred glass slides of World War I battlefields. I gingerly looked at some of those very same slides—still in their varnished wooden box together with the viewer that Fitzgerald used—during a research trip to the Ernest F. Hollings Special Collections Library at the University of South Carolina in search of Fitzgeraldiana. The black-and-white scenes they depict are mostly of men posed formally on battle-fields, a few in the company of a stray goat. No matter that the scenes are mundane; Fitzgerald felt the sting of missing out on his generation's defining moment. I think it's touching, then, that he endowed both Gatsby and Nick with the service record he lacked.

Overseas duty is the very first thing that Nick and Gatsby talk about when they meet at Gatsby's house in chapter 3, in one of the oddest entrances, by the way, of any main character in a work of literature. Gatsby slips oh so quietly into the novel that bears his name. Remember? Nick has been invited, via chauffeur-delivered formal letter, to cross over his lawn on a Saturday night to attend one of Gatsby's regular parties. Feeling socially awkward, Nick latches onto Jordan, the only person at the riotous gathering whom he knows. She tries to find Gatsby to introduce him to Nick, but our host is nowhere to be spotted in the crowd. Hours pass. Nick, now lubricated with champagne, is sitting at a small table with Jordan, "a man of about my own age and a rowdy little girl who gave way upon the slightest provocation to uncontrollable laughter."

> At a lull in the entertainment the man looked at me and smiled.
>
> "Your face is familiar," he said politely. "Weren't you in the Third Division during the war?"
>
> "Why, yes. I was in the Ninth Machine-Gun Battalion."
>
> "I was in the Seventh Infantry until June nineteen-eighteen. I knew I'd seen you somewhere before."
>
> We talked for a moment about some wet, gray little villages in France.

The very next moment, the daredevil Gatsby seals this World War I "band of brothers" relationship by inviting Nick to go out with him on Long Island Sound in the morning; always striving to ride high above the waves, Gatsby wants to try out his new hydroplane.

His lack of overseas military service put Fitzgerald at a disadvantage with contemporaries like Hemingway, John Dos Passos, and even Ring Lardner, who'd covered the war for *Collier's*. Like so many "sad young men" of the time, Fitzgerald had images of chivalric sacrifice filling his head. But the trenches of World War I would be neither Fitzgerald's fate nor his subject in fiction. Mizener writes in his biography of Fitzgerald that, in October 1918, Fitzgerald's unit received its overseas order and was sent to Camp Mills, Long Island. From there, they were marched onto a transport, only to be marched off again. That's as close as Fitzgerald came to seeing Europe while he was in uniform. Generously, though, Fitzgerald loads Gatsby's pockets with physical evidence of glorious overseas service: that medal of valor from "little Montenegro," that photograph of the recently demobbed Major Gatsby at Oxford. For the rest of his life, Fitzgerald craved similar souvenirs. (Edmund Wilson recalled that in the late 1920s, Fitzgerald "produced his old trench helmet which had never seen the shores of France and hung it up in his bedroom [in his house] at Wilmington.")[68]

Instead, Fate dispatched Second Lieutenant Fitzgerald off on a different sort of reckless adventure altogether. Before that Camp Mills farce, Fitzgerald had been sent to a series of army training camps in the South. In June of 1918, he wound up at Camp Sheridan near Montgomery, Alabama. There, as his ledger records, he "fell in love on the 7th of September."[69] That was a prudent two months after Fitzgerald, who was serving as an aide to several senior officers in the camp, had accompanied the officers to a dance at the local country club. On the dance floor was a gaggle of noisy young people waiting for the next song to begin. Fitzgerald spotted Zelda Sayre in the group. She was a seventeen-year-old blond beauty wearing a fluttery dress. Fitzgerald promptly abandoned the officers upon whom he was supposed to be attending, walked up to the group, and introduced himself to Zelda.

In Delmore Schwartz's classic 1937 short story "In Dreams Begin Responsibilities," an unnamed narrator experiences a moment out of time in which he enters a movie theater and sits down to watch a movie. Surreally, the movie turns out to be a black-and-white film chronicling the courtship of his (now miserably married) parents. At one point, the narrator shouts at the screen: "Don't do it. It's not too late to change your minds, both of you." Fitzgerald fans may feel that very same urge at this point in his life story.

Scott and Zelda partly created and all but destroyed each other. Along the way, they became the ultimate mascots of the Jazz Age. Scott called Zelda "the first American flapper," which I guess would make him the top jelly bean or sheikh (the latter name for a flapper's male counterpart derives from the 1921 Rudolph Valentino film). Together, they enjoyed ten pretty good to great years in their marriage. These were high-flying years, when money ran through their hands like water; years spent riding atop the roofs of taxicabs in New York and drinking "corn on the wings of an aeroplane in the moon-light"[70]; nights exhausted in rushing from party to party, bar to bar, in Paris, in Rome, and on the Riviera. They called each other "Goofo" and reveled in the fact that their golden beauty made them look like twins. When daughter Frances Scott Fitzgerald—Scottie—came along in 1921 to complete their vagabond nuclear family, Scott and Zelda barely slowed their pace. During that first decade with Zelda, Scott wrote three of his five novels and the bulk of his 160 or so short stories. He became the highest-paid short-story writer of the time, earning up to four thousand dollars a story in the late 1920s from the *Saturday Evening Post*. Then, Zelda's mental illness, their heavy drinking, the imagined and real infidelities, and all the other excesses that swirled into their folie à deux dragged them both down. The change in Zelda seen in her photographs over just sixteen months—from April 1930 (when she was admitted to her first sanitarium, the Malmaison Clinic outside Paris) to September 1931 (when she was discharged from Prangins Clinic in Switzerland)—is shocking. A plug has been pulled and all sparkle has drained out of her face; at only thirty-one, she's doughy and flat. To paraphrase Gertrude Stein, there's no longer a "there there." A terrible recurring case of eczema, which would plague Zelda on and off for years, accounts for some of the outer ravages; inside, she heard voices urging her to suicide. Shortly before her first hospitalization, Zelda thought the flowers in an outdoor marketplace were talking to her; at one point, Scott came home early to their Paris apartment and discovered her on the floor playing with a pile of sand. She practiced ballet before a mirror for nine, ten hours at a time until she passed out. Scott began missing shirts and under-wear; Zelda told him he was imagining things. Then, one day, he opened a closet to find it piled with weeks of soiled laundry that Zelda had tossed in and forgotten.[71] The diagnosis cover-ing these and so many other disturbing incidents was schizo-phrenia. In the 1931 photo taken at the time of her discharge from Prangins, either Scott or Zelda has written the word *recovered*, but Zelda never did recover. Schizophrenia is not curable, and in the 1930s it would have been near impossible to treat. By the time the Roaring Twenties were over, so too, effectively, was their marriage.

Fitzgerald always read his life as syncopated with the larger life of America: anyone familiar with his ethereal essay about New York, "My Lost City," knows that he viewed his own depression as conjoined with the nation's Great Depression. The onset of Zelda's full-blown schizophrenia also eerily coincided with the Great Depression. One of the earliest signs that something was seriously wrong was an incident in France where Zelda tried to wrest the steering wheel of their car away from Scott and drive over a cliff. This near tragedy happened in October 1929, the very same month the Wall Street stock market crashed. Though there were periods when Zelda lived again with Scott and Scottie, the knowledge that another spectacular breakdown hovered on the horizon must have made for the quintessential walking-on-eggshells atmosphere in their various rented homes.

Zelda was a patient at the Highland Hospital in Asheville when a fire broke out in the kitchen there on the night of March 10, 1948. The fire spread through the dumbwaiter shafts and killed nine women. Zelda, locked in her room and scheduled to receive electroshock treatments the following day, was one of the victims.

There are lots of impassioned and knowledgeable Zelda partisans out there,[72] some of whom blame Scott for Zelda's mental agony. I'm not one of them. I don't think anyone is to blame for Zelda's terrible suffering. I think Zelda fell victim to a lot of things: her husband's controlling tendencies, for sure, but also mental illness, which seems to have run in her family (her brother committed suicide), and way too much alcohol. In the 1920s, for the first time in American history, "nice girls" drank publicly, and Zelda was the head flapper, the girl who had to knock back the champagne and gin fizzes and try to keep up with the boys. There was no precedent for this behavior and, thus, no awareness of the toll it could take. Who knows how all that alcohol affected the trajectory of her schizophrenia, or bipolar disorder, which has also been suggested as the correct diagnosis for Zelda's mental illness?

Zelda's triple-threat career as a dancer, writer, and artist was stunted by her mental illness and, to a certain degree, by her own unfocused creative energies. She began studying ballet seriously very late: at twenty-seven. Nonetheless, in 1927, she was offered a spot as lead dancer in a ballet company in Naples, which she turned down. Her novel, *Save Me the Waltz,* barely sold any copies when it was published in 1932. Scott and Zelda became embroiled in a fierce argument about the novel before its publication: Scott insisted she revise or cut sections of it that he felt impinged too directly on his own novel in progress, *Tender Is the Night.* The published version of *Save Me the Waltz* (which Zelda wrote in three weeks) is sprinkled with occasional bright images and phrases, but it's an ornate jumble of a book. Zelda's paintings are charged and disturbing; unfortunately, her mother found them so disturbing that she destroyed most of them after Zelda's death.

The gravest accusations against Scott are that he mined Zelda's diaries and conversations for use in his own books, particularly *The Beautiful and Damned* and *Tender Is the Night.* Indeed he did. All writers are plagiarists, vampires, secret agents embedded within the family. At the end of that first dinner party at the Buchanans' mansion, Daisy tells Nick that when she woke up out of the ether after giving birth and found out that the baby was a girl: "I turned my head away and wept. 'All right,' I said, 'I'm glad it's a girl. And I hope she'll be a fool—that's the best thing a girl can be in this world, a beautiful little fool.'"[73] Zelda had said the very same thing after Scottie was born. Fitzgerald's grounding belief as a writer was that it was always necessary, always, to take notes. Apparently, even at the birth of his only child, he was mentally scribbling.

Though Fitzgerald was frequently a mean drunk and titanically self-absorbed (his constant complaints about money problems during the early years of the Great Depression—when he was still capable of earning three thousand dollars a short story—make you want to toss him over the Queensboro Bridge), he's redeemed, for me, by his loyalty. Granted, Scott had affairs in the 1930s, but they seem more sad than riotous. (Maybe that early Catholic influence squashed whatever sexual hedonism lurked within.) When he began living with Sheilah Graham in Hollywood, he told her that he could never divorce Zelda while she was still ill and needed him. As novelist Jay McInerney points out, during those Hollywood years Scott oddly re-created his little golden nuclear family, the family that had, by then, been split apart by illness and distance. In Sheilah Graham, Scott found himself another dazzling blonde who resembled the young Zelda; in his shy young secretary Frances Kroll Ring, he acquired an admiring surrogate just a few years older than his own daughter, Scottie—and one who happened to share her actual given name, Frances.

Arguing with Zelda devotees about Scott's responsibility for her ruin, however, is like arguing with Rush Limbaugh about Obamacare. That's why I kept mum the day I went out to Old St. Mary's Cemetery in Rockville, Maryland, to tape an interview with NPR senior editor Kitty Eisele about the strange story behind Fitzgerald's two burials. (More about that later.) It was a hot August day and the churchyard was empty. Occasionally we would spot a few folks in the adjacent railroad parking lot, and Kitty, microphone in hand and ever hopeful, would hustle over and ask them if they were there to pay their respects to Fitzgerald. One woman Kitty approached told us in a thick accent that she didn't know who F. Scott Fitzgerald was. Another woman certainly knew who Fitzgerald was and absolutely wanted no part of him. She said something dismissive like: "I like *Zelda*. I read her novel. Her husband stole from her and kept her down." I kept a weak smile pasted on my face. The air was still and heavy with the threat of an afternoon thunderstorm. No spirit voices made themselves heard that day to set the record straight.

Let's turn back to that first meeting between Scott and Zelda. (Don't do it!) It's one of the most famous meetings in all of literary romantic history. Shortly before that meeting, Scott had received word that Ginevra King was engaged to be married. That news may have intensified Zelda's allure, but she was plenty magnetic on her own. Scott courted her, as did, it seems, half the platoon. Zelda later told Harold Ober, Scott's literary agent, why she had married Scott: he made life "promisory" [*sic*].[74] Before they got to the altar (actually, the church office of St. Patrick's Cathedral in New York; Zelda was not a Catholic so they couldn't be married in the church proper), Scott had to prove to both Zelda and her stern father that he could support her by writing—a dubious proposition in any time.

Fitzgerald had been working on a novel about Princeton even before he'd enlisted; the long dull stretches in various army camps had been ideal for writing, and in May of 1918, he sent the manuscript of "The Romantic Egoist" to the publisher Charles Scribner's Sons. In August, it was rejected. Fitzgerald quickly revised the manuscript and re-sent it to Scribner's. In October 1918, it was again rejected. His best work makes writing seem effortless, but it hardly ever was for Fitzgerald. In

February of 1919, Fitzgerald, newly discharged from the army, took a train to New York City, determined to find distinction and to win Zelda by getting published. This was a risky strategy, particularly because Zelda insisted on her right to date other men in Scott's absence. We can only imagine his anxiety, masked by bravado, as he rode on that train alone up to New York City with only a belief in his own gifts to keep him steady.

Many years later, when Scottie declared her desire to be a writer, Fitzgerald would tell her that "all good writing is *swimming under water* and holding your breath."[75] Note those italics, which are Fitzgerald's. In the New York City of the dawning Jazz Age, the twenty-two-year-old Scott Fitzgerald dove in, swam under water, and held his breath. Then he broke to the surface with *This Side of Paradise*. Fitzgerald's first novel was one of those books that define an era; like most such books, it's now chiefly an interesting period piece. Five years after his much-heralded debut, Fitzgerald would write a masterpiece that, comparatively speaking, hardly made a ripple.

2

"In the Land of Ambition and Success"

For the past twenty years or so, I've been teaching a course at Georgetown on the literature of New York City. We start off with *The House of Mirth*, Edith Wharton's 1905 masterpiece about a woman tumbling down the social ladder, and we read our way through the twentieth century to post-9/11 novels like Joseph O'Neill's *Netherland*, the best of the many fictional reworkings of *The Great Gatsby*. My students also watch classic New York films (*A Tree Grows in Brooklyn, On the Town, Annie Hall*), read some urban history and sociology, and go on a one-day field trip to New York to "read the living text of the city" — which translates into taking a walking tour through the Lower East Side, Little Italy, and Chinatown and eating lots of knishes, cannoli, and soup dumplings. And, of course, we read *Gatsby,* one of the first Great American Novels to be set in a city.

Ever since I began teaching it, New York Stories has been the most popular course in Georgetown's English Department.

Naturally, my charisma as a teacher must be the reason, but a contributing factor is New York City itself. My students are fascinated by—and often a little afraid of—New York. Every year, roughly 80 percent of them say they want to move to the city after they graduate. New York is still the place to go to test yourself, especially when you're young.

That's certainly how Fitzgerald felt back in 1919. He was twenty-two years old and determined to make it in New York City, just like my students today. It wasn't his first time in the city; he'd been going into New York on his own ever since his days as a student at Newman and, later, Princeton. But this time Fitzgerald was arriving fresh out of the army, and he was set on conquering the publishing world, winning Zelda Sayre as his wife, and becoming a famous writer. New York City, back then, must have really been something. Fitzgerald, of course, put it best: looking back in his 1932 essay "My Lost City," one of the greatest pieces of writing on the city—ever— he said, "New York had all the iridescence of the beginning of the world."[1]

Just on the verge of the Roaring Twenties, New York was becoming the city we now know and that many of us love. It was the premier American city at a time when more and more Americans were migrating to metropolises. The 1920 census would show that, for the first time in the country's history, more Americans lived in cities than in rural areas. Skyscrapers ("pincushions," Henry James called them when he spotted some sprouting on his pilgrimage back to New York from England in 1904) were rising up in Lower Manhattan; by the end of the decade, many of the city's most distinctive and beloved buildings—among them the Daily News Building, the Radiator Building, the Chrysler Building, and the Empire State Building—were finished or under construction.[2] *Up*, the first word the toddler Fitzgerald uttered, is a word that he'd later use a whopping 202 times[3] in *Gatsby*. Clearly, 1920s New York was destined to suit Fitzgerald's high-flying aspirations.

But *Gatsby*, as we readers know, is relentlessly nostalgic, and so it's fitting that so many of the elegant landmarks of the novel's Manhattan date from the era of the city that immediately preceded the Jazz Age: the Plaza Hotel (1907), the Yale Club (1915), the old Pennsylvania Station (1910), the Queensboro Bridge (1909),[4] and the white marble Tiffany Building at Thirty-Fifth Street and Fifth Avenue, where Nick runs into Tom Buchanan for the last time and reluctantly shakes his hand. Tom, Nick speculates, is going into the jewelry store "to buy a pearl necklace—or perhaps only a pair of cuff buttons,"[5] potential purchases that remind us of Tom's wedding present to Daisy and of Meyer Wolfshiem, to whom Tom is linked in brutishness. That Tiffany Building, designed by Stanford White, still stands near the old B. Altman department store, which has been turned into a complex now used by the City University of New York, the New York Public Library, and Oxford University Press. The Tiffany Building wasn't so lucky in its new tenants: last time I checked, its ground floor was occupied by a Burger King. For better and worse, New York is all about change.

Literary scholar Ann Douglas talks about what was called the "airmindedness"[6] of the twenties: a sense that nothing was too high or too far to be out of reach. The skyscraper boom was certainly a product of this aspirational attitude, as were the new medium of radio (conquering the airwaves!) and the advent of airplane travel. How fitting that New York State's motto, prophetically adopted in the eighteenth century, is *Excelsior,* Latin for "Ever upward." Think also about the poetic epigraph on the title page of *Gatsby*—or, rather, let me tell you about that epigraph, since, judging by the deer-in-the-headlights reaction that request usually elicits from my students, few readers do more than glance at that little poem on the novel's title page:

Then wear the gold hat, if that will move her;
If you can bounce high, bounce for her too,
Till she cry "Lover, gold-hatted, high-bouncing lover,
I must have you!"

Like Lucky Lindy, high-bouncing Gatsby was a Jazz Age Icarus, brushing the clouds with his gold hat. It would be cool to credit Fitzgerald with an inspired discovery of a poem so precisely suited to both the striving spirit of the age and Gatsby's core ambition; however, no such bard as Thomas Parke D'Invilliers ever existed—or, more precisely, he exists only as a character in the pages of Fitzgerald's debut novel, *This Side of Paradise.* Fitzgerald must have been emulating one of his literary idols, T. S. Eliot, who'd concocted phony footnotes for his 1922 poem *The Waste Land,* when he thought of this literary gag.

There's something fizzy and irreverent about that fake poem at the threshold of *Gatsby.* Nowadays, when *The Great Gatsby* has ascended to the Great Books pantheon, it helps to decalcify the novel by remembering that Fitzgerald was quite young when he wrote it (twenty-six to twenty-eight) and that he had a streak of silliness in his makeup that it took oceans of hard liquor and years of hard luck to kill. Fitzgerald's letters into the early 1930s are packed with jokes and doodles and bogus quotes from the likes of Shakespeare's mother. Not only was Fitzgerald himself young, but he was writing to an audience of other young people. The 1920s saw the emergence of America's first youth culture, and Fitzgerald brought flappers and their "jelly-bean" boyfriends into the literary eye through *This Side of Paradise*, the defining novel of the Jazz Age. He didn't need permission to begin *Gatsby* by quoting a more established author; that cheeky epigraph from D'Invilliers signals to those in the know that the story that follows and the voice that Fitzgerald tells it in is fresh and all his own.

The rowdy crew of writers who would become Fitzgerald's compatriots in the 1920s—Edmund Wilson (whom he first met at Princeton), H. L. Mencken, George Jean Nathan, Dorothy Parker, Ring Lardner, and Ernest Hemingway, to name a few—would have gotten the joke. They were a boozy crowd who liked a good laugh, but all of them also were engaged in the very serious business of trying to modernize American literature, make it snappier and truer to the language of the city streets. We don't think of *The Great Gatsby* as a slangy or tough-talkin' novel; it is always, rightly, celebrated for its lyricism. But if you compare *Gatsby* to Fitzgerald's debut novel, *This Side of Paradise,* you'll see how the twenties loosened him up and how a wisecracking language percolated into *Gatsby*, making it more modern and urban. For all of its much-vaunted depiction of flaming youth engaged in risqué necking parties and wild drinking, *This Side of Paradise* reads like an Edwardian novel built on cinder blocks of purple prose. Even Fitzgerald's brief descriptions in that novel are a mouthful:

"The unwelcome November rain had perversely stolen the day's last hour and pawned it with that ancient fence, the night." Huh?

Gatsby, in contrast, is much less affected. Even though Ernest Hemingway is the guy always credited with stripping American sentences down to their essential parts and injecting streetwise lingo into his dialogue, there are more contractions and slang words in the opening pages of *Gatsby* than in the first chapter of Ernest Hemingway's 1926 novel *The Sun Also Rises*. Nick displays a jaunty side to his reflections by using contractions like *don't* and *I've*. Once he starts quoting remembered conversations with Daisy, Tom, and Jordan, his diction can verge on the ungrammatical: "It'll show you how I've gotten to feel about—things," says Daisy before she describes to Nick that famously cynical reaction upon learning that she had given birth to a girl.

Another mark of the striking modernity of *Gatsby*'s style is the fact that it shuns the kind of faux biblical pronouncements that abound in the work of Fitzgerald's contemporaries. I'll cite Hemingway again because he's such a fan of oracular-sounding prose, from *The Sun Also Rises*, which takes its title from Ecclesiastes, all the way through to his last leaden novella, *The Old Man and the Sea*. William Faulkner and Thomas Wolfe also revel in the kind of Old Testament–, Milton-, and Shakespeare-speak that *Gatsby* sidesteps. (Just mentally flip through Fitzgerald's titles in comparison to theirs: Faulkner's *The Sound and the Fury* and *Absalom, Absalom!*; Wolfe's *Of Time and the River* and *Look Homeward, Angel*.) Sounding like a prophet, though, can pay off: Hemingway and Faulkner both won Pulitzers (Hemingway, one; Faulkner, two), as well as the ultimate laurel wreath: the Nobel Prize for Literature. The only medals Fitzgerald ever held were the ones he invented for Major Jay Gatsby.

But I've gotten ahead of myself. Here I am talking about the twenties and New York City and the advent of modernity and I'm even anticipating the subsequent cold-shouldering of Fitzgerald by the prize committees, and, meanwhile, it's still 1919 and Scott hasn't even stepped off his train yet. So, back to that opening scene: Fitzgerald arrived in New York City on February 22, 1919. His train would have pulled into the old Penn Station (the grand structure modeled on the Roman Baths of Caracalla that was built in 1911 and demolished in 1963), because the Atlantic Coast Railroad Line, which then traveled between New York and points south, ran on Pennsylvania Railroad tracks north of Washington, DC.[7] When Fitzgerald stepped out onto the sidewalk in front of old Penn Station, New York City traffic did not screech to a halt; the skyscrapers failed to bow. Fitzgerald lasted in New York City fewer than five months. By the first week of July, he'd packed up his bags and hightailed it back to his parents' house at 599 Summit Avenue in St. Paul.

These days, we call such adult children "boomerang kids": twenty-somethings who can't make it in the real world and so return to the shelter of their childhood bedrooms and life with mom and dad. When you think about how badly young Scott had screwed up his life by this point, you have some sympathy for his parents, whose reaction to their son's failures was not recorded. To briefly review: Wealthy relatives step in to bankroll Fitzgerald's prep school and Ivy League education; in return, Scott essentially flunks out of Princeton because of excessive drinking and high jinks with the drama clique. He enlists in the army, but his stateside military career, while keeping him out of harm's way, is not the stuff of military legend. Then, to really make a mess of things, Fitzgerald gets engaged to a teenage Southern belle who isn't even Catholic! All that was needed to make the situation a total train wreck was for that on-again, off-again fiancée to become pregnant— and, indeed, for some weeks after Scott paid a quick visit to Zelda in Montgomery while he was living in New York, Zelda feared that she was. When Fitzgerald showed up on his parents' doorstep in midsummer of 1919 and announced that he was going to move into their top floor and work on his novel— a novel that had already been rejected *twice* by Scribner's— they must have wondered whether their only son would be sponging off them for the rest of their lives. Fitzgerald's parents let him in but refused to provide him with an allowance. That was a break for posterity. The image of F. Scott Fitzgerald at the age of twenty-two living at home *and* holding out his hand to Mom and Dad for spending money would have been too depressing.

What did Fitzgerald in on this first adult foray into New York is something my students and I talk about often in my New York literature course: the fear of being lost in the crowd. It's a specifically urban variation on the primary American nightmare of drowning, going under. You can see that terror running throughout most New York City literature and film, but there's an especially vivid depiction of it in a 1945 movie called *The Clock*, which stars Judy Garland and Robert Walker. The story takes place in New York City during World War II: Robert Walker is a soldier on forty-eight hours' leave; Judy

Garland is a secretary. They "meet cute" in Penn Station, the original majestic station that was the demobbed Lieutenant Fitzgerald's point of entry into the city. In the very first scene, Walker, a hayseed from the heartland, exits his train and is immediately dazed by the hustle and bustle of Penn Station. He steps onto an escalator—his *Gee, gosh!* expression lets viewers know that this is the first escalator he's ever ridden—and ascends to street level. That's when things get freaky. Walker is overwhelmed by the noise and towering skyscrapers on Thirty-Fourth Street; the camera angles wobble, and Walker looks like he's got the worst case of vertigo ever filmed pre-Hitchcock. Before he passes out, Walker manages to stumble back down into the safety of the station, where he meets his romantic destiny in the form of Judy Garland.

That recurring nightmare of being engulfed by the city in all its too-muchness runs through all types of New York stories. I think of Charles Dickens's 1842 travelogue *American Notes* in which he describes the prolonged shudder of walking through New York streets bursting with "pigs, pedestrians, and prostitutes." Jump ahead to the 1929 short story "Big Blonde" written by Fitzgerald's friend Dorothy Parker or to Ann Petry's 1946 novel about Harlem, *The Street*—both works of fiction bring to life the pressing claustrophobia of New York apartment houses and tenements. Even a valentine to the city like E. B. White's classic 1949 essay *Here Is New York* talks about "the collision… of…millions of foreign-born people"[8] in Manhattan. In modern novels like Ralph Ellison's *Invisible Man*, Tom Wolfe's *The Bonfire of the Vanities* and Paul Auster's *City of Glass*, New York is a labyrinth; in Spike Lee's *Do the Right Thing* it's a jam-packed tinderbox. I could go on and on, but I'll stop this disquieting overview with a line from E. L. Doctorow's very best novel, *The Book of Daniel*, about the Rosenberg case. There's a haunting sentence early in that novel that speaks to New York's power to swallow people whole. Our narrator, Daniel, is recalling his childhood in the Bronx of the 1940s and says of his family: "I could never have appreciated how obscure we were."[9]

In the New York City of 1919, Fitzgerald lost his footing and began to drown in obscurity. Upon his arrival, he had rashly wired Zelda: DARLING HEART AMBITION ENTHUSIASM AND CONFIDENCE I DECLARE EVERYTHING GLORIOUS THIS WORLD IS A GAME AND WHILE I FEEL SURE OF YOU[R] LOVE EVERYTHING IS POSSIBLE I AM IN THE LAND OF AMBITION AND SUCCESS.[10] But Fitzgerald's confidence soon fizzled. His master plan was to land a job writing for a newspaper by day and write short stories by night, but the office staff at the newspapers he called upon weren't bowled over by his peculiar clips: scores he'd written for revues at Princeton. Fitzgerald settled for a grunt job with the Barron Collier Advertising Agency at ninety dollars a month, writing slogans primarily for displays in streetcars. His catchiest jingle was for an ad campaign touting a steam laundry in Muscatine, Iowa: "We Keep You Clean in Muscatine."[11] A few years later, Fitzgerald's low-level familiarity with the flourishing world of advertising— another 1920s phenomenon—would inspire one of the most disturbing images in *The Great Gatsby:* the giant billboard in the valley of ashes that displays "the eyes of Doctor T. J. Eckleburg."[12] True writers salvage every experience, no matter how grim—that is, if they're lucky enough to first salvage themselves.

With every passing month of his New York odyssey, Fitzgerald grew more anxious about his failure to set himself above the crowd. He'd moved into a rented room at 200 Claremont Avenue, near Columbia University. It sounds, from Fitzgerald's description, like a typical postcollege dump: "one room in a high, horrible, apartment-house in the middle of nowhere."[13] The nearby intersection of 116th and Claremont Avenue is identified on a photograph in the New York City Municipal Archives as "the windiest intersection in New York City."[14] Certainly, the howling wind couldn't have enhanced the charm of the isolated location. The apartment building that had threatened to entomb the twenty-two-year-old Fitzgerald was torn down in 1926, but if you look at period pictures of the neighborhood or at old zoning maps of New York City, you understand Fitzgerald's depression. There's nothing much going on way up there in 1919. Fitzgerald could have walked over to Riverside Park and Columbia University; he probably took the subway at 125th Street (the Interborough Rapid Transit line, or, as some called it, the Interborough Rattled Transit) to get to work. When he wasn't drinking with old Princeton buddies, Fitzgerald sat in that apartment, night after night, writing short stories that were briskly rejected by the glossy magazines proliferating at the time.[15] Generations of fledgling writers have taken heart from Fitzgerald's oft-quoted recollection of having "one hundred and twenty-two rejection slips pinned in a frieze about my room." He sold one story, "Babes in the Woods," to the *Smart Set*, the *New Yorker*–type magazine founded by George Jean Nathan and H. L. Mencken, both of whom would later become friends of Scott and Zelda. One published story, though, wasn't enough to cling to in the welter of New York City.

As his dream of becoming a writer stalled and the engagement with Zelda dimmed into less of a definite thing, Fitzgerald became less real to himself. Many years later, describing what he said were "the four most impressionable months of my life" in "My Lost City," Fitzgerald refers to himself as "ghost-like," both "hovering" and "haunted." He also reaches for his essential nightmare image: the threat of drowning. "While my friends were launching decently into life I had muscled my inadequate bark into midstream."[16] One evening, while drinking martinis at the Princeton Club (which had temporarily merged with the Yale Club near Grand Central Terminal), Fitzgerald announced that he was going to jump out the window; the preppy humanitarians sitting in the lounge urged him on, pointing out that the windows were French and thus ideally suited for jumping through. After a quick visit to Montgomery to see Zelda, Fitzgerald reported for work at the Barron Collier Agency waving a revolver.[17] Clearly, he was sinking fast. When Zelda ended the engagement in June, Scott went on a three-week bender. Then he cut his losses and escaped from New York.

In the decades I've been teaching my New York Stories course, I've come to recognize a pattern that I, as a lover of the city, don't like very much. The pattern is this: Dreamers often come to bad ends in New York stories. The city attracts those who aspire to something greater, something different; oftentimes, it destroys them. Against-the-current types like Melville's Bartleby (who "prefer[s] not to"); Wharton's Lily Bart; Johnny Nolan, the starry-eyed dad in *A Tree Grows in Brooklyn;* the unnamed narrator of Ralph Ellison's *Invisible Man;* and idealistic Holden Caulfield are just a few of the fictional characters who've been chewed up and spit out by

New York. Fitzgerald wisely escaped before the rejection slips on the walls of that crummy apartment squeezed out all light and air. Gatsby wasn't so smart. He's drawn to New York as he's drawn to Daisy, and both attractions are fatal.

New York City exerts a gravitational pull on every character in *Gatsby*. As Nick eloquently reminds us at the novel's end, everybody in this jittery story has come to the city from somewhere else: "I see now that this has been a story of the West, after all—Tom and Gatsby, Daisy and Jordan and I, were all Westerners, and perhaps we possessed some deficiency in common which made us subtly un-adaptable to Eastern life."[18] We readers observe this pull at work most powerfully—and absurdly—in the climactic chapter 7 of the novel, whose opening is a mirror image of chapter 1. Again, the main characters—with the critical addition of Gatsby this time—are assembled in the Buchanans' floaty living room. We're told it's the hottest day of the year, and Daisy, after luncheon, seems to be driven a little mad by the heat. She cries out: "What'll we do with ourselves this afternoon...and the day after that, and the next thirty years?"[19] The preposterous response to this existential question is for all of them to jump into the two available roadsters and drive into Manhattan. *Who leaves an airy mansion on the Long Island Sound to drive into Manhattan on the hottest day of the year?*

There's clearly something that New York has that the characters think they need. The city, particularly during the Roaring Twenties, enjoyed the reputation of being tough and fast—in the sense of both speed and sexuality. No wonder Daisy feels perversely compelled to urge everyone on for that last fatal round trip to Manhattan; it's appropriate that New

York—the capital of Terrible Honesty, as critic Ann Douglas calls it (borrowing the line from hard-boiled-fiction writer Raymond Chandler)—should be the place where the truth will out about the limits of Daisy's love for Gatsby. (Her awful admission to Gatsby, "Oh, you want too much!...I did love him once—but I loved you too,"[20] takes place at the Plaza Hotel, no less, where the sounds of a wedding reception wickedly filter into the hotel suite where Gatsby and Tom and Daisy argue.) New York is about personal freedom and unsentimental sex; that's why Tom and Myrtle's love nest is located, not on Long Island or, heaven forbid, in the valley of ashes, but on West 158th Street. My students are often taken aback to realize that hooking up, looking hot, and acting blasé about sex aren't fresh ideas; they're at least as old as the Jazz Age. Only Gatsby holds himself apart from this Roaring Twenties hardness and hedonism centered in the city. His courtly love–style veneration of Daisy derives from a more chivalrous time, although a modern sexual freedom is also mixed into their relationship when you remember that they're cheating on Tom and that they slept together when they first met five years earlier.

For our narrator, Nick, New York offers a more melancholy gift, what E. B. White called, in *Here Is New York,* "the gift of loneliness and the gift of privacy."[21] Although he's arrived in the city to buckle down and learn the bond business, Nick tells us that he was "restless" after the war and couldn't stay put in the "middle-west."[22] Everyone in this novel is "restless"; it's one of the ways *Gatsby* captures the atmosphere of post–World War I America. Nick also can't settle down because he's fleeing the pressure of a tacit engagement to a girl back home. No big romantic story there; he's just not that into her. The oddest thing about this entanglement is that Nick himself doesn't tell us about it; Daisy and Tom both mention that they've heard rumors about his engagement at the end of that opening dinner party. Taken together with Nick's boast at the very end of chapter 3 that "I am one of the few honest people that I have ever known,"[23] alert readers should start wondering whether Nick is completely leveling with them. But whatever Nick's moral failings, he's saved—for me, at least—by his love of New York. *The Great Gatsby* pays three radiant tributes to New York: the Queensboro Bridge passage; the ending of the novel, in which New York is conflated with America as "something commensurate to [man's] capacity for wonder"[24]; and this lightly elegiac passage in which Nick sounds like a Jazz Age Walt Whitman:

"I began to like New York, the racy, adventurous feel of it at night and the satisfaction that the constant flicker of men and women and machines gives to the restless eye....At the enchanted metropolitan twilight I felt a haunting loneliness sometimes, and felt it in others—poor young clerks who loitered in front of windows waiting till it was time for a solitary restaurant dinner—young clerks in the dusk, wasting the most poignant moments of night and life."[25]

You can imagine Fitzgerald during the isolation of his months in the city in 1919 at one with those clerks and yet feeling desperately driven to set himself apart, to not waste his "most poignant moments."

And what about our unfathomable friend Gatsby? Cities in general, and New York in particular, are where he makes his money, through the drugstores and soda fountains where his bootleg liquor is sold and in the shady bond deals he's master-minding. Gatsby always seems more at home, though, in his car or hydroplane or mansion—gleaming places and machines that he controls. New York is too messy and unpredictable for Gatsby. Take that awkward business lunch with Meyer Wolfshiem in "a well-fanned Forty-second Street cellar."[26] The lunch culminates in an unplanned encounter with Tom Buchanan; earlier, Wolfshiem had gone off script by mistakenly raising the topic of a "business gonnegtion"[27] with Nick, and Gatsby got flustered. You'd think that Gatsby is fit strictly for a gated community in suburbia except for one thing: the novel conflates Gatsby with New York City. They're both over-the-top phenomena, mysterious and beautiful and fabricated. When Nick and Gatsby drive over the Queensboro Bridge in one of the most indelible scenes from the novel, Nick tells us:

> "Anything can happen now that we've slid over this bridge," I thought; "anything at all...."
> Even Gatsby could happen, without any particular wonder.[28]

Gatsby, the visionary con man, is as much an improbability as New York City, itself both a wonder and a con.

That mention of the lunch with Wolfshiem and that drive over the Queensboro Bridge compels me to consider one of the elephants-in-the-classroom topics that frequently come up these days: Where does the novel stand on issues of immigration and race? The answer is that *Gatsby* doesn't stand in one place about anything; rather, this is a novel that jumps and ducks and shimmies. I think one big reason why Fitzgerald set

The Great Gatsby in the mixing bowl of New York is that he wanted to weigh in, albeit ambiguously, on some core American issues, and the city was the center for debates in the 1920s about foreign influences, eugenics, and racial "pollution." Post–World War I New York was reeling from the colossal wave of immigrants that had begun pouring into the city in the 1880s. Between the late 1880s and 1919, more than seventeen million immigrants to the United States entered through New York City,[29] and many of them went no further than New York. Unlike earlier immigrant groups from Northern Europe, the second wave was composed of non–English speakers, many of whom sported darker complexions: Russian and Polish Jews, Greeks, Southern Italians, Poles, Hungarians, Romanians, Bohemians, and others from Southern and Eastern Europe. Then, as now, lots of native-born Americans were nervous about what these new immigrants would do to the country. And that was in addition to the African Americans who were arriving in the city as part of the Great Migration from the South. *The Great Gatsby* is more than a little nervous about all these newcomers. *Gatsby* hears the "foreign clamor" on the streets of New York, and it's not exactly music to the novel's ears.

It's strange for me to think that in 1919, as Fitzgerald was making the rounds of those newspaper offices and dragging his heels homeward at night to that upper Upper West Side apartment, he might have passed my own pregnant grandmother Helen (or Helena) Dobosz. She was a Polish immigrant, one of that second wave, who arrived in New York alone at seventeen and worked almost all her life as a cleaning lady. Her second child, my mother, was born in 1919 in a tenement on Avenue

C, about seven weeks after Fitzgerald quit New York and hurried back home to St. Paul. To hear most of my students talk about *Gatsby*, you'd think that all of New York in the Jazz Age was drinking champagne and dancing the Charleston. *Gatsby*, however, knows better; for better or worse, it notices people like my grandmother.

That Queensboro Bridge passage anxiously surveys the folks who wouldn't have been invited as guests into Gatsby's mansion: immigrants like my grandmother as well as African Americans, even those "New Negroes" with money in their pockets and plenty of attitude. Gatsby's car glides onto one lane of the Queensboro Bridge roadway, and it's left in the dust by a funeral cortege composed of people "with the tragic eyes and short upper lips of south-eastern Europe" and a "limousine... driven by a white chauffeur, in which sat three modish Negroes, two bucks and a girl."[30] Nick laughs at the black passengers' look of "haughty rivalry" as their car speeds by Gatsby's roadster, but the novel itself isn't laughing. If you know your New York geography, you catch the ominous tone of this fast-moving scene. That the new immigrants are linked with a funeral is bad enough, but consider that those snooty African Americans pass our two white guys (Nick and Gatsby) as all the cars are specifically said to be driving over Blackwell's Island. These days, Blackwell's Island is called Roosevelt Island and it's the site of upper-middle-class apartment developments, but in Fitzgerald's day it was a sinister place—home to a prison, a charity hospital, a smallpox hospital, and the Women's Lunatic Asylum of New York City. (Intrepid stunt journalist Nellie Bly went undercover, posing as a mentally disturbed woman, to expose brutal conditions in there in 1887; Fitzgerald identified

Bly as his model for Ella Kaye, the journalist who cheats the young Jay Gatsby out of his inheritance from his mentor, Dan Cody.[31]) The fact that such a grim island lurks beneath the glorious bridge and that the faster cars carrying immigrants and black folk are allied with death and disease betrays, to put it mildly, a worry about where an increasingly diverse America was headed. In Fitzgerald's 1926 story "The Swimmers," its hero, Henry Marston, surveys the onslaught of Americans in Paris and thinks: "All that was best in the history of man must succumb at last to these invasions, as the old American culture had finally exhausted its power to absorb the bilge of Europe."[32] I suspect that in his less attractive moments, Fitzgerald regarded the non-English-speaking immigrants swirling around him as "the bilge of Europe."

Readers have to work a little to unpack the Blackwell's Island symbolism, but no heavy lifting is required with the figure of Meyer Wolfshiem. As scores of Fitzgerald scholars have pointed out, the portrait of Meyer Wolfshiem was inspired by the real-life figure of Arnold Rothstein, the New York Jewish racketeer known as "the Brain" and "the Big Bankroll" who was rumored to have fixed the 1919 World Series. Fitzgerald recalled in a 1937 letter that he'd met Rothstein, although the particulars of that meeting have been lost to history.[33] (Gatsby himself owes something to Edward M. Fuller, one of Fitzgerald's Great Neck neighbors, who had been convicted, along with his brokerage firm partner William F. McGee, of stealing their clients' money. Another model for Gatsby lurks in the career of Max Gerlach, a bootlegger, mechanic, and car dealer who had a dealership on Northern Boulevard in Flushing, Queens, near the valley of ashes. Gerlach and Fitzgerald knew each other and there's a newspaper clipping in Princeton's F. Scott Fitzgerald Papers on which Gerlach has scribbled the Gatsby-like greeting: *How are you and the family, Old Sport?* Before she died, Zelda shored up the Gatsby-Gerlach association by suggesting that Gatsby was based on "a neighbor named Von Guerlach or something who was said to be General Pershing's nephew and was in trouble over bootlegging."[34] Gatsby, ultimately, can't be confined to a historical source. Unlike Wolfshiem, he's the stuff that dreams are made of, an amalgam of many people, most of all F. Scott Fitzgerald himself. To round out the early 1920s criminal sources for Gatsby's story, Sarah Churchwell, in her recent book *Careless People*, makes a case for the sensational Hall-Mills murders as an inspiration for the homicidal finale of *Gatsby*. (In September of 1914, the bullet-riddled bodies of an Episcopal priest named Edward Wheeler Hall and his janitor's-wife mistress, Eleanor Mills, were discovered near New Brunswick, New Jersey. Their deaths were much grislier than the trio of deaths in *Gatsby:* In addition to being shot, Mills had had her throat slashed and her tongue cut out. The murders were never solved.)

Back to the disturbing figure of Wolfshiem. With Rothstein as his base, Fitzgerald proceeded to embellish. Indeed, it's as though Fitzgerald were tinkering with a Mr. Potato Head, Anti-Semitic Edition, as he constructed the figure of Wolfshiem. The first piece is the nose, which Fitzgerald describes as "flat" and "expressive," in which "two fine growths of hair... luxuriated in either nostril."[35] Next comes the heavy accent, which marks Wolfshiem as a nativist's nightmare, an unassimilated outsider no doubt risen up from the "Yiddish Quarter" of the Lower East Side. The pièce de résistance is, as I've already noted, Wolfshiem's occupation. Like Shakespeare's Shylock and Edith Wharton's villain Simon Rosedale in *The House of Mirth*, Wolfshiem is, among other things, a moneylender whose distinctive cuff buttons (as they're called in the novel) silently communicate the warning *Let the borrower beware!*

Molars may not be as gruesome as a pound of flesh, but still, they're an offensive fashion accessory. Wolfshiem seems to have become a problem for Fitzgerald as the years passed. In her lovely memoir of her twenty months working as Fitzgerald's last secretary, Frances Kroll Ring remembers that when Fitzgerald was writing *The Love of the Last Tycoon*, he wanted to avoid making the villain (Brady) Jewish:

> He said he had, on occasion, been rebuked for his portrait of...Meyer Wolfshiem in *Gatsby*. Scott was stung by the criticism which he considered unfair.... He was a gangster who happened to be Jewish. But sensitivities were running high in this period (the late 1930s) and Scott did not want to have any link with prejudice or anti-Semitism.[36]

Ring, herself a Jew, also recalls that Fitzgerald was fascinated by a Passover story she told him about how her parents kept a live carp swimming in their bathtub at home until her father clobbered it with a hammer and her mother made it into gefilte fish. "Scott shook his head in disbelief at this fish story. Then a cunning light came into his eyes as he commented that he would never have brought the fish to such a savage end. He would simply have filled the tub with gin and let the fish drink itself into oblivion."[37]

Anti-Semitic? Check. Racist? Check. Nativist? Check.

(Let's set aside *sexist* and *homophobic* for the moment.) If you want to subject *The Great Gatsby* to a political purity test, it flunks. *Gatsby* is at once timeless and time-bound, a social novel of the 1920s as much as it is a free-floating Great American Novel. But view the novel in its entirety rather than in isolated passages, and its politics get more complicated. The novel clearly relishes more than it fears the modernity and mixing of New York City. Once again, think of Nick's New York tribute that starts: "I began to like New York, the racy, adventurous feel of it at night." The mythic landscape of *Gatsby* is laid out like a compressed Candy Land game board, in which the valley of ashes rubs shoulders with the Eggs; Myrtle and Tom's love nest nestles a couple of quick spaces away from the Plaza. That kind of compressed geography is possible only in a city. The very air of the novel is redolent of diversity: the jazz tunes that waft through *Gatsby* are products of the city and of what critics have called "artistic miscegenation" between black and white musicians and composers. (Ironically, Fitzgerald himself was not that much of a jazz aficionado; all the evidence—letters and lists of recordings—point to his strong love for classical music.) And only in New York could Gatsby's parties attract such a zany collection of nouveau riche immigrants as well as theater and movie stars. Many of the early silent film companies had studios in New York and on Long Island, among them Famous Players–Lasky, which built a studio in Astoria, Queens, in 1920 and made the first (silent) film of *The Great Gatsby* in 1926. The company later became Paramount, and it made two more film versions of *Gatsby*, in 1949 and 1974. Panning the static 1974 version, *New York Times* reviewer Vincent Canby invoked *Gatsby*'s death-by-drowning anxieties when he described the film as "lifeless as a body that's been too long at the bottom of a swimming pool."[38]

The strongest argument, however, against taking *Gatsby* to task over its political incorrectness — against giving free rein to what the late British historian E. P. Thompson so eloquently termed "the enormous condescension of posterity" — comes from the most unlikely of sources: Tom Buchanan.

Tom Buchanan. My heart leaps up at the prospect of thinking about Tom! A college football player whose glory days are behind him, Tom is all meat. Nick's opening description of Tom makes him sound like a bison: "You could see a great pack of muscle shifting when his shoulder moved under his thin coat."[39] Whenever he's indoors, Tom always seems too big for his surroundings. He's always breaking things: Daisy's little finger; Myrtle's nose; ultimately, Gatsby's dream.

Tom was loosely based on a real person: polo player and war hero Tommy Hitchcock Jr., who was a fellow St. Paul Academy alum and a genuine hero of World War I. (He had left St. Paul's early to join the Lafayette Flying Corps in France. When Hitchcock was shot down and captured by the Germans, he escaped by jumping out of a train. He walked over one hundred miles by night to reach the safety of Switzerland.) Hitchcock was Fitzgerald's lifelong ideal of a man of action, so to turn him into Tom, Fitzgerald had to scoop his spirit out, retaining the heft of Hitchcock's frame but filling it with straw.

Tom possesses Hitchcock's confidence (evident in period photos), but he hasn't done anything to earn it — except be born rich. In late November of 1924, Max Perkins wrote Fitzgerald a long and detailed response to the draft of *Gatsby* that he'd received a month earlier. (Upon reading the novel through the first time, Perkins had immediately responded with a quick note that began with what were surely some of the best words F. Scott Fitzgerald had ever heard: "Dear Scott, I think the novel is a wonder."[40]) In his longer letter, Perkins put on his editor's cap and told Fitzgerald that "Gatsby is somewhat vague."[41] But Perkins prefaced his criticism of Gatsby with this comment about Tom: "I would know Tom Buchanan if I met him on the street and would avoid him." Fitzgerald clearly agreed. He wrote Perkins back from the damp hotel in Rome where he and Zelda and Scottie had holed up for a few weeks that Christmas season:

"My first instinct after your letter was to let [Gatsby] go + have Tom Buchanan dominate the book (I suppose he's the best character I've ever done—I think he and the brother in 'Salt' and Hurstwood in 'Sister Carrie' are the three best characters in American fiction in the last twenty years, perhaps and perhaps not) but Gatsby sticks in my heart."[42]

Like Max Perkins, we readers also know Tom. We've sat next to him on a plane or train. He's our retired neighbor down the street, our office mate. He's that fellow in our carpool or someone's date seated at our table during a wedding reception. Or, as in Nick's case, he's our cousin's husband. Tom is That Guy Who's Read a Book. Maybe it's *Blink* by Malcolm Gladwell or *Battle Hymn of the Tiger Mother* by Amy Chua or *The Omnivore's Dilemma* by Michael Pollan. Or maybe it's *Mein Kampf*. In Tom's case, the book is *The Rise of the Colored Empires* "by this man Goddard."[43] It's given Tom what so many people seem to want: the one theory that explains the universe. And now, whether we want to hear it or not, Tom is (like his real-life counterparts) hell-bent on explaining that theory to us.

The Rise of the Colored Empires riffs on the title of an actual bestseller, *The Rising Tide of Color Against White World-Supremacy*, by Lothrop Stoddard, which Fitzgerald's own publisher, Scribner's, brought out in 1920. Scribner's, pre-Fitzgerald, was known as a conservative publishing house, and that conservatism extended to its political leanings; Max Perkins — and the authors he brought into Scribner's — did a lot to shake things up. Fitzgerald made up the name Goddard out of a combination of Stoddard and Madison Grant, another eugenicist who wrote a popular book called *The Passing of the Great Race* in 1916. As is often the case with such boorish readers, Tom has only roughly grasped the argument of the book. (Grant talked about the disappearance of Nordics, and Stoddard, a "scientific racist," called for a eugenic separation of the races, but he was also a critic of European colonialism.) Grant's and Stoddard's — or Goddard's — argument has been brining in Tom's brain for a while, and in that first scene at the Buchanans' mansion, Nick gives Tom an opening by speaking the trigger word *civilized*. Tom erupts:

"Civilization's going to pieces," broke out Tom violently. "I've gotten to be a terrible pessimist about things. Have you read 'The Rise of the Colored Empires' by this man Goddard?"

"Why, no," I answered, rather surprised by his tone.

"Well, it's a fine book, and everybody ought to read it. The idea is if we don't look out the white race will be — will be utterly submerged. It's all scientific stuff; it's been proved."[44]

Note that in his summation of Goddard's idea, Tom fumbles for a verb and comes up with the word *submerged*. There's that drowning image again. Somebody is going to wind up being submerged in this book, but it's neither Tom nor Nick; neither Daisy nor Jordan. No, the only white guy who doesn't make it out of the water alive is Gatsby. Who knows? Given his hard-to-place original surname, Gatz, and given the fact that he's described as "tanned," Gatsby might not even be pure Aryan stock. If so, it's appropriate, in Tom's view, that he's the guy who goes under while the others survive.

But hold on: Tom is a boob! He spouts racist nonsense, and the novel rolls its eyes at him for doing so. As Tom rants on, Daisy begins mugging like a Jazz Age Lucille Ball, winking and whispering asides to Nick. Jordan tries (unsuccessfully) to interrupt Tom's monologue, which she's no doubt sat through many a time before. Nick tells us, "There was something pathetic in his concentration, as if his complacency, more acute than of old, was not enough to him any more."[45] How gently understanding that sentence is. There are cultural changes in the air that Tom's thick antennae pick up on, but he doesn't know how to respond except by digging in his riding-boot heels and shoring up his white-male supremacy by quoting fragments from probably the only book he's read since graduating Yale—with a gentleman's C, no doubt.

Because Tom's tirade is played for laughs in the very first chapter of *The Great Gatsby*, it reassures us from the outset that the novel is inclusive, even progressive, in its politics. Then we run smack into Wolfshiem and watch in dismay as those speeding carloads of immigrants and African Americans roar past

Gatsby and Nick on the Queensboro Bridge. What to think, what to think? Certainly the novel carefully notices race and ethnicity; *Gatsby*, undeniably, is worried about an America on the move, and it checks out just where these "others" are headed and how fast they're going. Fitzgerald himself was reading Oswald Spengler's *The Decline of the West* in 1924 as he was intently working on *Gatsby*, and that two-volume threnody couldn't have helped his outlook on the future of Western civilization. But, but, but...that antic automobile race—which dramatizes Goddard's and Tom's very fears—concludes on a note of anticipation, not dread. Nick thinks: "Anything can happen now that we've slid over this bridge...anything at all...."[46] Maybe the most accurate thing to say about the politics of Fitzgerald's novel is that, as a product of the early to mid-1920s, *Gatsby* doesn't know yet what's going to happen to America. The novel keeps its mind open, even if it's a conflicted one. Only Tom and his "simple mind"[47] have all the answers. One of the many breathtaking achievements of *The Great Gatsby* is that it thoroughly engages its time without being a one-dimensional political novel.

New York City was the epicenter of all these American questions about immigration and race; democracy was literally being tested on its streets. Like Paris, New York was also a mecca for writers, artists, musicians, and architects who itched to "make things new." Fitzgerald, holed up writing in his parents' rented house at 599 Summit Avenue, didn't plan to stay away very long. Fortunately, the third time round turned out to be the charm for *This Side of Paradise*. At a September editorial board meeting at Scribner's, Max Perkins bulldozed the manuscript through the unanimous nay votes. (He threatened to quit if the other board members didn't change their vetoes.) Fitzgerald was over the moon. When he received Perkins's acceptance, he ran out of his parents' house and giddily waved the letter at passing cars. A couple of days afterward, Fitzgerald wrote to a Minnesota friend named Alida Bigelow who was away at college. He heads the letter "1st Epistle of St. Scott to the Smithsonian" and then proceeds to natter nonsense rhymes until, finally, he tells her the news: "Scribner has accepted my book. Ain't I Smart!"[48] You could see how Fitzgerald, even in his happy prime, could be a high-maintenance friend.

In preparation for his debut, Fitzgerald moved back to New York City, staying first at the Murray Hill Hotel and then at the Allerton. On the actual publication day, March 26, 1920, he briefly moved to New Jersey to his spiritual home, the Cottage Club at Princeton. *This Side of Paradise* sold out its first printing of three thousand copies in only three days. The novel became a phenomenon because it was lively and risqué (couples necked, petted, and drank) and announced a new spirit of the age. On the first of April, Fitzgerald moved into the Biltmore, which, at a minimum of two dollars and fifty cents a night (European plan), rivaled the Plaza as one of the priciest hotels in the city.[49] The reason for the move was his other big day: his impending marriage to Zelda Sayre. Fitzgerald's confidence, along with his wallet newly flush with fees from his short stories (which had also broken through to publication), had convinced Zelda that Scott was her man, and their engagement had been resumed over the winter of 1919–1920. On April 3, he and Zelda were married in the vestry of St. Patrick's Cathedral. Zelda was nineteen years old; Scott was twenty-three. Curiously, neither set of parents came to the wedding, but Zelda's three older sisters, two of whom lived in New York, attended. The "Affidavit for License to Marry," which an efficient archivist unearthed for me at New York City's Municipal Archives, lists Scott's occupation as "writer" and Zelda's as "———." Both their signatures are firm and flashy, although Scott made a bit of a mess, blotting his last name. Probably he was nervous. Following the short ceremony (not even a lunch afterward, according to Zelda's aggrieved sister Rosalind), Scott and Zelda walked out of the vestry and became the toasts of the town.

When guests complained about the loud parties at the Fitzgeralds' honeymoon suite at the Biltmore, the couple moved a block south to the Commodore (also two dollars and fifty cents a night, European plan), where, pulling one of the many pranks that would make them celebrities, they spun for an hour in the revolving door, a relatively new device. Life was indeed a whirl of parties, drinking, high jinks (those infamous dips in New York City's fountains), theater outings, dancing, and more drinking. Their behavior brings to mind college kids on a prolonged spring break (they were, after all, as young as college kids, although better-looking than most). Though the conventional opinion about Zelda is that her beauty eluded the camera's eye, I think that oft-circulated 1923 photo of the Fitzgeralds on the cover of *Hearst's International* magazine is stunning. With her marcelled hair, Zelda looks like a Jazz Age golden sphinx. Zelda joked that she was wearing her "Elizabeth Arden face" for that photo, and clearly, New York had worked its sophisticated magic on this Alabama beauty. When Zelda arrived in New York for their wedding, Scott had panicked about her Southern belle costumes. Ever anxious, like Gatsby, about self-presentation, Scott prevailed upon a female friend, Marie Hersey, to help teach Zelda how to dress in a more cosmopolitan manner. Zelda hated the Jean Patou suit she bought on this first foray into New York shopping, and Scott-bashing biographers point to this incident as support for their reading of him as an overbearing control freak, but the makeover scene is a standard episode in coming–to–New York stories (especially female ones) as disparate as Mary Cantwell's *Manhattan, When I Was Young* and Patti Smith's *Just Kids*. New York has always held out the promise of fresh starts, of reinvention. By the time Zelda learned to powder on her Elizabeth Arden face, she had become the top girl of the twenties.

Nothing puts a damper on a good time like a deadline, however, and Fitzgerald had a lot of them. There were short stories to write for the high-paying glossies and a new novel to think about. (Scribner's established the pattern of publishing collections of Fitzgerald's short stories in between his novels; Fitzgerald would write approximately 160 stories during his lifetime.) Because New York was too distracting, he and Zelda moved in the summer of 1920 to an eighteenth-century farmhouse in Westport, Connecticut, near Long Island Sound. This was the first time Fitzgerald had the opportunity to take a prolonged look out over those fateful waters. Ever restless, Scott and Zelda moved back to the city in the fall, to an apartment at 38 West Fifty-Ninth Street. A trip to Europe followed. (In the Fitzgerald Papers at Princeton, there's a 1921 letter from Archbishop Dowling of St. Paul to a Monsignor O'Hearn requesting an audience with the pope for Fitzgerald. "Mr. Scott Fitzgerald...desires greatly to see our Holy Father when he visits Rome this summer." Maybe Pope Benedict XV got a whiff of Fitzgerald's published material, because the requested audience never came about.) The following October was marked by Scottie's birth, in St. Paul, Minnesota. In 1922, Fitzgerald's second novel, *The Beautiful and Damned* (the one that's always acknowledged as "the New York novel"), was serialized in *Metropolitan* magazine and then published in book form. Sales of this story about the marriage of drifting Manhattan socialites were good, topping fifty thousand copies.

At White Bear Lake in Minnesota, where the Fitzgeralds were living at the Yacht Club in the summer of 1922, Scott did some preliminary work on what would be his third novel. At this point, that third novel was envisioned as taking place in the nineteenth-century Midwest and having some kind of Catholic theme. In mid-July, he wrote a brief letter to Maxwell Perkins (still addressing him as "Mr. Perkins") about various business matters, but in the last sentence of that letter he gives Perkins—and readers—the very first intimations that *Gatsby* is materializing: "I want to write something *new*—something extraordinary and beautiful and simple + intricately patterned." Then, as though he's a bit nervous about what he's just confessed, Fitzgerald reins in this confession of ambition by signing the letter primly, "As Usual, F. Scott Fitzgerald."[50]

The only fragment left of this ghost *Gatsby* is "Absolution," a short story about a young boy and the Catholic priest on the edge of a nervous breakdown who's hearing his confession. It was published 1924 in the *American Mercury*, a magazine started that year by H. L. Mencken and George Jean Nathan. Along with "Absolution," three other stories in what critics call the *Gatsby* cluster were published in magazines in the mid-

1920s: "Winter Dreams" (*Metropolitan,* 1922), "The Sensible Thing" (*Liberty,* 1924), and "The Rich Boy" (*Redbook,* 1926). All four of these stories fixate on the act of reaching for someone or something that is just out of one's grasp. In "Absolution," the fraying priest, Father Schwartz, makes a short speech that sounds as though Fitzgerald intended it to be a warning to a young Gatsby figure. Wandering around his study, Father Schwartz approaches Rudolph Miller, the frightened eleven-year-old boy who's trying to make a confession, and asks him:

"Did you ever see an amusement park?"

"No, Father."

"Well, go and see an amusement park." The priest waved his hand vaguely. "It's a thing like a fair, only much more glittering. Go to one at night and stand a little way off from it in a dark place—under dark trees. You'll see a big wheel made of lights turning in the air, and a long slide shooting boats down into the water...."

Father Schwartz frowned as he suddenly thought of something.

"But don't get up close," he warned Rudolph, "because if you do you'll only feel the heat and the sweat and the life."

When Spanish-born artist Francis Cugat created the dust jacket for *The Great Gatsby,* he ended up enshrining that image, first invoked in "Absolution," of distant amusement-park lights. Surely this is the most famous dust jacket in the relatively short history of dust jackets. They may eventually go the way of record-album covers, but fortunately for posterity, Cugat's brief career as a dust-jacket designer coincided with the giddy beginning of art in the age of mechanical reproduction. A portrait painter and a set designer, Cugat was also the older brother of Xavier, the bandleader. Cugat was paid one hundred dollars for the *Gatsby* dust jacket, the only one he ever did. (Don C. Skemer tells me of a joke in the antiquarian book trade about the *Gatsby* first edition being a $750 book with a $150,000 dust jacket.) Maybe Cugat gave up on the dust-jacket racket because it involved too much work for too little pay. As sketches that came to light in the 1990s show us, Cugat labored over other ideas for the *Gatsby* cover. These earlier sketches are clearly inspired by the valley of ashes. At first, they seem to be in a more realistic mode, depicting a few tumbledown houses under clouds. Then you notice that the clouds have eyes and mouths.[51] At the time Cugat was invited to design the cover, he would have heard, presumably from Max Perkins, that the novel—still in progress—was called *Among the Ash Heaps and Millionaires.*

Like so much else about *The Great Gatsby*, what happened next is mysterious and contingent. At some point in August 1924, Fitzgerald, still in France, saw Cugat's dust-jacket design and went gaga for it. "For Christ's sake don't give anyone that jacket you're saving for me," he wrote to Perkins. "I've written it into the book."[52] But if Perkins mailed him one of Cugat's sketches, what image did Fitzgerald see and write into *Gatsby*? If it was the valley-of-ashes sketch with the surreal cloud creatures, then Cugat may have inspired Fitzgerald to conjure up the eyes of Dr. T. J. Eckleburg. If Fitzgerald saw the later image of a sad femme fatale face floating over a nighttime

The original book jacket for The Great Gatsby: *"Celestial Eyes" by Francis Cugat.* (PRINCETON UNIVERSITY LIBRARY)

cityscape ablaze with amusement-park lights, it seems the likely source of Nick's allusion to Daisy as a "girl whose disembodied face floated among dark cornices and blinding signs."[53] Like so many other questions about *The Great Gatsby,* this one about the long-distance "collaboration" between artist and writer is impossible to answer unless some lost correspondence between Perkins and Fitzgerald comes to light. I do know this for certain: Francis Cugat, who may have only *heard* about *Gatsby* from Max Perkins, was one of the sharpest early readers of the novel. Fitzgerald said of the assessments of *Gatsby,* "Of all the reviews, even the most enthusiastic, not one has the slightest idea what the book was about."[54] In Cugat, however, Fitzgerald had the extraordinary luck to be matched with an illustrator—an artist—who got that the book was about reaching out, aspiring, for a mirage.

Like everyone who's read and reread *The Great Gatsby* in the standard Scribner's paperback edition, I've looked at Cugat's cover so often that it's one of those overly familiar images, like the American flag or the Eiffel Tower, that you no longer really see. But my vision was restored by a close encounter with the real thing. In late summer of 2013, an art curator at the Firestone Library at Princeton wheeled the framed poster-size gouache painting that Cugat called *Celestial Eyes* into the rare-book room. The real painting is even more abstract than paperback reproductions suggest: there are lots of yellow flares and letters of the alphabet—*s*'s and *p*'s and *f*'s—floating around the deep blue night sky; many minor Ferris wheels swirl in the foreground and many shadowy tenement buildings loom in the background. But above all, what hit me was that Cugat nailed the sense of longing that infuses *Gatsby*. Those brooding eyes with the nudes swimming in their irises will forever hover in the distance. That beautiful woman can't be grasped; she'd dissolve through your fingers if you tried. These are not the heavenly eyes of God; they're the celestial eyes of a pagan deity who floats above a secular "bright lights, big city" world.

After about twenty minutes of close study of Cugat's painting, I tried to turn my attention to the archival box of Fitzgerald's letters that was on the library table. My eyes kept drifting back to the painting. I finally had to ask for *Celestial*

Eyes to be removed from the room. It's impossible to ignore. (Hemingway seems to be the lone dissenter in his opinion of Cugat's dust jacket; in *A Moveable Feast*, he describes it as "garish" and says, "It looked like the book jacket for a book of bad science fiction."[55])

Like *The Great Gatsby* itself, Cugat's painting was almost literally tossed into the dustbin of history...or, more precisely, into Scribner's trash can. Charles Scribner III later donated the painting to Princeton. (Scribner is a member of the class of 1973.) He was able to do so because his cousin George Schieffelin fished *Celestial Eyes* out of a container of publishing "dead matter" in the Scribner's building and took it home. The painting was passed on to family members until it came safely to rest, with the Scribner's archive, at Princeton.[56]

There's no way Cugat could have known that Zelda Fitzgerald, herself an embodiment of the "eternal feminine" of his painting, seems to have been an enthusiast of carnivals and amusement parks. Novelist John Dos Passos wrote about his adventure of riding in a Ferris wheel with an exhilarated Zelda. Dos Passos's recollection is intriguing, not only because it's so harsh but because of the practical reason why he and Zelda were thrown together in the first place. It was September of 1922, and the Fitzgeralds had left baby Scottie with family back in St. Paul to hunt for a house to rent outside New York City. (Preparing to move back to the city from St. Paul, Fitzgerald wrote to Max Perkins: "I never knew how I yearned for New York."[57]) On the day Dos Passos joined the Fitzgeralds, they all drove out to Great Neck, Long Island, where they called on a drunken Ring Lardner. On the drive back, Zelda insisted that they stop at an amusement park. Scott stayed in the car, sulking and drinking, while Zelda and Dos Passos went on the ride. Dos Passos later wrote:

> The gulf that opened between Zelda and me, sitting up on that rickety Ferris wheel, was something I couldn't explain. It was only looking back at it years later that it occurred to me that, even the first day we knew each other, I had come up against that basic fissure in her mental processes that was to have such tragic consequences. Though she was so very lovely I had come upon something that frightened and repelled me, even physically.[58]

Talk about the dangers of getting up too close. Anyone who's read "Absolution" will hear Father Schwartz's warning echoing between the lines of Dos Passos's sad little story.

Dos Passos doesn't seem to have been along for the ride the day the Fitzgeralds found their rental house, 6 Gateway Drive in Great Neck, which Zelda described as a "nifty little Babbit-home."[59] Like so many of the homes and apartments associated with the Fitzgeralds, it looks like a nondescript dwelling in period photos. Built in 1918, the small house with a red-tiled roof and cream-colored walls still stands, and over the decades, it's been enlarged and beautifully upgraded. The Fitzgeralds rented it for three hundred a month[60]; its sale price today is in the millions, but none of the online realty sites that routinely list property information mention the fact that F. Scott Fitzgerald began sketching out *The Great Gatsby* there, in the summer of 1923, in a "large bare room" over the garage outfitted with "pencil, paper and oil stove."[61]

As biographer Matthew J. Bruccoli details, "that slender

riotous island"[62] that the Fitzgeralds found themselves living on provided plenty of raw material for the book. In 1938, Fitzgerald recalled the mostly New York– and Long Island–based sources for *Gatsby*'s chapters in a list he scribbled on the endpaper of his copy of André Malraux's newly published book about the Spanish Civil War, *Man's Hope:*

> I. Glamour of Rumsies + Hitchcoks
> II. Ash Heaps. Memory of 25th. Gt Neck
> III. Goddards. Dwanns Swopes.
> IV. A. Vegetable Days in N. Y.
>   B. Memory of Ginevras Wedding
> V. The meeting all an invention. Mary
> VI. Bob Kerr's story. The 2nd. Party.
> VII. The Day in New York
> VIII. The murder (inv.)
> IX. Funeral an invention[63]

Determined to lay off the booze, Fitzgerald fueled himself with pots of coffee and cranked out a lot of stories in the late winter of 1923 and early spring of 1924 in order to gain uninterrupted time to write his next novel. Most of those stories are forgettable, the exception being "The Sensible Thing," one of the *Gatsby*-cluster tales that deal with Fitzgerald's signature theme: the attempt to recapture a lost vision of happiness. "The Sensible Thing" draws much from Fitzgerald's miserable months in New York City in 1919. In it, failed architect turned insurance salesman George O' Kelly lives on 137th Street in a one-room sublet. George is in love with a fickle Tennessee belle named Jonquil Cary, and the story hinges on the question of her faithfulness to

George. While he was furiously generating (lesser) short stories for cash, Fitzgerald, as always, was reading. Great Neck is where, probably upon Lardner's recommendation, Fitzgerald plunged into Dostoevsky's *The Brothers Karamazov* and Dickens's *Bleak House* (the latter became his favorite Dickens novel).[64] Other works of literature that to some degree affected the alchemical composition of *Gatsby* were Joseph Conrad's *The Nigger of the Narcissus* (to which critics credit the invention of Nick Carraway as a partially involved narrator) and the works of Willa Cather, particularly, as Fitzgerald respectfully told her in a letter written in late March or early April of 1925, the novels *My Antonia* and *A Lost Lady* and the short stories "Paul's Case" and "Scandal." That letter was resurrected in the *New Yorker* in the wake of the Baz Luhrmann–generated *Gatsby* frenzy of May 2013; in it, Fitzgerald confesses to a case of "apparent plagiarism" in describing Daisy's allure in terms similar to those that Cather used for the love object in *A Lost Lady*. Cather, whom Fitzgerald idolized, was gracious about the apparent plagiarism (Fitzgerald told her he had written his Daisy passage before he read *A Lost Lady*). I'd nominate Cather's odd story "Paul's Case," published in *McClure's Magazine* in 1905, as an even more potent if more diffuse influence on *The Great Gatsby*. The tale of a sensitive boy from Pittsburgh who craves beauty and the finer things, "Paul's Case" follows the brief ascent (through crime) of the main character, who succeeds in winning himself a few precious days of luxury at the Waldorf hotel in Manhattan before he dies. Cather anticipates the yearning and the tragic arc of another poor boy, James Gatz from South Dakota, reaching out for his own version of the green light.

Fitzgerald was working hard and trying to cut back on his

drinking because he felt scared. All artists are insecure; their reputations are at the mercy of their last books, or plays, or paintings, or films. *Can I pull it off again?* After *This Side of Paradise* set the standard so high, Fitzgerald was privately tormented by that question in the early 1920s. By the early 1930s, his torment was dramatized in public. Fitzgerald was struggling with *Tender Is the Night* and had already abandoned a couple of novels, including one whose subject was matricide. (One novel in progress that did see the light of publication— and shouldn't have—was Fitzgerald's medieval romance *Philippe, Count of Darkness*. Amateur historian Fitzgerald aimed to explore the beginnings of the feudal system through the exploits of a swashbuckling hero modeled on Hemingway. *Redbook* began serializing this disaster in October 1934. The headnote for the second installment reads like an *Onion* spoof: "The brilliant thought quality and style of the creator of *The Great Gatsby* are very much in evidence in this majestic story of 819 A.D."[65] *Philippe, Count of Darkness* bit the dust after installment three, although a fourth installment was posthumously printed in November 1941, no doubt because Fitzgerald's recent death had made the creaky tale a curiosity.)

In 1923, Fitzgerald's self-doubts were already congealing. His big effort of the past year, a play called *The Vegetable*, debuted and expired in Atlantic City in November of 1923. (Zelda reported to a friend that "in brief, the show flopped as flat as one of Aunt Jemimas famous pancakes."[66]) Under the sway of his friend H. L. Mencken, Fitzgerald had ventured into what was for him the foreign territory of political satire. *The Vegetable* tells the story of an ordinary man who wants to be president but can't even make it as a postman. Its subject is outize American ambition. *The Vegetable* played this subject for laughs; *The Great Gatsby* would treat the same subject with reverence.

So from the late winter of 1923 through the early spring of 1924, Fitzgerald sat at his desk in that chill room over the garage on 6 Gateway Drive, challenging himself to make something magical. One of *The Great Gatsby*'s most repeated words is *unutterable*; alone in his writing studio, Fitzgerald may have wondered if he could find the words for his own unutterable visions. Writing to Perkins (by now "Dear Max") in a crucial letter dated April 10, 1924—exactly a year to the day before *The Great Gatsby* would be published—Fitzgerald apologizes for the slow progress he's making on his new novel, especially because he's thrown out much of what he wrote the previous summer. He says he hopes to have the novel done by June, but then backtracks: "And even [if] it takes me 10 times that long I cannot let it go out unless it has the very best I'm capable of in it or even as I feel sometimes, much better than I'm capable of."[67] Fitzgerald, as was his way, then lambastes himself for all his bad habits—among them "drinking," "raising hell generally," "laziness," "Referring everything to Zelda," and "word consciousness—self doubt." Toward the end of the letter, he swings back to self-confidence, then returns to self-loathing, then back, finally, to nervous self-affirmation:

> I feel I have an enormous power in me now, more than I've ever had in a way but it works so fitfully and with so many bogeys because I've *talked so much* and not lived enough within myself to delelop [*sic*] the necessary self reliance....In my new novel I'm thrown directly on

purely creative work—not trashy imaginings as in my stories but the sustained imagination of a sincere and yet radiant world. So I tread slowly and carefully + at times in considerable distress. This book will be a consciously artistic achievement + must depend on that as the 1st books did not....

Please believe me when I say that now I'm doing the best I can.[68]

I don't see how anyone who reads Fitzgerald's letters and the biographies (even the ones written by Zelda partisans) can possibly come away without feeling two things: first, some contempt for Hemingway (the man, not his work), and, second, a deep respect for Maxwell Perkins (the man *and* his work). As A. Scott Berg showed in his magnificent 1978 biography *Max Perkins: Editor of Genius*, Perkins was a literary visionary, graced with extraordinary reserves of patience and generosity toward even the neediest and most erratic writers under his wing. Surely, there must have been times when Fitzgerald—who used Perkins as a therapist and a banker as well as an editor—just plain wore him out.

If the writing room where Fitzgerald chopped and reconceived his earliest version of *The Great Gatsby* was spare, the views of nearby Manhasset Bay were to die for. On summer nights, Scott and Ring Lardner could sit outside the Lardner house on 325 East Shore Road and look across the dark water or over at the blazing parties under way at the neighboring mansion of *New York World* publisher Herbert Bayard Swope, who happened to be friends with gangster Arnold Rothstein. Here's how Ring Lardner Jr., around eight years old at the time, later mapped out the geography and the atmosphere of that charmed period:

"There was a porch on the side of our house facing the Swopes' and Ring and Scott sat there many a weekend afternoon drinking ale or whiskey and watching what Ring described as an almost continuous house-party next door."

The location of the Swopes' house was just right for the view of Daisy's pier across the bay.[69]

Besides Lardner, other neighbors were New York show-business types like Ed Wynn, Eddie Cantor, and Groucho Marx. (Jews were allowed to rent and buy homes in Great Neck, one of the only Gold Coast towns to have such progressive real estate policies.) Fitzgerald rubbed shoulders at parties out in Great Neck with theatrical and artistic types like Gloria Swanson, Marc Connelly, Dorothy Parker, and Rube Goldberg; after all, as we readers know from *Gatsby*, Great Neck was an easy commute to the bright lights of the city. On a good evening, a roadster could cruise straight down Route 25 (Northern Boulevard), through Corona (the valley of ashes), Astoria, and Long Island City, over the Queensboro Bridge, and onto Broadway in about an hour. Fitzgerald was a notoriously slow and bad driver. New York City traffic pamphlets of the time put the speed limit on Northern Boulevard at forty miles an hour, so it probably would have taken him longer to make the commute.[70]

My family made that commute—in reverse—most weekends when I was growing up in the 1960s. On those weekend rides "out to Long Island," we never veered over to Port Washington or Great Neck proper. When we rode out on Northern Boulevard, we passed the shops that lined Manhasset's Gold

A map of Great Neck from The New Yorker, *1927.* (JOHN HELD JR., THE NEW YORKER MAGAZINE, 1927, REPRINTED COURTESY OF CONDÉ NAST)

Coast, but we rarely stopped. We were in search of cheaper entertainments: a dose of history (Teddy Roosevelt's Sagamore Hill) or dinner at Howard Johnson's or, in the summer, a swim at Oak Beach. We sometimes did go off the beaten path on "literary" field trips (Washington Irving's home, Sunnyside, in the Hudson Valley was a favorite), but though my dad was a great reader, I don't remember him ever mentioning *Gatsby* or any of Fitzgerald's other books. Born in 1920, my father was too young for Fitzgerald's "first flowering"; by the time the revival gathered force, my dad's love of serious literature was mostly nostalgic and he was reaching for World War II adventure stories and thrillers. So, though I'd passed within miles of it on those childhood weekend rides, I'd actually never laid eyes on Fitzgerald's "courtesy bay." That's how it came to be that in 2013, my husband, my fourteen-year-old daughter, and I took a Father's Day weekend road trip up from Washington, DC, out to Long Island for what turned out to be an amiable floating tourist trap billed as the *Great Gatsby* Boat Tour.

"Ahoy!" calls out a young woman (already buzzed?) as she and the rest of what seems to be a wedding party clamber aboard the small vessel—think the *Minnow* of *Gilligan's Island* fame—that's going to carry us out on the waters between East Egg and West Egg and into Long Island Sound. Rich, Molly, and I have already staked out our spots on the bench that runs around the inside of the boat and are eyeing our fellow passengers filling the spaces. There's a woman beautifully dressed in full 1920s regalia: a tan-and-black flapper dress, cloche hat, and long ivory-bead necklace. She's reluctantly followed by Olive, a gray and white standard poodle who's being tugged aboard by her human. Meanwhile, the wedding party is getting louder; they're mugging for cell-phone selfies and shouting witticisms like "Hello, old sport!" Wine bottles are being unscrewed as the boat's engines rev up. A young dude on the starboard side is busy dissing both Fitzgerald and Hemingway to the woman sitting next to him. "What's the takeaway?" he asks her, in reference to *The Sun Also Rises*. As the dock recedes to the point of No Exit, I'm not thinking about either Fitzgerald or Hemingway; I'm thinking about Sartre and the apt remark from that play: "Hell is other people."

Our guide is a cheery middle-aged woman who tells us that she lives in the area and got the idea for this "floating" walking tour of *Great Gatsby* sites when she lost her job in the publishing industry. She also tells us she took Baz Luhrmann and his wife, costume designer Catherine Martin, out on Manhasset Bay to tour the Eggs in 2008 in preparation for Luhrmann's *Gatsby* film. Despite these credentials, she's relying heavily on notecards to give the bare bones of Fitzgerald's biography. One thing our guide mentions endears her to me: she says she didn't get *Gatsby* the first time she read it, but now, every time she rereads it, she wishes it were longer.

Whatever. Hardly anyone on the boat is listening. It's a beautiful bright summer's day out on the water and almost everyone else is leaning back, drinking whatever alcohol they've brought with them, and enjoying the view of wretched excess that the waterside mansions of Great Neck (West Egg) and Manhasset (East Egg) continue to provide. We gaze at a pretty white colonial mansion that we're told Groucho once rented and that's now owned by Bill O'Reilly. (Molly, an ardent Rachel Maddow fan, snorts loudly.) Our attention is directed to Sid Caesar's relatively modest rambler and then we gawk at what was, long ago, publisher Jock Whitney's timbered lodge, now updated and preposterously enlarged: this thing could accommodate every reader who bought a copy of *Gatsby* in 1925. Our guide informs us that she's heard rumors that actor Adam Sandler bought the place for his parents. I smile, thinking of the wild rumors that swirled around Gatsby. The rich and their doings out on this spit of land are still generating gossip.

As the boat heads out into Long Island Sound, we pass a boarded-up house on the very tip of West Egg—a spot that enjoys simultaneous views of the Manhattan skyline and an East Egg castle across the bay, which the first mate tells me belongs to the guy who owns the Arizona Beverage Company. (An iced-tea salesman in East Egg; Tom Buchanan would be disgusted.) But it's the boarded-up house that should give anyone who's read *Gatsby* a moment's pause. Our guide tells us that a murder was committed in the house, and for legal reasons, it can't be sold. A murder house in what looks to me to be the location of Gatsby's fictional house? C'mon. It's only the fact that this boat tour is so blasé about making any connections whatsoever to *Gatsby* that leads me to believe in this eerie correspondence.

After spending the first fifteen minutes of the tour fumbling with notecards and hazy facts ("Fitzgerald was born in...I want to say, Minnesota?"), our guide commands those few of us still tuning in to "enjoy!" and totters off to join the flapper and her escort, who've just popped open a bottle of champagne. Rich, Molly, and I exchange shrugs; for this we got up at dawn and drove seven hours? Across the deck, Olive has put her head between her paws, and one of the wedding party appears to be seasick. The facial expressions of the seasick woman and Olive the poodle mirror each other.

I try to breathe deep and accept my powerlessness as recommended by the online daily meditation program I sporadically log on to. At least I've finally seen the Eggs. As a spatially challenged person, I'm always trying to figure out where West and East Eggs are in relation to Manhattan, and I still sometimes stumble in classroom lectures. Overall, though, this excursion reaffirms my armchair-traveler inclinations. (I've been mentally drawing lines through my bucket list of literary sites — ~~Haworth Parsonage, Jane Austen's Bath~~ — as we sail around the Eggs.) Fitzgerald's language creates the fantasy of Gatsby's Long Island; even if I could take a time machine back, I'd probably be disappointed. Though I'd still like a summer's night swigging gin gimlets with Ring and Scott on Ring Lardner's porch.

Earlier in the tour, when we sailed by the narrow inlet that separates West Egg and East Egg, the guide pointed out a business park dominated by a boxy utilitarian building and told us that was the spot where Lardner's house once stood. Swope's mansion is also gone, the place that hosted the likes of George Gershwin, Robert Moses, the Vanderbilts, Irving Berlin, and the Marx Brothers. (Bill O'Reilly and the rumored presence of Adam Sandler's parents are indisputably a comedown.) As our little boat pulls into the dock, I decide to ask the guide if it's possible to see the outside of 6 Gateway Drive. I know the place still stands because I've seen real estate photos: it's a Mediterranean-style stuccoed house that, given its crucial role in American literary history, deserves a marker. (According to

Fitzgerald scholar Ruth Prigozy—who tried to get such a marker placed—there's a rule that allows only one historic-house marker per author.[71]) Given that my expectations have plummeted during the past ninety minutes, I'm surprised by the guide's practical knowledge of the house and the surrounding property. She tells me that a Rite Aid drugstore now abuts the property. If we approach 6 Gateway Drive through the Rite Aid parking lot, we can take some pictures of the house "before the police arrive." I look at Rich and Molly. Then, as one, we thank the guide, step onshore, and walk off toward an ice cream parlor we spotted earlier. Some places are best to dream of, not visit.

The great *New Yorker* writer A. J. Liebling said of New York City that its "geography was [its] destiny," meaning that from its early New Amsterdam days, the city, situated at the top of a grand natural harbor where two rivers met, could not avoid its happy fate as a commercial center. For *The Great Gatsby* as well, geography was destiny: Great Neck provided Fitzgerald with a perfect landscape in which to make Gatsby's transcendent longing materialize. Before the Fitzgeralds resolved, once more, to economize—this time by relocating to Europe in early May of 1924 (going by way of a ship that was "dry," Bruccoli points out, to underscore Fitzgerald's dedication to his writing regimen)—Scott soaked up New York City and environs. Neither he nor Zelda ever lived in New York again: they bounced between Europe and America a few times over the next seven years, in 1928 renting a grand house called Ellerslie in Delaware for six months and then returning to France. By September 1931, when the three Fitzgeralds came back to the

United States for good, Zelda had suffered her first break-down and institutionalizations. On the very last page of one of their family photo albums, there's a crooked black-and-white snapshot of the Empire State Building, which had officially opened three months earlier. On each side of the photo, Scott or Zelda or Scottie has printed in block capital letters: HOME AGAIN.

New York City was Scott and Zelda's best home. Their sojourn there was bound up with the first happy years of their marriage, the Jazz Age, and Scott's early success. *The Great Gatsby* is sprinkled with fleeting insider references to locales and haunts (the "poolroom on 43rd" where Wolfshiem and

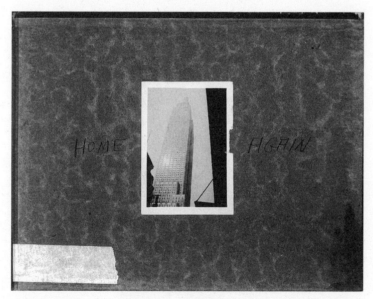

A photograph of the Empire State Building from Fitzgerald's personal album, inscribed with the words "Home Again." (MATTHEW J. & ARLYN BRUC-COLI COLLECTION OF F. SCOTT FITZGERALD, UNIVERSITY OF SOUTH CAROLINA LIBRARIES)

Gatsby first met; those cool "big movie houses on 50th"; "the old Metropole") that attest to the fact that, during his time in New York, Fitzgerald—like Poe and Whitman; like Alfred Kazin and Joan Didion—became "a walker in the city." *Gatsby* is so much a product of New York that on the day it was published, Fitzgerald was prompted by a tone-deaf comment made by one of his uncles to add this postscript to a nervous letter to Max Perkins:

> I had, or rather saw, a letter from my uncle who had seen a preliminary announcement of the book. He said:
> "it sounded as if it were very much like his others."
> This is only a vague impression, of course, but I wondered if we could think of some way to advertise [*The Great Gatsby*] so that people who are perhaps weary of assertive jazz and society novels might not dismiss it as "just another book like his others." I confess that today the problem baffles me—all I can think of is to say in general to avoid such phrases as "a picture of New York life" or "modern society"—though as that is exactly what the book is its [*sic*] hard to avoid them.[72]

3

Rhapsody in Noir

I love that, as that clueless letter from his uncle shows, even F. Scott Fitzgerald had to suffer family members who didn't get what he was doing. I also love that Fitzgerald acknowledges to Perkins that *Gatsby* is a modern New York story. But I don't think Fitzgerald was just talking about geography when he writes that *Gatsby* is "a picture of New York life." He's saying something about the mood and the form of the novel— qualities that the New York City of the 1920s specifically gave him. He's pointing to something contemporary about *Gatsby*'s shadowy atmosphere of criminals, bootleggers, and violence. I also think, to use a word Fitzgerald himself used in reference to his novel, that he's referring to *Gatsby*'s *intricate* structure: its compressed sense of time and hyperawareness of deadlines; its voice-over style of narration and its deliberately tangled story lines. Fitzgerald wouldn't have applied the term *noir* to these aforementioned elements in *Gatsby*; *noir* didn't emerge as a term for a certain kind of dark film until after World War II. Fitzgerald, however, did toss around the distinctively Jazz Age term *hard-boiled*. I'm convinced that, in referring to *The Great Gatsby* as a modern New York novel, Fitzgerald is also saying that there's something hard-boiled about it, an aspect to his poetic masterpiece that derives from the very same urban American sources that inspired the gals-guts-and-guns school of fiction that evolved into the pulp magazines of the early to mid-1920s.

The Great Gatsby as a near relation of the hard-boiled novel? Jay Gatsby as an "associate" of such tough guys as Three Gun Kerry and Race Williams? Those readers who segregate literary categories the way Tom Buchanan segregates races will find this suggestion preposterous, even offensive. But as critic Alfred Kazin pointed out in his landmark collection of critical essays on Fitzgerald published in 1951, Fitzgerald "constantly crossed and recrossed the border line between highbrow and popular literature."[1] There's plenty of incriminating evidence of significant "gonnegtions" between the hard-boiled school and *The Great Gatsby*. Think, first of all, about our hero's name: Jay *Gat*sby. A *gat* is twenties slang for a gun. Certainly, Gatsby must have been packing, at least in the early years of his rise in Meyer Wolfshiem's employ. Chew on the coincidence that the premier pulp magazine of the 1920s and 1930s was *The Black Mask,* founded by Fitzgerald's good friends H. L. Mencken and George Jean Nathan in 1920 as a popular venture that would support their "classier" literary publication, the *Smart Set*. (Mencken and Nathan also founded two soft-core "naughty" magazines to generate income: *Saucy Stories* and *Parisienne*.) Also take into account that Fitzgerald was on very cozy terms with the word *hard-boiled*. In 1934, in a preface to the Modern Library edition of *The Great Gatsby,* he called himself "a hard-boiled professional." And, most suggestively, the word *hard-boiled* appears in the very first chapter of *Gatsby*. Take another look at Nick Carraway's introduction in chapter 1. As Nick is presenting his family tree for our inspection, he mentions a great-uncle who founded his family's line in America and made a fortune: "I never saw this great-uncle but I'm supposed to look like him—with special reference to the rather hard-boiled painting that hangs in Father's office."[2]

Nick's use of the word *hard-boiled* is fairly new; *hard-boiled* was a term coined by soldiers during World War I to refer to particularly tough drill sergeants. Fitzgerald may well have heard the word—or used it himself—during his sojourns in all those army training camps. Before World War I, the term variously meant "practical," "stingy," and "tough to beat," as in a hard-boiled egg. Nick's comment that his uncle's portrait is hard-boiled could invoke all those meanings. *Hard-boiled* in the specific sense of "practical" and "tough" is an adjective that also applies to Nick himself. Though we tend to think of Nick as a Gatsby double, he's much less sentimental, especially in his treatment of women. He breaks up, long distance, with that fiancée back home, and casually dumps the office girl he has a fling with during his New York summer. He's especially efficient in his treatment of Jordan Baker: "You threw me over on the telephone," Jordan says. "I don't give a damn about you now but it was a new experience for me and I felt a little dizzy for a while."[3] At the close of the novel, our Nick is even tough enough to shake Tom Buchanan's hand—the hand of the man who fingered Gatsby to his murderer, George Wilson. As critics and scholars unanimously affirm, one of the extraordinary advances that Fitzgerald made in *Gatsby* was his decision to have the main character's tale told from the outside by an observant narrator. That inside-outside perspective preserves the central air of mystery that surrounds Gatsby (we're never completely clear on what he's done to make his money), but it also provides us readers with two radically different sensibilities: Gatsby's idealistic reading of romantic love and American possibility versus Nick's relatively more practical, more hard-boiled grounding.

Some of the contemporary reviewers of *The Great Gatsby* zeroed in on its hard-boiled elements, which by now are mostly buried under fossilized layers of Great Books–type reverential criticism. Fanny Butcher, reviewing the novel for the *Chicago Daily Tribune* on April 18, 1925, was generally enthusiastic, although she granted that "it is bizarre. It is melodramatic. It is, at moments, dime novelish."[4] Reviewer Baird Leonard, writing in the April 30, 1925, issue of *Life*, summarized *Gatsby* as though it were a short story written by Damon Runyon:

> It is the story of a super-four-flusher whose parties at his Long Island place were attended by thousands and whose untimely coffin was followed by two....When you get through with the story, you feel as if you'd been some place where you had a good time, but now entertain grave doubts as to the quality of the synthetic gin.[5]

The notice for *The Great Gatsby* that Scribner's placed in the April 4 issue of *Publishers' Weekly* lures potential readers with promises of both hard-boiled intrigue and romance. The copy reads: "The story of Jay Gatsby, who came so mysteriously to West Egg, of his sumptuous entertainments and of his love for Daisy Buchanan."[6]

All that for just two dollars! The *Gatsby* announcement, by the way, is wedged between notices for one of Putnam's spring titles, *The Women of the Caesars* (which was translated by Fitzgerald's Princeton mentor Christian Gauss), and Abraham Flexner's *Medical Education: A Comparative Study*. In that same issue of *Publishers' Weekly*, splashy advertisements sing the praises of *The Constant Nymph*, a romance by Margaret Kennedy, and Edna Ferber's *So Big*, which won the Pulitzer Prize for the Novel in 1925.

The titles of two of the first European translations of *The Great Gatsby*—one, in Norwegian, *The Yellow Car*; the other, in Swedish, *A Man Without Scruples*—invite readers to expect a suspense tale. In his own lifetime, Fitzgerald sparked much less interest from foreign readers and reviewers than either Hemingway or Faulkner. Fitzgerald, culturally speaking, didn't seem to translate well; judging by the reviews he did get, Fitzgerald was regarded as "too American" in an overeager and superficial way. Other marks against Fitzgerald, according to European critics, were that his writing lacked intellectual content and, during the 1930s, a leftist political point of view. Typical of this kind of Old World patronizing attitude toward Fitzgerald was V. S. Pritchett's sniffy retrospective comment in 1951 that Fitzgerald "was not a thinker but was simply impressionable."[7]

The British firm William Collins, Sons published *This Side of Paradise, The Beautiful and Damned,* and Fitzgerald's short-story collections. William Collins himself, however, turned down *The Great Gatsby,* claiming that "the British public would not make head nor tail of it."[8] His prediction was borne out a year later when Chatto and Windus published the novel and it made "no stir at all."[9] *Gatsby* received only six reviews from the British press, as opposed to sixteen for *Tales of the Jazz Age*.[10] *Gatsby*'s first appearance on the Continent was in France in 1926: Victor Llona did the translation (universally regarded as dreadful) for Kra's Collection Européenne. Fitzgerald himself paid the translator's fee, and sales were poor. Only half of the first printing of eight thousand copies were sold. Curiously, Norway and Sweden—these days, literary centers of the hard-boiled mystery novel—were the only other foreign countries to translate *The Great Gatsby* when it was first written. The titles of those two translations are the ones that suggest a fascination with the hard-boiled elements in the novel.

I'm jumping ahead a couple of decades, but now seems like the right moment to bring up my favorite film version of *The Great Gatsby* made in 1949, directed by Elliott Nugent, and starring Betty Field as Daisy and Alan Ladd as Gatsby. This version of Gatsby reads the novel as an underworld crime saga and the movie itself is noir in terms of its sensibility if not, strictly speaking, its camera techniques. So as not to rile the film scholars, I'd call it noir-*ish*. These days—thanks to the renewed interest in *Gatsby* films stirred up by Baz Luhrmann— you can download the 1949 film from the Internet. By happy necessity, in the summer of 2012, I had the thrill of watching it the old-fashioned way, on a reel-to-reel projector, in a dim basement screening room of the Library of Congress.

In the film's very first shot of Alan Ladd as Gatsby, he's leaning out of a speeding black roadster and machine-gunning down some rivals in the bootlegging business. (This scene immediately follows the bizarre "prologue" to the movie where a now-married Nick and Jordan stand over Gatsby's grave and spout a 1940s-era regretful tribute to the 1920s: A redeemed Jordan, played by the dark-haired character actress Ruth Hussey, begins the sermon, and Nick soon joins in: "It seems like another world, Flaming youth...The speakeasy...Prohibition...rum runners...the gang wars.") Ladd is pretty good as Gatsby: he's handsome and vacant enough, which seem to me to be two qualities essential to Gatsby the cipher. By 1949, Ladd was a huge star, known for doing elegant turns on the tough-guy role in films such as *This Gun for Hire*, *The Glass Key*, and *The Blue Dahlia* (stories by mystery masters Graham Greene, Dashiell Hammett, and Raymond Chandler, respectively). In one of those big, exotic party scenes that every *Gatsby* director clearly loves to film, we're treated to Indians in feathered headdresses, women on horseback trotting through Gatsby's mansion, and other guests strolling around in saris and turbans. During that scene, Ladd's Gatsby slugs a guest who fingers him as Gatz. There are lots of smart touches in this 1949 *Gatsby*—including a very young and very hysterical Shelley Winters as Myrtle (a role she was born to play), a Wolf-shiem wittily renamed Lupus, an Owl Eyes who quotes Keats's femme fatale poem "La Belle Dame Sans Merci," and a steaming valley-of-ashes set that looks like it was designed by Samuel Beckett.

Two elements, however, deserve special attention in this prolonged glance at the noir-ish *Gatsby*. First, this *Gatsby* film obsesses about Dan Cody, a character who's largely ignored in the other extant film versions and in most discussions—scholarly or popular—of the novel. In the Ladd film, the camera lingers on the water with a young Gatsby aboard Dan Cody's yacht. Cody, played by Henry Hull, looks and sounds like Mephistopheles. He's forever spouting every-man-for-himself business aphorisms: "If a smart man sees anybody ahead of him, he just moves in anyway"; "You got money, you just take." Capitalism here is thus equated with selfishness and thuggish behavior, especially striking given that *Gatsby* is often misread as an endorsement of the philosophy that greed is good. Cody is creepy, but even more intriguing is that all the dames in this film—at least in their first appearances—are femmes fatales. When Cody dies and Ella Kaye gains control of his fortune, she threatens Ladd's Gatsby: "Don't forget, I'm at the wheel now."

At the end of the film, right before he's shot in his Greco-Roman-style pool, Ladd's Gatsby, supine in a terrific tight-fitting bathing suit, makes a hard-boiled redemption speech to Nick, played competently enough by Macdonald Carey. Ladd's Gatsby says: "I'm through four flushing, trying to be something I'm not, a gentleman.... I was a sucker.... I'm going to pay up, Nick." The death scene is the other striking element in this film because it dwells obsessively on Gatsby's final throes in the pool. (This film overall is a very damp version of *Gatsby;* for example, in the rainy reunion scene between Gatsby and Daisy at Nick's house, Jordan jokes, "Anyone got a rowboat handy?") Ladd's Gatsby is shot, swims, tries to pull himself up, and then is shot two more times before he goes under. His death by drowning is drawn out and intense. At the eleventh hour, though, this version of *Gatsby* steps back from the black pit of noir despair and scurries to save its sinners: Daisy insists that Tom, played by beefy Barry Sullivan, warn Gatsby of

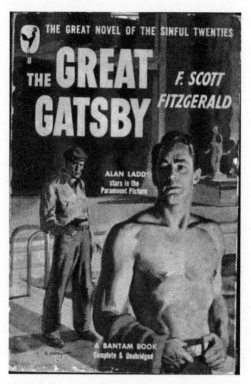

The Bantam paperback cover of Gatsby, *featuring Alan Ladd.* (MATTHEW J. & ARLYN BRUCCOLI COLLECTION OF F. SCOTT FITZGERALD, UNIVERSITY OF SOUTH CAROLINA LIBRARIES)

Wilson's approach; Tom stolidly complies, but Ladd's Gatsby ignores the insistent ringing of the telephone. Jordan, as indicated already in the prologue to the story, renounces her cheatin' ways and thus proves herself worthy of Nick's love.

Because this hard-boiled B-movie version of *Gatsby* wasn't available on the Internet until recently, I chose a clip from a different noir film to play for the audience gathered to hear my take on *The Great Gatsby* on the chill evening of October 23,

2008. I was in Perry, Iowa, that night as an emissary of the Big Read project. The Big Read was launched by the National Endowment for the Arts in response to an alarming 2004 NEA report called "Reading at Risk" that showed that less than half of American adults had ever read a work of literature in their leisure time. To make matters even more depressing, *literature* was defined pretty inclusively: romance novels, serial-killer suspense stories, and dirty limericks were eligible. The NEA decided to combat this threat to an informed democracy by sponsoring "one town, one book" events in libraries and civic centers all over America. Interested communities selected from a list of fiction titles put together by the NEA (among them *Fahrenheit 451*, *The Maltese Falcon*, *To Kill a Mockingbird*, and *The Great Gatsby*) and received critical materials for reading groups and lectures by "experts" like me.

Tonight, it's Perry's turn. The local citizens have been reading and rereading *Gatsby*, learning 1920s dances at a soiree at the Golf and Country Club, watching the 1974 film, and buying bright green T-shirts printed with a caricature of a smiling Fitzgerald in a tiny roadster. I've arrived in Perry to give the keynote address that will cap off the whole effort.

Perry, which I will explore over two days, is a Midwestern treasure: a tiny railroad town about thirty miles outside of Des Moines that boasts a Carnegie Library Museum and the Hotel Pattee, opened in 1913. Both buildings have been restored to their original splendor by a wealthy local benefactor. The hotel, where I'm staying in a needlework-theme room, houses a wooden bowling alley in its basement and a very nice bar. After my talk, I'll enjoy a couple of rounds of bracing gin and tonics with the locals, including Perry's mayor, a sharp middle-aged woman who's refreshingly outspoken in her political views. At that point in that particular October, everybody is more caught up in the looming presidential election than in *Gatsby*, but that's okay. I like this town whose motto is Make Yourself at Home! I can see the attractions of living here (the effect of those two gin and tonics?), except there's no work. As I'll learn the following morning when I visit the local high school, the nearby Tyson chicken plant is one of the chief employers in the area.

I'm self-conscious about my role as Great Books booster. I'll continue to be self-conscious about this role over the next few years as I serve as an itinerant preacher for the greatness of *Gatsby* at other Big Read events in places like Bowling Green, Kentucky, and Peoria, Illinois. The sponsoring librarians are almost always dynamic, smart women who tirelessly promote the pleasure of reading books, but they're beating on against the powerful current of all manner of electronic gadgetry (although I'm certainly not opposed to people reading e-books). The new public library in Peoria, where I'll speak a couple of years later, is mostly filled with computers, Blu-Rays, and DVDs. (The same is true of the new public library in my own Northwest Washington, DC, neighborhood.) I assume most of my audience that night in Perry will be white; indeed, the whiteness of the crowd any time I talk about *Gatsby* outside of a school setting underscores the fundamental problem with talking about any novel as one of "our" Great American Novels, one that "we" should all read. In the immortal (if apocryphal) words of Tonto, "Who you calling 'we,' white man?" The Big Read program has tried to acknowledge the racial and ethnic realities of America by putting works like Zora Neale Hurston's

Their Eyes Were Watching God and Amy Tan's *The Joy Luck Club* on the master list, but the crowds for *Gatsby*, at least, still skew as white as those billowing curtains in the Buchanans' living room. The crowd in Perry that night is also overwhelmingly female, and middle-aged to elderly, which means that the folks assembled in the meeting room on the second floor of the Town/Craft Center look a lot like the crowds who gather for most literary and NPR events. Since almost everyone will have already read *Gatsby* in high school, I can deviate from the *Gatsby*-as-vitamin-for-the-brain pep talk that I fear I'm expected to deliver as cultural emissary from the capital. Indeed, the printed program for my talk in Perry confirms my suspicions: it stresses a message of literary uplift. Printed on the back cover in bold letters are bullet points courtesy of the NEA: **Good readers make good citizens** and **Good readers generally have more financially rewarding jobs.** (I like the cautious use of that adverb *generally*.)

True enough. Yet I also want to point out that all great art is wayward and dangerous: it messes with our imaginations and plants outsize fantasies in our brains. Jimmy Gatz, after all, might have been better off had he not read Benjamin Franklin's *Autobiography*, the inspiration for that youthful self-improvement list that his father posthumously finds in Jimmy's paperback copy of *Hopalong Cassidy*. I want to recognize that disruptive, rogue quality in *Gatsby*, and so I've given my talk the mildly contrarian title of "*The Great Gatsby:* Just How American Is This Great American Novel?"

Maybe the edgy title worked because the town hall is packed that fall evening. Or maybe I just don't have much competition in Perry that night. After I'm introduced, I cue the librarian/

technical assistant. On the movie screen behind me, Billy Wilder's classic 1950 noir *Sunset Boulevard* begins to roll.

If you've seen it, you'll remember the opening: To the accompaniment of sirens and Franz Waxman's jittery score, police motorcycles and sedans packed with tabloid photographers careen down a palm-lined road. *Sunset Boulevard* is stenciled in white letters on a curbside. The cops and newshounds screech up the driveway of an ornate mansion, "the home of an old-time star." Some of the men run to the front door; others out to the back, where there's a pool. The body of a young man is floating in the pool. The camera angle changes and it's as though viewers are standing on the bottom of the pool, looking up at the victim's open-eyed face. All this time there's been a voice-over: a man has been calmly talking to us, explaining what we're seeing. As we viewers gaze up at the wet corpse, the voice-over quips: "Poor dope, he always wanted a pool. Only the price turned out to be a little high." The next scene takes us back a few months, into a crummy apartment in LA where a writer is banging away on a typewriter. Turns out the writer is William Holden, the actor we've just seen floating facedown in the pool. We realize, as the narrator switches to *I,* that we've been listening all this time to a dead man.

The lights come on in the Town/Craft Center and I make a feeble joke about the mistake of opening my talk with such a mesmerizing film clip, because now everybody just wants to go home and watch *Sunset Boulevard.* Nervous laughter because everybody knows it's true. Even I want to ditch the lecture and watch *Sunset Boulevard.* But I forge ahead because it's obvious, from the quick conversations I've been having with the Perry-ites before my talk, that almost everybody who has reread *Gatsby* still wants to talk about it as a beautiful and sad love story. ("Do you think Daisy ever loved Gatsby?" adults at these Big Read events and high-school and college students always reliably ask.) I do *not* want to talk about the novel as a love story, not tonight. I want to talk about the novel as a noir that surveys the rotten underbelly of the American Dream. Take that cheery assurance that **Good readers make good citizens** and stuff it down a drain. Billy Wilder's off-kilter opening helps me make the case for this reading even before I open my mouth because, as the Perry audience can see for themselves, both Wilder's and Fitzgerald's pools are fed by the same dark sources.

I begin ticking off the clues: hard-boiled corruption infests the atmosphere of *Gatsby*. There's bootlegging, the financial shenanigans of Gatsby and Wolfshiem and company, and the moral decay of Gatsby's parties. "Think about it!" I exhort the good citizens of Perry. "All novels develop from a series of choices. Fitzgerald *chose* to make Gatsby a gangster. He could have affirmed the idea of a meritocracy by having Gatsby rapidly rise up the corporate ladder, be a banker or a grocery-store mogul like his own wealthy McQuillan grandfather. Instead, Gatsby has more in common with Don Corleone than he does Ben Franklin. Like *The Godfather, The Great Gatsby* skews the American dream of material success as the reward for honest hard work and enterprise." (A few years later, Fitzgerald's cynical move of making *Gatsby* "mobbed up" will strike me with fresh force. In the summer of 2013, I'll take a tour of the Breakers, the Gilded Age mansion of Cornelius Vanderbilt II in Newport, Rhode Island. It's a place whose real-life extravagance makes Gatsby's fictional house seem like a starter mansion. As I walk through the morning room with its platinum wallpaper and stroll into Mr. Vanderbilt's bathroom with its thick marble tub equipped with a special spout for heated salt water, the tour guide speaking through my headset earnestly assures me that Vanderbilt "worked very hard all his life." We Americans want to believe that material excess is excused by very hard work; that the rich deserve their wealth. *The Great Gatsby* simultaneously affirms that idea— Jimmy Gatz's youthful self-improvement list— and snorts at its naïveté.)

For the record, most of the novel's other characters are also crooked in some way: Jordan Baker cheats at golf and tells lies about leaving roadsters out in the rain; Myrtle Wilson is an adulterous floozy; those "careless" Buchanans "smash up things and creatures."[11] Even Nick, as we've seen, isn't completely on the level as a narrator. Add to all this moral ambiguity the seediness of so many of the settings in the novel: Myrtle and Tom's love nest, Gatsby's own decadent parties, the valley of ashes with the Wilsons' dirty garage and Michaelis's shabby Greek coffee place.

In addition to all the ways in which he plays with the conventions of a crime story in *The Great Gatsby,* Fitzgerald wrote (and read) straightforward mystery tales too. His very first appearance in print was a short story for the September 1909 issue of *Now and Then,* a literary magazine put out by the St. Paul Academy. "The Mystery of the Raymond Mortgage" is a stiff-jointed Sherlock Holmes replicant. Fitzgerald later joked about a hole in the plotting: "Through some oversight, I neglected to bring the [mortgage] into the story in any form."[12] In the aftermath of *Gatsby,* Fitzgerald began toying with an idea for a novel (catchy working title: "The Boy Who Killed His Mother") about a foul-tempered young man whose father is serving time in prison for a violent crime; our antihero is driven to commit the same act against his domineering mother. Fitzgerald struggled with this crime story for four years, on and off. Also in the immediate wake of *Gatsby*, Fitzgerald published an entertaining whodunit called "The Dance" in the June 1926 issue of *Redbook* magazine. Narrated by a woman, this short story devotes a good amount of space to singing the praises of New York City. "All my life," the narrator tells us, "I have had a rather curious horror of small towns.... I was born in New York City, and even as a little girl I never had any fear of the streets or the strange foreign faces."[13] The narrator's skittishness about the festering secrets of small town life is validated after another young woman is killed in the middle of a country-club dance. (Fitzgerald tries his hand here at a variant of the locked-room mystery and pulls it off. "The Dance" was deemed good enough by mystery aficionados to be reprinted in *Ellery Queen's Mystery Magazine* in 1953.)

I invite my audience in Perry that night to think of *Gatsby*'s connection to Dashiell Hammett's 1930 hard-boiled masterpiece *The Maltese Falcon*, with its vision of debased knights chasing the grail of the fake falcon. While it's not clear exactly when Hammett read Fitzgerald, we know he did, and the two men admired each other's work. In 1936, while he was recuperating from that diving accident and trying to dry out at the Grove Park Inn in Asheville, North Carolina, Fitzgerald hired a private-duty nurse named Dorothy Richardson. He liked her and so put together one of his trademark "required-reading" lists for her. Amid titles like Stendhal's *The Red and the Black,* Renan's *Life of Jesus,* Ibsen's *A Doll's House,* and the complete poetic works of Keats and Shelley, Fitzgerald also listed *The Maltese Falcon* by Dashiell Hammett. Later on, in Hollywood, Fitzgerald made even more reading lists for his poorly educated lover Sheilah Graham. One of the many filed away in the Fitzgerald Papers at Princeton is entitled "Revised List of 40 Books." This list includes additions scribbled in pencil by Fitzgerald, among them Proust (all seven volumes), *Daisy Miller, Farewell to Arms,* and *Maltese Falcon.* (Fitzgerald apparently committed the crime of petty theft in supplying the books he recommended to Graham. Don C. Skemer, curator of manuscripts at Princeton, where Graham donated her *College of One* books, tells me that many of them have MGM Library bookplates inside their front covers.)

Hammett, for his part, respected and defended Fitzgerald against those who jeered at him during his long personal and professional nosedive of the 1930s. In her notoriously unreliable memoir *An Unfinished Woman,* Lillian Hellman tells a story that I hope is true. On a night out on the town in 1939, Hellman and Hammett stroll into the Stork Club on Fifty-Third Street in New York City. They sit down at a table that gradually fills up with other folks, including Ernest Hemingway. Hemingway and Hammett get plastered and Hemingway starts showing off by trying to bend a spoon with only his muscular arm. He succeeds. As Hammett gets up to leave the table, Hemingway grabs his arm and challenges him to do the spoon trick. Hammett refuses, saying: "Why don't you go back to bullying Fitzgerald? Too bad he doesn't know how good he is. The best."[14] According to Hellman, Hemingway's grip on Hammett's arm loosens and his grin melts away.

Mutual admiration apart, what Fitzgerald and Hammett shared—along with so many of their Lost Generation cohorts—was a vision of the modern world where God was an empty illusion. Whether the object of worship is unmasked as a phony bird (the falcon) or whether belief itself is dismissed in a contemptuous phrase like Hemingway's "Isn't it pretty to think so?," 1920s fiction in general, and the hard-boiled novel in particular, is godless and vacant.

Raymond Chandler, who, like Hammett and Fitzgerald, also served in World War I, nails this desolate vision at the end of his 1939 hard-boiled classic *The Big Sleep* when his detective hero Philip Marlowe says, "The world was a wet emptiness." Take away the moisture, and Marlowe might as well be describing the valley of ashes. You hear the despair in Nick's voice all the time he's going back over Gatsby's story: Daisy, the meritocracy, money, celebrity—they're all gods that have failed Gatsby. Only Gatsby himself, in Nick's understated testament of faith, "turned out all right at the end."[15] Chandler, by the way, was another hard-boiled detective writer who admired Fitzgerald. In a 1950 letter to the publicity director at Houghton Mifflin, Chandler commented that Fitzgerald:

had one of the rarest qualities in all literature, and it's a great shame that the word for it has been thoroughly debased by the cosmetic racketeers, so that one is almost ashamed to use it to describe a real distinction. Nevertheless, the word is charm—charm as Keats would have used it. Who has it today? It's not a matter of pretty

writing or clear style. It's a kind of subdued magic, con-
trolled and exquisite, the sort of thing you get from good
string quartettes [*sic*].[16]

Let's turn away from the theological gloom that pervades
Gatsby and its hard-boiled relations and consider a more tangi-
ble fixation they both share: cars. *The Great Gatsby*, like most
hard-boiled detective stories and the film noirs that were made
from them, is car crazy. The simple historical reason is that
America in the 1920s was turning into a car culture; thanks
to Henry Ford's assembly lines, automobile ownership was
becoming democratized. Ann Douglas writes that by 1929, one
out of every five Americans had a car (as opposed to one out of
thirty-seven Englishmen, one out of forty Frenchmen, and one
out of forty-eight Germans).[17] But in the hard-boiled universe,
cars are not just modes of transportation, they're fully loaded
assault vehicles that allow their passengers to satisfy all manner
of forbidden drives.

A woman in the driver's seat is particularly bad news in a
hard-boiled story. To the extent that Daisy embodies the newly
acquired personal freedoms of the flapper—she drinks and
sleeps around—she's already a figure who makes many of the
men in the novel edgy, even as they're captivated by her. And
let's not forget that the liberated sportswoman Jordan Baker
derives her androgynous moniker from two automobile makes:
the Jordan sports car and the electric Baker.[18] It's when Daisy
gets behind the wheel of Gatsby's yellow roadster, however,
that she indisputably achieves femme fatale status. To be
behind the wheel is to be in control, and for a woman to occupy
that place is as upsetting to the conventional hierarchies as that

image of the white chauffeur driving the three African American passengers across the Queensboro Bridge. ("Don't forget, I'm at the wheel now," Ella Kaye ominously warns young Gatsby in the 1949 film.) Who can say for certain whether Daisy's hit-and-run murder of Myrtle, her husband's mistress, is just an accident or a subconscious homicidal drive realized? What is crystal clear is the fact that *The Great Gatsby*, like so many hard-boiled novels and film noirs, is obsessed with the image of a woman behind the steering wheel. (*The* iconic noir woman-driver image is Barbara Stanwyck in *Double Indemnity* smiling behind the wheel in a sexually satisfied way as fall guy Fred MacMurray strangles her husband.)

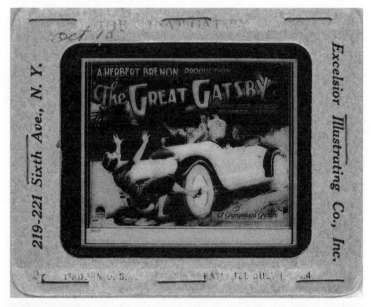

A glass slide from the 1926 silent movie. (MATTHEW J. & ARLYN BRUCCOLI COL-LECTION OF F. SCOTT FITZGERALD, UNIVERSITY OF SOUTH CAROLINA LIBRARIES)

Early illustrators of *The Great Gatsby* recognized the sexually transgressive seating arrangements within "the death car,"[19] as the tabloids call Gatsby's yellow roadster. In the Bruccoli Collection of Fitzgerald's papers, manuscripts, and assorted other material at the University of South Carolina, there's a glass slide of a marvelous advertising still from the lost 1926 silent movie of *The Great Gatsby;* it depicts Myrtle Wilson falling backward under the wheels of Gatsby's car as Gatsby himself is leaping up, aghast, in the passenger seat. Daisy, in contrast, stares grimly ahead, hands gripping the steering wheel, pedal to the metal. In the Fitzgerald Papers at Princeton, there's a brilliantly comic (but unattributed) newspaper cartoon pasted into the *Great Gatsby* scrapbook that Fitzgerald kept of reviews and interviews. The cartoon captures the final act of *Gatsby* in one frame: a cloche-hatted Daisy sits behind the wheel of a gigantic jalopy that is rolling over a mountainous (but strangely unfazed) Myrtle. Behind the two women, Gatsby's corpse lies stretched out on the pavement, and George Wilson is about to blow his brains out. These 1920s illustrators wanted to grab their viewers' attention; unlike us English teachers, they knew better than to wax rhapsodic about the novel's language or the larger American themes in the story. Instead, they went straight for sensation, and nothing was more sensational than the image of an out-of-control woman driver.

Gatsby itself swerves fully into pulp style at the time of Myrtle's murder: the episode is told from the points of view of a variety of witnesses. The only time the language of *The Great Gatsby* becomes ugly is in the jarring sentences that describe Myrtle's broken body: "her left breast swinging loose like a flap," her mouth "ripped at the corners."[20] It takes a while for the novel to catch its breath, recover from this pulp crudeness, right itself, and get back to poetry. Writing to Max Perkins from Rome in January of 1925, Fitzgerald strenuously protested a softening of Myrtle's gory death: "I *want* Myrtle Wilson's breast ripped off—it's exactly the thing."[21] I think of how, as so often in the larger story of *The Great Gatsby*, life followed art when a mentally ill Zelda in the fall of 1929 grabbed the steering wheel away from Scott on that road in France and tried to veer toward their deaths. That particular swerve was never righted.

I opened my talk in Perry that night with the clip from *Sunset Boulevard* because one of the most crucial connections between *The Great Gatsby* and the hard-boiled novels and film noirs is that image of going under, drowning (even if, technically speaking, the bullets finished off both Jay Gatsby and William Holden's Joe Gillis first). Hard-boiled and noir characters are always going belly-up in pools (Ross Macdonald's *Black Money*), oceans (James M. Cain's *Double Indemnity*), oil sumps (Rusty Regan in *The Big Sleep*), and lakes (Chandler's *The Lady in the Lake*). They're always dissolving into sweat (the 1950 Rudolph Maté film *D.O.A.*) and tears (Michael Curtiz's 1945 film of *Mildred Pierce*). They also all uniformly drown themselves in liquor. It makes complete noir poetic sense that when Gatsby finally takes his very first dip of the season in his pool, he promptly dies. "Poor dope, he always wanted a pool." Dreamers in the hard-boiled universe are always poor dopes. There's a line that perfectly explains why; it lodged in my brain years ago and comes from a hard-boiled novel or a noir or a critical book or an essay and has eluded all my attempts to track down its source. Still, since that line specifically details the way in which these guys are poor dopes, I'm going to go ahead and quote it: "They chased their dreams to the edge of the Pacific, only to be conned one more time."

Obviously, Gatsby doesn't go west to chase his dream (although he does wash up in West Egg); instead, he chases his dream to the edge of the Atlantic, "the great wet barnyard of Long Island Sound."[22] Then he's conned one more time—by his reading of Ben Franklin, by Daisy, by America—and goes under. Since *Gatsby* is not the story of one man's rise and fall but, in its prescient way, of a national "shipwreck" that's looming on the outer edge of the 1920s, there's a sense in which he, like almost everyone in this novel, is sunk from the very beginning. That initial scene in the Buchanans' house reads like the literary equivalent of Curtiz's great noir rendering of James M. Cain's *Mildred Pierce*. In that movie's opening shot, Mildred's beach house is filmed to look as though it's underwater, suggesting the impending oblivion at the end of the story. Listen, once more, to how carefully Fitzgerald describes the damp décor in the Buchanans' own "beach house": "A breeze blew through the room, blew curtains in at one end and out the other like pale flags, twisting them up toward the frosted wedding-cake of the ceiling, and then rippled over the wine-colored rug, making a shadow on it as wind does on the sea."[23] Can you hear the echoes of Homer's "wine-dark sea" in those lines? The revelers at Gatsby's party in chapter 2 also are described as though they're under the waves, drowning in liquor:

The groups change more swiftly, swell with new arrivals, dissolve and form in the same breath—already there are wanderers, confident girls who weave here and there among the stouter and more stable...and then excited with triumph glide on through the sea-change of faces and voices and color under the constantly changing light.[24]

Nick, talkative though he may be, also belongs to this pale company of the drowned: like Holden's Joe Gillis, Nick is a dead man talking. Physically, he may still be breathing, but emotionally, he's used up. (Baz Luhrmann's otherwise silly champagne bubble of a film wisely latched onto this empty aspect of Nick when it placed him at the opening of the film in a sanitarium recovering from a nervous breakdown and "dipsomania." In what is surely meant to be a doff of the hat to Fitzgerald's legendary editor, Luhrmann calls this joint the Perkins Sanitarium.) And what does Nick talk about with his precious breaths? He tells a story about his friend Jay Gatsby, who was a fellow soldier in World War I. As I've said, the modern use of the term *hard-boiled* came out of that war, and in almost every classic hard-boiled story, the most stable and intense relationship is not between the hero and the woman he loves but between two men, comrades in arms. The 1949 *Gatsby* movie stresses the buddy element running through the story by surrounding Ladd's Gatsby with gangster underlings who'd served with him in the Great War. Hard-boiled novels and the noirs that were made from them are male buddy stories that explore what makes a man a man in a newly fallen world. That Tom Buchanan is the guy who's cut out for this compromised world (given that he strides off, untouched, at the end of *The Great Gatsby*) is a grim predictive vision of the "hollow men"—all show, no substance—who are primed to flourish in the modern age. Before Gatsby's delayed entrance into his own party and into the novel that bears his name, he flits around like a ghost. He abruptly materializes at Nick and Jordan's table and, a chapter later, he'll just as suddenly vanish on Nick in that Forty-Second Street lunch cellar after Nick introduces him to Tom Buchanan. Gatsby's very first silent apparition in the novel—at night, on his lawn—establishes the eerie postmortem atmosphere. Remember, Gatsby is dead already when Nick begins telling us his story. After taking his eyes off Gatsby for a moment, Nick finds "he had vanished, and I was alone again in the unquiet darkness."[25]

Fitzgerald knew that he had created a story in which the primary relationship was between two men. Writing to H. L. Mencken in a letter dated May 4, 1925, Fitzgerald, in his typically spelling-challenged style, confessed that "the influence on it has been the masculine one of The Brothers Karamazof, a thing of incomparable form, rather than the femineine one of The Portrait of a Lady."[26] When *Gatsby* turned out to be a commercial failure, Fitzgerald quickly came to believe that he had "paid" for making Nick and Gatsby the focus of the novel. In a letter to Maxwell Perkins dated April 24, 1925, Fitzgerald bemoans weak sales and blames the title, which he says is "only fair, rather bad than good...*And most important*—the book contains no important woman character and women controll [*sic*] the fiction market at present."[27]

Hard-boiled fiction is a man's world; the only big roles for women are the femme fatale (Daisy) and the corpse (Myrtle). Not only are these male buddy stories, they're stories about soldiers. The classic hard-boiled novels of the 1920s and 1930s were written by men who had served in the war. The most prominent example is Raymond Chandler's masterpiece *The Big Sleep*, where Philip Marlowe and the other tough guys consistently address each other as "soldier." The hard-boiled formula also venerates older "manly men" like Gatsby's mentor, Dan Cody, that "pioneer debauchee" whose photograph hangs on the wall above Gatsby's desk. In Dashiell Hammett's Continental Op stories and novel, the Op works for a detective agency headed by a boss known only as the Old Man. To cite *The Big Sleep* again, Philip Marlowe risks life and limb because he comes to respect his elderly (military) client General Sternwood. Hard-boiled novels stress the loyalty that good men show to each other—certainly a central motif in *Gatsby*. Recall that scene on the final page of the novel where Nick visits Gatsby's "huge incoherent failure of a house"[28] on the night before he returns to the Midwest. He tells us that what we would call a graffiti artist has been at work: "On the white steps an obscene word, scrawled by some boy with a piece of brick, stood out clearly in the moonlight, and I erased it, drawing my shoe raspingly along the stone."[29] That's Nick's job as narrator: to clean up the blots on Gatsby's name. If not for Nick's overwhelming loyalty to his fallen friend, there would be no story.

So does Nick want to be more than buddies with Gatsby? Given the explosion of queer studies in the academy over the past two decades, it's become commonplace to talk about *The Great Gatsby* as an unrequited homosexual love story in the *Death in Venice* line. There's certainly enough support in the novel for the homosexual reading of Nick. After most public *Gatsby* lectures I've given in the past few years, someone will pipe up and ask about that curious moment at the end of chapter 2 where an underwear-clad Nick and the photographer McKee wind up together. Just as suggestive is the fact that a phallic joke precedes that scene: Nick and McKee step into the apartment-house elevator, and the "elevator boy" snaps at McKee, "Keep your hands off the lever."[30] Nick's relationships with women are brief and evasive and he guardedly falls for Jordan Baker, whose look, name, and sporty occupation are mannish in the context of the 1920s.

I think my definitive response to the Gay *Gatsby* readings is "Could be." I'm so wed to the reading of *Gatsby* as a hard-boiled novel that Nick's love for Gatsby seems in keeping with the bromance nature of that genre. To put it another way, Nick doesn't have to be gay to explain why he's in thrall to Gatsby's memory. If he did, then Sam Spade, Philip Marlowe, and Mickey Spillane—each of whom risks his life to do right by a murdered partner or male friend—would also have to be gay...as, admittedly, many queer theorists of detective fiction have argued is the case. That Nick loves Gatsby is a certainty beyond dispute. Love and loyalty are what motivate him to tell Gatsby's story two years on. To me, what's even more crucial than Nick's sexuality is this realization that, like every noir narrator worth his near empty bottle of gin, Nick tells us a story *that has already happened*. He's "borne back ceaselessly into the past."[31]

There you have it: the big reason why it matters for us readers to recognize *Gatsby*'s hard-boiled identity. Since Nick's story is retrospective, the outcome is already decided. Despite the hopes for civic uplift that the NEA might have nurtured in choosing *The Great Gatsby* for the Big Read, Fitzgerald's masterpiece is, in many ways, a very un-American novel indeed. Reinvention? No dice. The past always reaches out to grab the dreamer, and the poor dope always drowns in the end. (The title of the classic 1947 noir starring Kirk Douglas, Robert Mitchum, and Jane Greer could have been a good alternative title for *Gatsby: Out of the Past*.) As literary critic Morris Dickstein has pointed out, the essential movement of *Gatsby*'s story is backward, "like an inquest."[32] We start with Nick's present-time narration in 1924, then we're drawn backward to the summer of 1922, then to Gatsby and Daisy's meeting in 1917, and, finally, to those go-for-broke last paragraphs that telescope all the way back to "the old island...that flowered once for Dutch sailors' eyes—a fresh, green breast of the new world."[33]

The shadow side of *The Great Gatsby*'s all-American story—the one that preaches a chamber of commerce sermon about limitless potential—is a noir with a distinct *No Exit* atmosphere to it. What Raymond Chandler dubbed "the smell of fear" wafts into the novel from its earliest pages, in which the final disasters are foretold. Take the fact that there are not one but two car crashes ominously preceding the hit-and-run that kills Myrtle and, essentially, Wilson and Gatsby as well. In chapter 3, at the end of the first party scene, Owl Eyes emerges from a wrecked coupe that's lost a wheel in Gatsby's driveway. As the crowd of drunken stragglers blames Owl Eyes for the accident, he protests that: "I wasn't driving." And, indeed, at that same moment, the drunk driver extricates himself from the car. Anyone who's read *The Great Gatsby* at least once before should sense something familiar in this scene involving a car crash and wrongly accused driver: it anticipates Gatsby chivalrously taking the blame for Daisy's carelessness at the wheel that costs Myrtle her life. One chapter later, we hear about yet another car wreck in which, once again, a wheel is lost. This time, infidelity is involved. Shortly after his marriage to Daisy, Tom and a chambermaid from the Santa Barbara Hotel are in a smashup. Since only her arm is broken, that chambermaid gets off more lightly than poor Myrtle will. Car references abound, but the other one that I'll single out is that conversation—in hard-boiled patois—that Nick and Jordan have about the breakup of their relationship. Jordan reminds Nick of a conversation they once had about driving a car. "You said a bad driver was only safe until she met another bad driver? Well, I met another bad driver, didn't I?"[34] "Bad driving" is clearly a code, tough talk for reckless behavior. The instances of bad driving that anticipate the car wreck that kills Myrtle in chapter 7 give it a fated feel.

Fate is the essential ingredient in hard-boiled and noir narratives; so are coincidence and repetition. This short novel twice tells the story of Gatsby and Daisy's initial meeting; scenes are repeated, such as the party at the Buchanans' house that opens chapters 1 and 7. Even objects make repeated appearances: Meyer Wolfshiem's nasty cuff links and Daisy's pearl wedding necklace are reprised in Tom Buchanan's final appearance in the novel when he goes into that jewelry store on Fifth Avenue (probably Tiffany) "to buy a pearl necklace—or perhaps only a pair of cuff buttons."[35] Christopher Hitchens wrote a gorgeous appreciation of *The Great Gatsby* in the May 2000 issue of *Vanity Fair*, but Hitchens got one thing wrong. Talking about how the novel rises above its "abysmal weakness of plot and plausibility," Hitchens offered this instance of a hard-to-swallow plot device: "A man of Gatsby's supposed force and vitality just takes a house and waits for the girl to come, luckily discovering after brooding at length on a green light that the adored one's cousin lives next door!"[36] To which I protest, "But of course! It's Fate!" The convoluted plots of classic hard-boiled novels and noirs rest on such coincidences that are proof, not of a benevolent God (as they would have been in the nineteenth-century novel), but of ultimate dead ends. Coincidence in *Gatsby* speaks to the foolishness of embracing that other late Victorian chimera: the notion that "I am the master of my fate: I am the captain of my soul."[37] All appearances to the contrary, Gatsby is stuck in the passenger seat, not sitting behind the steering wheel, of his own story.

I think Fitzgerald absorbed the techniques and the attitude of the emerging genre of hard-boiled fiction while he was intermittently living in and close to New York City from the late winter of 1919 to the spring of 1924. So much of the sturdy fabric of *Gatsby*—the criminal underworld, the tough-guy lingo, the obsession with the past, the violence, the doom-laden sense of fated-ness, the voice-over narration, the death by drowning—were staples of the hard-boiled genre that was hatched in America and, specifically, in New York City, in the twenties. Many of the classic noirs of the 1940s and 1950s would take their stories from those hard-boiled tales, including the Alan Ladd *Gatsby* of 1949. The hard-boiled element in *The Great Gatsby* accounts for some of the dark magic of this very strange and un-American Great American Novel.

After *The Great Gatsby* was published in April of 1925 and then quietly sank under the waves by autumn of that year, Fitzgerald, who was living in Paris with Zelda and Scottie, answered a fan letter sent to him by New York critic, Marya Mannes, who must have also said something enthusiastic about her hometown:

> You are thrilled by New York—I doubt you will be after five more years when you are more fully nourished from within. I carry the place around the world in my heart but sometimes I try to shake it off in my dreams. America's greatest promise is that something is going to happen, and after awhile you get tired of waiting because nothing happens to people except that they grow old.[38]

Fitzgerald missed out on the chance to grow old—although, as we know from Nick's self-pitying birthday dirge in *Gatsby*, both he and his creator regarded thirty as the absolute end of youth. When Fitzgerald and his family returned for good to America in 1931, he and Scottie mostly lived in and around Baltimore while Zelda spent time as a resident or outpatient of various sanitariums. Then, in the summer of 1937, Scottie was sent to boarding school and, during vacations, to live with the family of Fitzgerald's literary agent, Harold Ober, while Fitzgerald moved to what had become America's premier hard-boiled city, Los Angeles. He was lured out there by a six-month contract with Metro-Goldwyn-Mayer to work on scripts. This was his third trip out to work for the movies, which chewed up and spit out many a fine writer. Like a hard-boiled fall guy, Fitzgerald would "chase [his] dreams to the edge of the Pacific, only to be conned one more time."

In Hollywood, the story of the last act of Fitzgerald's life acquired many of the details—if not the full-blown plot—of a classic noir. When he first moved out to Los Angeles, he took a furnished apartment at the tawdry Garden of Allah complex. Owned by silent film star Alla Nazimova, the Garden of Allah was home to a lot of hard-drinking writers (Robert Benchley, Dorothy Parker) and movie stars (Errol Flynn, Greta Garbo, Humphrey Bogart) and was distinguished by its fabled pool, constructed in the shape of the Black Sea to commemorate Nazimova's Russian roots. In those early months Fitzgerald was unmoored and lonely; there are accounts of him eating by himself at the MGM commissary and there's also this sad little postcard he sent to himself: "Dear Scott—How are you? Have been meaning to come in and see you. I have [*sic*] living at the Garden of Allah. Yours, Scott Fitzgerald."[39]

Life picked up, however, when he fell for a young blonde with a dappled past: the fledgling Hollywood gossip columnist Sheilah Graham who, like Jay Gatsby, also "sprang from [some] Platonic conception"[40] of herself. In his unfinished Hollywood novel, *The Love of the Last Tycoon*, Fitzgerald wrote that his hero, Monroe Stahr, was attracted to the lovely Kathleen Moore because she had "the face of his dead wife." Graham bore a resemblance to Zelda and came to feel that Fitzgerald was reliving his youth with her.[41] Graham would eventually write five books about their three-and-a-half-year affair; her son (allegedly with Hollywood star Robert Taylor) wrote still another.

Graham had something of the aura—and the personal history—of a 1930s tough dame. In addition to her son from her liaison with Taylor, she also had a daughter out of wedlock, Wendy Fairey, with the British positivist philosopher A. J. Ayer. Before Graham met Fitzgerald, she'd been in an open marriage: her impotent, older husband encouraged the eighteen-year-old Graham to date the wealthy stage-door Johnnies who flocked to see her perform as a chorus girl. By the time she arrived in Hollywood, Graham was already working her way up the social ladder—she'd gotten engaged to the Marquess of Donegal. Unlike Zelda, who's been turned into something of a martyr figure by some of her admirers, Graham was no victim. Much as she loved Fitzgerald (there's a 1939 codicil to her will in one of the archival boxes in Princeton in which she leaves everything to him), she also profited by writing about their relationship for decades after his death.

But Graham also seems seductively forthright in her accounts of life with Scott; indeed, she won me over halfway through *Beloved Infidel,* her first and best-known memoir about their romance. I wanted to meet up with her at Musso and Frank's and dish over martinis. Graham's voice is smart and disarming, and her books abound with the kind of small details that make a subject come alive. Fitzgerald, we learn, liked canned turtle soup for lunch and Hershey bars for a snack. We also hear about his ugly behavior when drunk. Off the sauce, he drank gallons of sweetened coffee and Coca-Colas; at night he put himself to bed with sleeping pills and popped Benzedrine to wake up in the morning. "At present, he is drinking at least a pint of gin a day," Graham writes in notes she made to herself in 1939 prior to what must have been a tense conversation with Fitzgerald's doctor. "It is stupid for you to regard me as the villainess of the piece because I can't bear to see him drunk."[42] Graham seems to have genuinely cared for Fitzgerald in both a romantic and nurturing way. In the spring of 1938, she found him a beach house out in Malibu; she thought the salt air would restore him to health and she wanted to distance him from his drinking buddies. Fitzgerald, though, hated the damp and avoided the sun. According to Graham, he "never swam or even waded in the inviting surf."[43] Here's how she describes Fitzgerald at the beach:

"Scott, at Malibu. He is in an ancient gray flannel bathrobe, torn at the elbows so that it shows the gray slip-over sweater he wears underneath. He has the stub of a pencil over each ear, the stubs of half a dozen others—like so many cigars— peeping from the breast pocket of his robe. One side pocket bulges with two packs of cigarettes."[44]

How odd. There are so many photos of Fitzgerald in his prime in bathing costumes, sitting, often with Zelda and Scottie, by a pool or an ocean. Maybe that diving accident in 1936 ruined his love affair with swimming. Or maybe, as Fitzgerald neared the end of his life—as he became more exhausted by his own personal struggle to keep his head above water—he regarded the ocean as a more threatening force. I think of a similar story about the aging Raymond Chandler living with his dying wife, Cissy, in their house in La Jolla overlooking the ocean. As Judith Freeman recounts in *The Long Embrace*, her superb book on Chandler and Cissy, a visitor paid a call at the beach house and noticed that Chandler's desk in his small study was turned toward an interior courtyard window, away from the fabulous ocean view. When the visitor asked Chandler about the odd position of the desk, he said he didn't like the ocean: "Too much water, too many drowned men."

Fitzgerald moved from that beachfront rental house back to

Scott and Scottie in the Mediterranean. (MATTHEW J. & ARLYN BRUCCOLI COLLECTION OF F. SCOTT FITZGERALD, UNIVERSITY OF SOUTH CAROLINA LIBRARIES)

Hollywood. He died of a heart attack (possibly his third) on December 21, 1940. By the time of his death, because of his weakened condition, he had moved in with Sheilah Graham to her ground-floor apartment on North Hayworth Avenue, although, for appearances' sake, he kept his apartment at 1403 North Laurel Avenue. The past repeated itself in that address: Fitzgerald had been born on Laurel Avenue—in St. Paul—forty-four years earlier. North Laurel Avenue in Los Angeles is half a block south of Sunset Boulevard. Of course, that proximity would have meant nothing to Fitzgerald or any of his loved ones in 1940, but I wonder if Billy Wilder, who was acquainted with a washed-up writer named F. Scott Fitzgerald during that Hollywood period, might have been taking mental notes.

4

A Second-Rate, Midwest Hack and the Masterpiece He Wrote

The Great Gatsby is just under fifty thousand words and nine chapters long. In the Scribner's authorized paperback edition, it runs 189 pages. Fitzgerald always thought that *Gatsby*'s brevity was a contributing factor in its disappointing sales. Then, as now, readers want plenty of book for their buck. The irony is that, by the late 1950s, *Gatsby* had become a mainstay of high-school and college syllabi, in part, because it is so short. *A Tale of Two Cities, The Old Man and the Sea,* and *Ethan Frome* also owe some of their classroom popularity to the fact that they don't require English teachers to prod students along on a forced march through vast stretches of prose.

The climax of *The Great Gatsby* occurs in chapter 5. In the Scribner's authorized text, Daisy and Gatsby are reunited on page 91, which is a hairbreadth short of the precise numeric dead center of the novel. That's how obsessively overdesigned this novel is. Daisy has been lured to tea at Nick's cottage; she's wearing a tricorner lavender hat that matches the "dripping bare lilac trees"[1] on Nick's lawn; Gatsby, a nervous wreck, flies out the back door upon her arrival and then, formally, knocks at the front door. It's a slapstick moment whose comedy is undercut by the fact that Gatsby stands at Nick's front door now looking like a drowned man. No matter how many times you reread *Gatsby*, the awkwardness of the first moments of the reunion with Daisy is excruciating. Nick himself can't stand the tension, so he waits in the hall and "overhears" Gatsby's mute, ghostlike entrance into the sitting room and Daisy's first words of greeting, so stiff they could've been cribbed from a 1920s etiquette lesson for "How to Properly Greet an Old Flame":

> For half a minute there wasn't a sound. Then from the living room I heard a sort of choking murmur and part of a laugh followed by Daisy's voice on a clear artificial note.
> "I certainly am awfully glad to see you again."
> A pause; it endured horribly. I had nothing to do in the hall so I went into the room.[2]

After some pained moments of conversation and tea drinking, Nick slips out the back and leaves the lovers to their privacy. By the time he returns, Daisy is crying and Gatsby has been temporarily restored to life: "There was a change in Gatsby that was simply confounding. He literally glowed."[3] Thus, we readers are shut out of one of the most momentous reunions in all of literature.

The remainder of chapter 5 — one of the shortest chapters in the novel — is taken up by the tour of Gatsby's mansion. As evening descends, Nick says his good-byes to Gatsby and

Daisy. We're told that Gatsby is once again looking unsure of himself, perhaps because what memories of Daisy he's stored up "in his ghostly heart"[4] haven't been matched by her fleshly reality. (Siren Daisy, however, still keeps Gatsby in thrall with her voice: "that voice was a deathless song."[5]) Then Nick walks out of Gatsby's mansion and down the marble steps "into the rain,"[6] leaving them alone together.

Nick tells us that for several weeks afterward he didn't see Gatsby or talk to him on the telephone, that there was "a short halt"[7] in their relationship. How bold of Fitzgerald to pause at dead center of *Gatsby* to allow the principal players their privacy, away from Nick and, of course, us readers.

Fitzgerald himself wanted a time-out in the spring of 1924. He had ground out eleven short stories in the six months between November 1923 and April 1924 in order to pay his debts and buy the freedom to concentrate on his novel in progress. A ledger entry for April 1924 reads: "Out of the woods at last + starting novel."[8] The mental strain, however, ran Fitzgerald down; he complained of coughs, itches, stomach problems, and insomnia.[9] In a letter written in the early weeks of 1924 to fellow Scribner's novelist Thomas Boyd, Fitzgerald said: "I've been sweating out trash since the failure of my play but I hope to get back to my novel by March 1."[10] Still, the release from short-story writing would mean nothing if Fitzgerald couldn't extricate himself from the tipsy social life of Great Neck, an area dubbed by some "the Riviera on Long Island Sound." In that same letter to Boyd, Fitzgerald notes that "Rebecca West + a rather (not *too*) literary crowd are coming out Sunday for a rather formal party + Zelda's scared."[11] According to Fitzgerald biographer and friend Andrew Turnbull, West turned out to be a no-show at that dinner, so "Fitzgerald got a pillow, painted a face on it, crowned it with an enormous plumed hat, and put it in the seat of honor. All during the meal he insulted this effigy of the authoress and teased it about her books."[12] Ring Lardner was Fitzgerald's partner in crime on Great Neck; on one memorable occasion, the two had a long boozy lunch with neighbor Rube Goldberg. The lunch culminated in Fitzgerald and Lardner giving Goldberg, who'd passed out, a patchy haircut that he had to cover with a hat. Another time, the pair went out to the Doubleday estate in Oyster Bay where Joseph Conrad was rumored to be a guest. They performed a drunken dance on the lawn in order to lure the great writer out but were asked to leave, pronto. If the fun paled on Long Island, there were always forays into New York. When a plainclothes policeman insulted Zelda at a dance at Webster Hall, Fitzgerald punched him. Such was the Fitzgeralds' celebrity that the headline in the paper the next day read: "Fitzgerald Knocks Officer This Side of Paradise."[13]

A liquor-fueled life of high jinks, long lunches, and parties, amusing as it may be, is death to serious work; there's a reason why writers burrow themselves into artist colonies or country retreats. The house in Great Neck was supposed to be Fitzgerald's very own artist colony, but he was a social creature, and, from boyhood on, he'd always cared too much about being liked. It was just too hard for Fitzgerald to go cold turkey on the invitations his hard-won popularity was generating. In "How to Live on $36,000 a Year," the comic piece he wrote for the *Saturday Evening Post* that appeared on April 5, 1924, Fitzgerald struck a pose of bafflement as he tried to figure out how that then-considerable sum had flown out the windows of his Great Neck house during the previous year. "Restaurant Parties" and "Entertaining" were each budgeted at $70 a month, and the Fitzgerald food bill (presumably including hosting dinners at their house) came to a whopping $202 a month. It's a testament to Fitzgerald's charisma that he didn't alienate his readership with this piece, given that, according to the Internal Revenue Service tables for that time, the average net income in America was $3,226.

An escape was needed. In early May of 1924, the Fitzgeralds impulsively vacated the Great Neck house and sailed to Europe, leaving loyal Ring Lardner to deal with the practical business of closing up their rented house on Gateway Drive.

After a brief stop in Paris they moved to the Riviera, which was then a winter resort and, therefore, unfashionable and cheap in the summer. Near the town of St. Raphael, they rented the imposing Villa Marie for seventy-nine dollars a month and settled in with an English nanny for Scottie, a cook, and a maid. Scott certainly didn't become a recluse—he went to the beach with Zelda and socialized in the evenings—but he did spend a large portion of the day shut inside the villa working on his novel. Consciously or not, all the time he was writing *Gatsby*, Scott situated himself close to water: Great Bear Lake in Minnesota, where he began the ur-*Gatsby* manuscript; the Long Island Sound; and now the Mediterranean. While Scott was inside writing, Zelda spent hours on the beach. It was out there by the sea that she began an affair with a French aviator, Edouard Jozan. Fitzgerald's ledger notes "the Big crisis—13th of July."

What actually happened between Zelda and Jozan is as shrouded in mystery as what happens between Daisy and

Gatsby during the "several weeks"[14] that Nick loses track of his friend. By the way, Fitzgerald came to regard the silence he inserted after the reunion between Daisy and Gatsby as a mistake. A month after *The Great Gatsby* was published, Fitzgerald wrote to Edmund Wilson, "The worst fault in it, I think is a Big Fault: I gave no account (and had no feeling about or knowledge of) the emotional relations between Gatsby and Daisy from the time of their reunion to the catastrophe."[15] He echoes this mea culpa in a contemporaneous letter to H. L. Mencken, addressed "Dear Menck": "There is a tremendous fault in the book—the lack of an emotional presentment of Daisy's attitude toward Gatsby after their reunion (and the consequent lack of logic or importance in her throwing him over)."[16]

I don't put much stock in these self-deprecating comments. Fitzgerald was always an energetic breast-beater, and in those letters he sounds to me like he's trying to act "grown up" about the criticism his novel has received, including the quibbles from his friends. Though both Wilson and Mencken were fairly enthusiastic about *Gatsby,* they were also men of letters who took themselves extremely seriously; no letter or review was complete without some negative comment. Mencken was kinder about *Gatsby* in a personal letter he wrote to Fitzgerald than he was in the review that was printed in the *Baltimore Sun* and *Chicago Tribune:* "No more than a glorified anecdote.... Certainly not to be put on the same shelf with, say, *This Side of Paradise.*"[17] (Some friend!) By May of 1925, Fitzgerald was in full self-castigating mode, frantically trying to figure out what he had done wrong to account for why the sales of *Gatsby* were so sluggish. The silence at the heart of the relationship between

Gatsby and Daisy was one of his anxious answers; so was Gatsby's enigmatic character; so was the brevity of the novel; so was the title (it was "just so so," he wrote to Max Perkins); so was the fact that it was "too masculine, too muscular" to appeal to women readers. Fitzgerald's soul took a beating at the reception of *Gatsby*, just as his heart took a beating when Zelda's affair with Jozan was revealed.

I don't agree with Fitzgerald's self-criticism about the damaging effects of that central silence. Anything "real" that took place between Gatsby and Daisy during those crucial weeks could never measure up to what Gatsby had envisioned in his imagination all those years. Above all, this is a novel about the titanic power of dreams; it's not a novel about the spell of sex or the naughty giddiness of an illicit affair. I don't want to know how Daisy's body felt to Gatsby or how she smelled when he buried his face in her hair. I know how Gatsby felt: he felt let down. We're told he's already looking a bit confused by the limited reality of Daisy by the time Nick leaves him and Daisy on the evening of their reunion. Moreover, passing over Gatsby and Daisy's relationship in silence further intensifies the relationship that is dramatized in the novel: Nick's enduring love for the dead-and-gone Gatsby.

Back to that tempestuous summer of 1924: It's not clear if Zelda asked Fitzgerald for a divorce or not. (That there was great sadness in the marriage is evidenced by the fact that Zelda tried to commit suicide by taking an overdose of sleeping pills a few weeks after the July "crisis.") To my mind, the most crucial—and unanswerable—question about the affair is the one that concerns *Gatsby:* How much of the trauma of Zelda's betrayal seeped into the plot of Fitzgerald's novel in progress?

You can hear Fitzgerald's shell-shocked tone in the last paragraph of an August 1924 letter he wrote to Ludlow Fowler, a Princeton classmate who, significantly, had served as the best man at his wedding: "I feel old...this summer—I have ever since the failure of my play a year ago. That's the whole burden of this novel—the loss of those illusions that give such color to the world so that you don't care whether things are true or false as long as they partake of the magical glory."[18]

Some writers are surprisingly clumsy at describing their own work, but not Fitzgerald, at least not here. In this one sentence, Fitzgerald gives a better explanation of what *The Great Gatsby* is really *about* than anyone else has come up with to date. Sadly, Fitzgerald is talking not only about his novel, but about the end of something with Zelda.

As biographer Matthew J. Bruccoli points out, the typescript of *Gatsby* was not sent to Scribner's until late October, so Fitzgerald had at least three and a half months to write his grief over Zelda's betrayal into the novel. The Jozan affair would later resurface in a more convoluted fictional form in *Tender Is the Night*, but at the time Fitzgerald was writing *Gatsby*, his wounds were raw. Writing, once again, must have provided a refuge, even though the novel he was working on turned out to be one in which practically everywhere a reader looked, someone was cheating on someone else. Would that have been the case if the novel had been written before July 1924?

Or say that Fitzgerald had already completed much of the first draft of *Gatsby* by that July...imagine how newly and painfully resonant certain scenes in the novel would be. After Daisy publicly professes her love for Gatsby by telling him, "You always look so cool,"[19] Tom, looking on, is "astounded."

In an elegant variation on the epiphany that has sparked many a torch song, we're told that "his mouth opened a little and he looked at Gatsby and then back at Daisy as if he had just recognized her as someone he knew a long time ago."[20] How could Fitzgerald *not* have put himself in Tom's shoes, as well as in the shoes of the other cuckolded husband, George Wilson? A few pages on in that same chapter 7, Wilson is described as "hollow-eyed" and "sick," since he, like Tom, has just "wised up"[21] to his wife's infidelity. And then there's poor betrayed Gatsby. Let's briefly return to the climactic scene where Daisy reveals that her love for Gatsby, unlike his for her, is limited:

> "Oh, you want too much!" she cried to Gatsby. "I love you now—isn't that enough? I can't help what's past." She began to sob helplessly. "I did love him once—but I loved you too."
>
> Gatsby's eyes opened and closed.
>
> "You loved me *too?*" he repeated.[22]

If Fitzgerald had written these bitter scenes pre-Jozan, then rereading them and revising them with Zelda's help—as he did with the entire manuscript of *The Great Gatsby* before sending it to Perkins in October—must have been humiliating. And if he wrote all or some of these passages in the aftermath of Zelda's affair with Jozan, that chronology could account for their punch-in-the-gut intensity.

Who knows? I want to extricate myself from these provocative but unanswerable biographical questions and, as Nick does with Gatsby, call a short halt to our sojourn with the Fitzgeralds. A shattered Scott is sitting alone at his desk in the

Villa Marie, "drag[ging] the great Gatsby out of the pit of my stomach in a time of misery,"[23] as he later recalled in a seven-page autobiographical memo he wrote in 1930 while Zelda was hospitalized in the Prangins Clinic in Switzerland. Let's turn from the flawed affairs of humankind to the near flawless—but very, very weird—novel that Fitzgerald did manage to produce.

Yes, I said "very, very weird." All great works of art are weird, especially in the archaic sense of that word as meaning "uncanny," but I think *The Great Gatsby*, proportionally, contains more than its share of oddities. I've already investigated a few of the stranger aspects of the novel: its defiant insistence on breaking the fundamental rule of good fiction by telling rather than showing and the many striking ways in which it qualifies as an early hard-boiled story. The more you reread *Gatsby*, the curiouser and curiouser it gets. Here's an abbreviated catalog of some other peculiarities of *The Great Gatsby:*

(1) *Gatsby* is neither a character-driven nor a plot-driven novel; instead, it's that rarest of literary animals: a voice-driven novel. Decades ago, my mother, who's never been a reader, asked me what *Gatsby* was about. I remember that this very short conversation took place in the kitchen of the Queens apartment I grew up in, so I must have been reading *Gatsby* for the first time, in high school. I'm sure I said something like: "Well, it's about a man who falls in love with a woman, but she marries a rich guy, and so the man, who's named Gatsby, tries to make a lot of money and throw parties to win her back. And he does, but then he dies." The end. I have no doubt that my mother shook her head ruefully and probably said

something about how the rich always come out on top (even if they're dead).

If the plot of *The Great Gatsby* disintegrates upon retelling, the characters—apart from the all-too-real Tom Buchanan and, for a few indelible paragraphs, Meyer Wolfshiem—barely register as flesh-and-blood entities. Daisy is a green light and a voice that's "full of money"; Nick is also a voice—one that guides us deep into the world of the novel. We don't know what Nick looks like or how he dresses or what he eats. And what about Gatsby? In that famous letter about the first draft of *Gatsby* in which Max Perkins raves about Tom, he expresses reservations about the character of Gatsby. Perkins's long critique begins: "Gatsby is somewhat vague. The reader's eyes can never quite focus upon him, his outlines are dim."[24] In response, Scott did a strange thing: he asked Zelda to draw sketches of Gatsby so that he could see him more clearly. He tells Perkins in his letter of December 20, 1924, that after he's "had Zelda draw pictures till her fingers ache, I know Gatsby better than I know my own child."[25] Imagine how precious those sheets of paper would be today. Given that the Fitzgeralds moved around so much, those pictures probably got tossed in some hotel wastebasket in Europe in 1924, but the tantalizing mention of Zelda's sketches of Gatsby probably has sent many a researcher flipping through papers in Fitzgerald collections at Princeton and the University of South Carolina, hoping for a *Da Vinci Code* moment where one of Zelda's lost sketches falls out of an old ledger and we can finally see Jay Gatsby plain.

Or not. Fitzgerald knew Gatsby intimately, but even with Zelda's help, he never gives a complete physical profile of his central character. Gatsby is a smile, "one of those rare smiles with a quality of eternal reassurance in it, that you may come across four or five times in life."[26] He's his pink suit, rainbow of shirts, and yellow car; his verbal tic of "old sport." Gatsby is also his aura of solitude; look over the novel again and you'll be struck by how many times — at his dock, at his parties, outside the Buchanans' house, and in his pool — Gatsby is alone. Most of the actors who've played Gatsby on-screen have been blond and thus bear a passing resemblance to Fitzgerald, but during the late 1930s, when he was working in Hollywood, Fitzgerald mentioned that if the studios ever made another *Gatsby* film, he thought a very different kind of physical presence — the dark and mustachioed screen idol Clark Gable — would be a good choice to play Gatsby.

Gatsby is the ultimate enigma, the absent center of the novel. Nick projects as much onto Gatsby as Gatsby projects onto Daisy. This is a novel about illusion, after all, as Fitzgerald eloquently said in that letter to Ludlow Fowler. Among *The Great Gatsby*'s early readers, Edith Wharton, for one, thought that its "hero" was much too mysterious. In a letter thanking Fitzgerald for the copy of the novel he'd sent to her, Wharton writes:

> I am touched at your sending me a copy, for I feel that to your generation, which has taken such a flying leap into the future, I must represent the literary equivalent of tufted furniture & gas chandeliers. . . .
>
> My present quarrel with you is only this: that to make Gatsby really Great, you ought to have given us his early career . . . instead of a short resume of it. That would have

situated him, & made his final tragedy a tragedy instead of a "fait divers" for the morning papers.

But you'll tell me that's the old way, & consequently not *your* way.[27]

In the decades since *The Great Gatsby* first appeared, Wharton's gentle but firm criticism of Gatsby's character has been taken up time and again, especially when a new film or ballet or opera or play of *Gatsby* is launched and the received wisdom is resurrected: that the novel is impossible to film or stage because its power is so dependent, not on plot or character, but on language.

And so it is.

Fitzgerald's language, filtered through Nick's voice, is above all else what makes *The Great Gatsby* so extraordinary. Fitzgerald undermines the coarse materiality of rich, careless people like Tom and Daisy in a detached poetic style that elevates but doesn't obliterate ordinary American language. As is true in the sonnets of Fitzgerald's beloved John Keats, almost every word of this intensely compressed masterpiece counts. On the very last page, where all vestiges of a plot are completely abandoned and Nick stands in the starlight outside Gatsby's vacant house—striking the very same pose in which he first spotted Gatsby—we get sentence after sentence packed with intricate meditations. In one of the most famous sentences of those last few pages, Nick, thinking of the Dutch explorers who sailed into New York harbor, says, "For a transitory enchanted moment man must have held his breath in the presence of this continent, compelled into an aesthetic contemplation he neither understood nor desired, face to face for the last time in history with something commensurate to his capacity for wonder."[28] That's a sentence to spend a lifetime periodically contemplating: the historical sweep of it, the mournfulness.[29] In *Gatsby*'s most profound moments, Fitzgerald summons up a voice—call it the omniscient American voice—that renders the American Dream irresistible and heartbreaking and buoyant, all at once.

(2) Another "funny" thing about *Gatsby* is that it's funny. Because of its Great Book status and the breathtaking power of the more solemn passages in the novel, first-time readers overlook the fact that there's a lot of comedy in this novel. Some of Fitzgerald's contemporaries, however, got the joke. In 1925, the only magazine interested in serializing *Gatsby* was *College Humor*, a glossy publication that featured cartoons and satiric pieces by the likes of Robert Benchley and Groucho Marx. Fitzgerald turned down the ten-thousand-dollar offer because he was afraid that readers would get the mistaken idea that Gatsby was a football player and that that would hurt book sales.

The major work that Fitzgerald wrote right before *Gatsby*— as opposed to those short stories he dashed off to pay the bills—was a play called *The Vegetable*. It was intended to be funny—a political satire. Burton Rascoe of the *New York Tribune*, for one, thought the play was a hoot: "I chortled and guffawed over it; it is utterly mad and ridiculous, irreverent, bubbling, disrespectful, witty, malicious and gay."[30]

At the beginning of *Gatsby* especially, Fitzgerald is still drawing on his comic talents. To catch the humor, it's best to read—or hear *Gatsby* read—out loud. In a letter to me,

Eleanor Lanahan, Scott and Zelda's granddaughter, recalled some of the many times she'd read *The Great Gatsby*, chief among them at a public reading onstage:

> I've read it aloud, with many others, on the stage of the Fitzgerald Theatre in St. Paul, under the stage direction of Garrison Keillor, which is the very best way to experience the book. Each time I read it differently. In St. Paul, for the very first time, I realized how much humor it has.[31]

I had similar experiences both times I saw *Gatz*, the seven-hour reading/dramatization of the novel at New York's Public Theater. The audience at those performances laughed out loud at some of Fitzgerald's snappy conversations and the unexpected turns some of his sentences take. In the famous Queensboro Bridge passage, New York City is described as "rising up across the river in white heaps and sugar lumps all built with a wish out of non-olfactory money." *Money that doesn't smell? Manhattan?* Surely Fitzgerald jests. The humor fades as sunlight drains out of the novel and the chill of autumn enters the air—which leads me to the next and perhaps the most incredible oddity of all.

(3) Page for page, *The Great Gatsby* is as elaborately patterned as other modernist masterworks, such as T. S. Eliot's *The Waste Land* and Joyce's *Ulysses*. (Fitzgerald sent a copy of *The Great Gatsby* to T. S. Eliot, who must have been pleased at the homage to *The Waste Land* in the image of the valley of ashes.) Unlike those encrypted texts, however, *Gatsby* can be enjoyed without the aid of an Enigma machine. In fact, *Gatsby* goes

down so smoothly that many readers don't catch on that the novel is wildly overdesigned.

As Matthew J. Bruccoli observed in his preface to the authorized text of *The Great Gatsby:* "One gauge of F. Scott Fitzgerald's achievement is that many admiring readers are unaware of the complexity of *The Great Gatsby* because the novel is such a pleasure to read."[32] Granted, the green light is hard to ignore, as is the billboard featuring the eyes of Dr. T. J. Eckleburg, which practically has neon lights around it proclaiming, *Symbol!* But otherwise, Fitzgerald has a pretty deft touch when it comes to symbol patterns and narrative structure. I honestly don't know how many readings it took for me to catch on that Gatsby and Daisy's reunion took place in the dead center of the novel. Nick's voice and the story he tells are so absorbing that, through many years of rereadings, I barely noticed the placement of that scene.

Remember that Fitzgerald told Max Perkins in that famous letter of 1922 that he wanted his next book to be, among other things, "intricately patterned." Boy, is it ever. I've taught *Gatsby* almost every year for the past three decades and I always think I know most of what there is to know about the novel's complex scaffolding of symbols, including the central image of water... until I realize, once again, that I don't. Sometimes, something new will snag my attention in a passage that I've read dozens of times before; sometimes, my students point out details I've missed that are hiding in plain sight. About ten years ago, I was talking about the drowning motif in class, and a student piped up with the epiphany: "Everybody at Gatsby's parties is drowning in liquor." Only last year, my graduate teaching assistant gave a lecture on *Gatsby* to our freshman class and pointed out the passage on the penultimate page where Nick erases the "obscene word, scrawled by some boy"[33] on the white steps of Gatsby's mansion. She made the connection between Nick's action and his role as a narrator who cleans up Gatsby's story. I was dumbfounded. I should have caught the significance of that moment long, long ago, but I'd always been so focused on the gorgeousness of the final page of *Gatsby* that my eyes had slid right past that detail. Classroom moments like that are golden. While working on this book, I was startled to realize that at the Buchanan dinner party in chapter 1, Daisy tries to distract everyone's attention from Tom's phone conversation with Myrtle by claiming to have heard a bird out on the lawn: "'I think [it] must be a nightingale come over on the Cunard or White Star Line. He's singing away—' Her voice sang: 'It's romantic, isn't it, Tom?'" An English nightingale (echoes of Keats!) making the Atlantic passage on the White Star Line would be replicating the very same route as the *Titanic,* which sank ten years before the Buchanans and Jordan and Nick sat down to dinner. Why put all that detail into Daisy's silly remark if we readers aren't meant to think of one of the most notorious sinking disasters in history?

Sampling even the topmost crust of the mountain of *Gatsby* criticism, I've come away feeling as though I could spend the rest of my life trying to understand the astounding degree to which Fitzgerald "overwrote" *Gatsby*. For starters, there are the ten or so major symbol systems I try to cover in classroom lectures. Time is a big one. The indefatigable Bruccoli totted up 450 time words in *Gatsby;* hours of the day and seasons are noted constantly, and time even enters into titles of songs. At the conclusion of the disappointing party at Gatsby's house that Daisy and Tom attend, the band plays "Three O'Clock in the Morning," a "neat sad little waltz of that year."[34] There's also the oft-acknowledged comic intrusion of the clock in the reunion scene between Gatsby and Daisy: Gatsby leans his head so far back against the mantelpiece in Nick's sitting room that he's literally hit over the head with time. Bizarrely, Edmund Wilson, in his *New Republic* review of the 1926 Broadway play of *Gatsby,* thought that the adaptation "succeeded in improving on Fitzgerald" by having Gatsby knock over a highball glass rather than the clock and then apologize for "upsetting the vase." Wilson clearly needed another rereading of *Gatsby* to catch the importance of the clock.

Like sand in an hourglass, time is running out from the very first pages of this novel: an ultimate "deadline" casts its shadow over Gatsby. Other symbol patterns have to do with temperature ("You always look so cool"), geographical direction (East Egg versus West Egg), names (including the flower names of Daisy and Myrtle), music, vision, vehicles (cars, hydroplanes, trains), birds, color (whole constellations of meaning swirl around greens, grays, reds, and blues), and medieval-quest romances and mythology (Gatsby as Icarus; Gatsby as Apollo the sun god; Gatsby as Prometheus; Gatsby as that old warhorse of many a term paper, a Christ figure). For an overview of the plethora of other symbols in the novel, check out the glut of *Gatsby* research papers for sale on Internet sites like GradeSaver.com and Tutionster.com (whose ad depressingly promises its customers "Academic Help by PhD Experts!"). You can imagine a modern-day Tom Buchanan disposing thusly of his freshman English requirement at Yale.

The *major* symbol patterns, however, are just the beginning of the fun. As in those wonderful art deco designs of the 1920s, there are repetitive subpatterns within the larger patterns: geometric cubes within cubes, stories within stories. Consider, once more, that dominant symbol of time. Each of the first three chapters in the novel features a party, and each of those parties occurs at a progressively later time in the day. The Buchanans' dinner takes place at sunset, followed by the late-afternoon-to-evening bacchanal at Tom and Myrtle's love nest, followed by Gatsby's party at which he makes his delayed entrance past midnight. The cumulative effect is to heighten suspense until the moment we readers finally meet Gatsby in the flesh at the third party.

But, as the infomercial pitchmen always say, Hold on, there's more! That party structure extends throughout the entire novel! Every chapter of *The Great Gatsby* is built around a party of some sort, including dinners and lunches and the final poorly attended "party" that is Gatsby's funeral. Some scholars attribute this dramatic structure—which should seem contrived but doesn't—to Fitzgerald's extensive playwriting experience at Princeton and on through his flop of *The Vegetable*.

Speaking of something else that should feel contrived but doesn't, there's a pattern of unrequited desire running through *Gatsby*. One person in every couple in the novel stretches out to grasp the other, who remains forever out of reach. The emblematic image of this yearning is Gatsby in the darkness stretching out his arms for the green light at the end of Daisy's dock. Nick exactly mimics this gesture in the last chapter of the novel: he stands alone, under the stars, in front of Gatsby's mansion, looking out over the water. Nick not only steps into his dead friend's shoes but tries to grasp Gatsby by telling his story. Jordan, in turn, languidly reaches for the emotionally unavailable Nick. Even the minor characters take part in this highly choreographed dance of unrequited desire: Wilson's clutching for Myrtle is mirrored by Myrtle's clutching for Tom; Tom possessively reaches for Daisy. And Daisy? Daisy reaches for no one, not really, not even Pammy, her daughter. Daisy's self-containment is in keeping with her narcissistic identity as a femme fatale.

Simply put, the intricacy of *The Great Gatsby* is staggering. Once you become aware of how deliberate even the most throwaway moments in the novel are, you develop a double vision toward *Gatsby,* admiring its smooth surface while sensing the fathoms that abide beneath. I'll just mention one more example of what I've come to think of simply as *Gatsby's* "too-muchness." In chapter 2, as Myrtle, Tom, and Nick are riding in a "lavender"[35] cab on their way to the apartment on 158th Street, Myrtle suddenly insists they pull over so that Tom can buy her a puppy from a sidewalk vendor. It's one of those quick comic moments, given that the vendor bears "an absurd resemblance to John D. Rockefeller" and the "very recent" puppies he's claiming are Airedales instead appear to be "of an indeterminate breed."[36]

Later, in the smoky apartment, Myrtle happily natters on, listing all the things she's "got to get." That list includes "a collar for the dog, and one of those cute little ash trays where you touch a spring, and a wreath with a black silk bow for mother's grave that'll last all summer."[37] Everybody at the party is too drunk to pay any attention to Myrtle. The last time we glimpse the little dog, it's "sitting on the table looking with blind eyes through the smoke and from time to time groaning faintly."[38] (Edith Wharton, a staunch dog lover, told Fitzgerald in that thank-you note for *Gatsby* that she couldn't stop thinking about the fate of the poor puppy.) But it's Myrtle's shopping list that really merits a mulling over. The dog collar Myrtle wants to buy is ironically indicative of how she's treated by Tom Buchanan, the ashtray invokes Myrtle's lower-class origins in the valley of ashes as well as her approaching ashes-to-ashes fate, and the cemetery wreath is a grim foreshadowing of her death.[39] Symbol stacking for symbol stacking's sake is tedious, but that's not what's going on in *Gatsby*. Fitzgerald was a romantic egoist, a lapsed Catholic, a dreamer; by temperament and upbringing, he saw meaning in the mundane. The distinctive oddity—or miracle—of *Gatsby* is not that it contains so many symbols but that (green light and Eckleburg excepted) it manages to read as though it barely contains any.

(4) Reviewing Myrtle's shopping list takes me to the eeriest facet of *The Great Gatsby*: its predictive quality. This Ouija board aspect of *Gatsby* is a guaranteed discussion starter on a slow day in freshman English. I can offer no explanations, only observations:

One of the lines in the novel that jars me out of the 1920s every time I read it is Nick's one-sentence description of the discovery of Wilson's body near Gatsby's pool: "It was after we started with Gatsby toward the house that the gardener saw Wilson's body a little way off in the grass, and the holocaust was complete."[40] That word *holocaust* is arresting, particularly given that this is a novel in which the word *swastika* appears in connection with a Jewish character wearing human molars as cuff links. My students are not stupid, but like many of the best and brightest young Americans, they're often a little vague as to time lines in world history. When I remind them that *Gatsby* was written in 1925 and that the Nazis didn't come to power in Germany until 1933, they're confused. They always want to know: What are all these World War II–era words and images doing floating around in *Gatsby*? I tell them that words like *holocaust* and *swastika* didn't have the meanings in 1925 that they do now, but still, we all agree, it's strange to find them in a novel about Jazz Age New York.

The Great Depression is another world event that the novel seems to foretell. The lights are turned out in Gatsby's mansion in chapter 7 and the parties are over, just as the giddy national party that was the Roaring Twenties got shut down on Black Tuesday, October 29, 1929. Certainly Fitzgerald wasn't alone in suspecting that the good times couldn't roll on indefinitely, but his novel predicts a crash, for Gatsby, at least, of total wipe-out proportions.

There's also a personal reach to the predictive aura of *The Great Gatsby*. I've already mentioned that Fitzgerald's first burial hewed pretty closely to Gatsby's dismal send-off. After Fitzgerald died in Hollywood on Saturday, December 21, 1940, his body was taken to a funeral home, Pierce Brothers Mortuary, in a run-down neighborhood in Los Angeles. A cosmetic mortician went to work on Fitzgerald, and he was put on view in, of all places, "the William Wordsworth room." A visitor recalled that he was laid out to look like "a cross between a floor-walker and a wax dummy. Except for one bouquet of flowers and a few empty chairs, there was nothing to keep him company except his casket."[41] Dorothy Parker, one of the few friends present, blurred the lines between life and art when she ironically quoted Owl Eyes' comment on Gatsby: "The poor son-of-a-bitch."

Fitzgerald's body was then shipped back to Maryland, where Catholic authorities denied him burial in the Fitzgerald family plot in St. Mary's churchyard. On December 27, 1940, biographer Andrew Turnbull attended the viewing at the (still operating today) Pumphrey Funeral Home in Bethesda, followed by the Episcopalian burial service at the Rockville Union Cemetery. (As a boy, Turnbull had come to know Fitzgerald, Zelda, and Scottie when they all lived at La Paix, the estate owned by Turnbull's parents.) Here's a snippet of his eyewitness account. Too bad Fitzgerald couldn't appreciate the *Gatsby*-esque coincidences:

> It was a meaningless occasion, having no apparent connection with the man, save as one of life's grim jokes designed to make us think....In the airless hall and communicating rooms of the funeral parlor were a few spindly poinsettias....The casket was open, and the suave funeral director ushered us up to it. All the lines of living had gone from Fitzgerald's face....His clothes suggested a shop window.
>
> We sat on stiff chairs in the overlit room as friends and relatives arrived in twos and threes—the Murphys, the Perkinses, the Obers...Ludlow Fowler, John Biggs, Zelda's brother-in-law Newman Smith—twenty or thirty in all. At the last, there was a flurry of boys and girls— Scottie's friends on their way to or from some party.... The coffin was closed. The roll of a carpet sweeper was

heard gathering stray leaves and petals, and then the voice of the clergyman droning the Protestant burial. It was as if nothing were being said *of* him or *to* him that the heart could hear.

Afterwards, we drove to the cemetery in the rain.[42]

(5) Here's the final item in my list of oddities about *The Great Gatsby: Gatsby* is the only great novel that Fitzgerald ever wrote.

I've just lost all you *Tender Is the Night* fans—and I know how fervent you can be because I've run into quite a few, one time en masse on a Baltimore sidewalk. Last winter, I got word that the row house in the Bolton Hill section of Baltimore where Fitzgerald was living when *Tender Is the Night* was published had just been put on the market and that there would be a real estate agent's open house on Super Bowl Sunday. Since there are so few Fitzgerald sites that are accessible to the public, I decided to drive up from Washington and have a look.

That Sunday of the open house turned out to be wet and lightly snowy; the Ravens were playing the 49ers and the whole city was a study in black, purple, and gold. Nevertheless, by the time I arrived, a big crowd of people (lots of them in black, purple, and gold) had already gathered on the street in front of the tall gray row house on Park Avenue. Nobody was happy. It turned out a contract had already been signed and the open house was canceled.

I know from reading various biographies of Fitzgerald and from listening to an interview that Scottie gave to Matthew J. Bruccoli that this row house, whose appearance falls somewhere between *modest* and *stately*, had hosted illustrious showbiz visitors such as George Burns and Gracie Allen (whom Scottie said her father was "crazy about") and Clark Gable, who came to lunch.[43] The open-house crowd lacked any obvious star power, but I was happy to see a lot of college-age men and women milling about—not the usual demographic of literary tourists. One couple told me they'd driven down from central Pennsylvania that morning; a few other people identified themselves as members of the Fitzgerald Society. Indeed, the sidewalk turned out to be lousy with Fitzgerald experts. (I imagined the shade of Fitzgerald floating around inside the row house, laughing and double-checking the locks.) One woman told me she'd written a play about Zelda, another was working on a book about Sheilah Graham, and an older man claimed he'd been instrumental in relocating Scott and Zelda to their current resting place in the Old St. Mary's churchyard. Almost everyone I chatted with told me they just had to get in because they loved *Tender Is the Night*. Not being so devout, I was content to leave and let a Baltimore native, NPR web producer Beth Novey, take me on an impromptu tour around the outside of other Fitzgerald landmarks: the dreary Cambridge Arms Apartments, where Scott and Scottie rented an apartment to be close to Zelda, who was then in the psychiatric hospital Sheppard Pratt; and the still elegant Belvedere Hotel, where Fitzgerald gave Scottie her sixteenth-birthday tea dance, at which he got blotto.

I want to like *Tender Is the Night* more than I do. Maybe, someday, I will. The novel contains so many stretches of lovely writing, but I have to stand with those critics who label it a beautiful failure. I don't think it touches *The Great Gatsby*. The plot of *Tender Is the Night* is murky, and its omniscient narrator possesses none of the resonance of Nick's distanced yet enthralled voice. Fitzgerald spent nine years after the publication of *Gatsby* working erratically on his next novel as he was trying to find—and finance—the best care for Zelda, raise Scottie, and battle his own alcoholic demons. When *Tender Is the Night* was first published, it sold about twelve thousand copies. By 1934, Americans had a diminished appetite for reading about rich folks on the Riviera. As he had with *Gatsby*, Fitzgerald obsessively ruminated on what he had done wrong in *Tender Is the Night* that might account for its poor sales. He focused on the structure of the novel; its middle section was composed of flashbacks, which had confused some readers. Throughout the remainder of the 1930s, Fitzgerald worked on revisions. As an author's copy of *Tender Is the Night* in the collection of Princeton's Firestone Library attests, Fitzgerald even tore pages of the novel out of their binding in order to rearrange them. In 1951, literary critic and Fitzgerald friend Malcolm Cowley, relying on notes that Fitzgerald had made, brought out another version of the novel, this one told in a straightforward, chronological manner. It bombed, and Scribner's reverted to Fitzgerald's original. Whatever Fitzgerald had in mind for the ultimate incarnation of *Tender Is the Night*, I think it's safe to say his vision was never realized.

Fitzgerald's other novels are second-tier works. *This Side of Paradise* is a time-sensitive literary sensation; it made Fitzgerald the sage of the Jazz Age, but, unlike *Gatsby*, it doesn't transcend its time. *The Beautiful and Damned* is interesting because of its glimpses of 1920s New York life and the Fitzgeralds' already wobbling marriage, but it's a thinly written story with

SO WE READ ON

wooden main characters. That leaves us with *The Love of the Last Tycoon*, which is maybe a great novel in the making, but only in the making. Fitzgerald planned his Hollywood novel to be short and symmetrically designed, like *Gatsby;* he left about forty-four thousand words of a projected sixty thousand in a very, very rough draft that was posthumously edited and shaped into an unfinished novel by Edmund Wilson. Like Dickens's *Mystery of Edwin Drood,* it's an appetite-whetting fragment.

Readers expect that if a writer has hit it out of the ballpark once, he or she can do so again and again, but in fact, literary history is studded with singletons. In modern American literature alone, we have the classic examples of *The Catcher in the Rye, Invisible Man,* and *To Kill a Mockingbird.* Skipping down a few notches on the value scale, there's Margaret Mitchell's *Gone with the Wind,* which won the Pulitzer Prize for Fiction in 1937. MGM put Fitzgerald to work on the screenplay of that novel in the winter of 1939, a job that deeply impressed Scottie, who told her father, to his horror, that she thought Mitchell's novel was one of the "masterpieces of all time." Fitzgerald always thought of himself as a poet, and poets burned out early, particularly the Romantic poets he loved. The years of drinking and terrible personal stress ate away at Fitzgerald's creative and physical stamina, and besides, the muses are notoriously fickle.

Note, though, that I started out this reflection on *The Great Gatsby*'s singularity by saying that it's the only great *novel* Fitzgerald wrote. I think that some of his other writings fall into the masterpiece category, among them the *Crack-Up* essays, some of his short stories (especially the ones belonging to the *Gatsby* cluster), and his letters—many of which are emotionally raw and radiant with humor and self-awareness. There are substantial volumes in print of Fitzgerald's letters to Zelda, to Maxwell Perkins, to Ginevra King, to Harold Ober, and to Scottie. Probably, like many of us, he was his best self in his writing, but I dare anyone to read Fitzgerald's letters and *not* come away feeling, as Nick does about Gatsby, that "there was something gorgeous about him, some heightened sensitivity to the promises of life."[44]

But it's time I wrapped up this short halt and returned to the Riviera in the summer of 1924, where love lies bleeding in the sand. After the exposure of Zelda's affair with Edouard Jozan, Fitzgerald, nevertheless, continued to bend his head down at his desk, working on *Gatsby*. In September 1924, Fitzgerald turned twenty-eight, and the first draft of the novel was finished. He wrote in his ledger: "Hard work sets in." Fitzgerald was talking about the hard work of revision, with which Zelda helped. He also sent off a letter to Max Perkins on September 10 in which he says: "the novel will absolutely + definately [*sic*] be mailed to you before the 1st of October....It is like nothing I've ever read before."[45] In October, the ledger notes: "Working at high pressure to finish." In November, the typescript was sent to Max Perkins, and the ledger proclaims: "Novel off at last."

Before and after that joyous announcement, Fitzgerald was rewriting and chopping and rewriting. As gifted an artist as Fitzgerald sometimes was, he was just as gifted a craftsman. There were times when Fitzgerald, usually under pressure to make a quick buck with his short stories, coasted on his creative powers. Otherwise, he was the archenemy of the Allen Ginsberg "first thought, best thought" school of impulsive writing. Literature, he told a young family friend in 1938 who'd sent him a story to critique, "is one of those professions that wants the 'works.' You wouldn't be interested in a soldier who was only a little brave."[46] Fitzgerald was talking about the emotional courage that good writing demands as well as another kind: the nerve to look steadily at drafts of one's work, rip them apart, and start over again. His urge to rewrite often shades into obsession. *This Side of Paradise* went through two major revisions before the third try was the charm with Scribner's. As we've seen with *Tender Is the Night*, Fitzgerald sometimes kept on revising even *after* publication. To an extent, this was also the case with *Gatsby*.

Among the many treasures in the Fitzgerald Papers at Princeton, there's a rather beaten-up copy of *The Great Gatsby* that's especially tantalizing to those readers trying to fathom Fitzgerald's creative process and intentions. This first edition of *Gatsby* is Fitzgerald's own personal copy. We know it's his because inside the front cover, on the right-hand page, Fitzgerald has written:

> *F. Scott Fitzgerald*
> *(His copy and not to be Lent)*
> *May 1925*

This *Gatsby* is missing its dust jacket, and its binding is falling apart. Someone has spilled what looks like coffee on page 65 (at the end of chapter 3, where Nick is leaving his first party at Gatsby's house). It looks like someone tried to flick the coffee away from the page with a thumb.

A tireless rereader of his own novel, Fitzgerald has marked

up in pencil almost every thick, soft page of this *Gatsby*. There are underlinings as well as cryptic vertical lines drawn next to passages; there are notations where Fitzgerald seems to be reminding himself of the source of gestures and bits of dialogue (next to the description of the photographer McKee, for instance, Fitzgerald writes, *Lewellen Jones*). In still other places, Fitzgerald scribbles the names of reviewers and friends— Burlingame, Rosenfield, Ring—who commented on those specific passages in their reviews and letters. And then there are the changes; lots of little changes. Precisely because almost every one of the changes is so incidental, I find them touching. Fitzgerald is such a perfectionist, he just can't let go. These changes were picked up in subsequent editions so that *Gatsby* got closer and closer to Fitzgerald's Platonic ideal of the novel. In chapter 3, he changes Nick's military affiliation (*why?*) from the First Division to, as he abbreviates it, the "3d." Myrtle's mouth, in death, is described in the first edition as being "ripped a little at the corners," but Fitzgerald deletes *a little*. In chapter 2, where Nick describes Tom's shameless public behavior with Myrtle—"his acquaintances resented the fact that he turned up in popular cafés with her"—Fitzgerald underlines *cafés* and writes *restaurants* in the right-hand margin. (Until I slowly paged through Fitzgerald's own edition of *Gatsby*, I hadn't realized that he chose to hold that profane party at Myrtle and Tom's apartment on a Sunday, the Sabbath— another subtle way in which this modern novel undermines pious convention.) A *they are* is changed to a *they're;* the fictional Muhlbach Hotel is changed to the real Sealbach (which will be corrected to the Seelbach—Fitzgerald couldn't spell to save himself). A metal light fixture in Wilson's garage is changed to a wire one, and on and on Fitzgerald goes, ceaselessly revising his own novel.

These changes were mere tweaks compared to the revisions that Fitzgerald undertook prepublication, as he was writing *Gatsby* in 1924. I'm not going to walk too far into the weeds here, because scholars of *The Great Gatsby* can and have devoted lengthy articles as well as books to its editing history. I do want, however, to briefly acknowledge the process—informed by sweat and panicky second-guessing and disciplined craftsmanship—through which Fitzgerald shaped his drafts into the final version of *Gatsby*.

The arc of *Gatsby*'s evolution begins at White Bear Lake in 1922, when Fitzgerald first begins writing a Catholic novel set in the Midwest of the nineteenth century (he tossed out most of that eighteen-thousand-word draft, except for what became the short story "Absolution"). The arc extends over to the very edge of *Gatsby*'s publication.

Fitzgerald did not type; he wrote in longhand, usually in pencil. (There's a ten-second film clip dating from the early 1920s, now instantly viewable on the Internet, that shows Fitzgerald, dressed in a suit, sitting outside under a tree and writing on a small table. At the very end of the clip, he holds his head in his hand, as though he's in the throes of creative struggle.) When Fitzgerald completed the manuscript of *Gatsby*, it was turned over to a secretary, and that typescript of the novel—which Fitzgerald also revised—was the document that was sent to Max Perkins at the end of October 1924. That original typescript, as well as the carbon copies of it, has not survived, but the manuscript has, thanks to the Fitzgeralds' daughter, Scottie.

In the early 1940s, the executor of Fitzgerald's estate, Judge John Biggs Jr., who had been Fitzgerald's friend and classmate at Princeton, urged Scottie to sell some of her father's papers and manuscripts to the university in order to cover Zelda's care and pay back her own college loans. Zelda was ready to follow this well-intentioned direction, and it was in her power to do so. (Scott's will declared that all his books, writings, and possessions were Scottie's property until such time as Zelda regained her sanity. But since Zelda was never declared legally insane, the estate technically belonged to her, as Scott's widow.) Scottie, however, argued forcefully for keeping all her father's papers together in one archive. They were offered to his alma mater, Princeton, which came up with the figure of one thousand dollars for the entire lot.

In *Scottie,* her forthright and moving biography of her mother, Eleanor Lanahan writes that David Randall, Scribner's manager of rare books, stepped in at this point to challenge Princeton's lowball offer. Julian Boyd, then Princeton's University librarian, refused to raise the bid and, according to Randall, said something along the lines of "Princeton was not a charitable institution, nor was its library established to support indigent widows of, and I quote, 'second rate, Midwest hacks,' just because they happen to have been lucky enough to have attended Princeton — unfortunately for Princeton."[47]

In 1949, Princeton did up the offer to twenty-five hundred dollars. As the sale was going through, Scottie surprised everyone by deciding to make the papers "an outright gift."[48] That gift consisted of fifty-seven boxes of correspondence, proofs, records, books, and manuscripts, including the autograph manuscript of *The Great Gatsby.* The F. Scott Fitzgerald Papers at Princeton have since grown to eighty-nine archival boxes and eleven oversize containers. The collection also includes Sheilah Graham's papers and books. To Fitzgerald scholars, the Fitzgerald Papers and the related material is priceless. (For those more inclined to speculate about the cold-hard-cash value of the Princeton collection, consider this random fact: a first edition, with dust jacket, of *Gatsby* was offered for sale in May 2013 by the Jones Brothers, an online rare-book site, for the startling price of $194,000.) In celebration of the centenary of F. Scott Fitzgerald's freshman year at Princeton (and coinciding with the release of the Baz Luhrmann film), Princeton recently digitized the autograph-manuscript copy of *The Great Gatsby*. Princeton has also digitized the surviving two pages of the ur-*Gatsby* (which had been attached to a letter to Willa Cather) and the corrected galleys of what Fitzgerald was calling, by December of 1924, "Trimalchio." With the aid of the magnification function and, perhaps, reading glasses, Fitzgerald's cuts, cross-outs, additions, and marginalia are available for viewing on your home laptop.

Digitization is a marvel, but the multitude of Fitzgerald fans fervently hoping to genuflect in person before the original manuscript are kept at a protective distance. Princeton must remain unmoved. Don C. Skemer, Princeton's current curator of manuscripts, tells me that access to Fitzgerald's manuscripts were restricted by Scottie, the donor, as part of the gift agreement with Princeton. "Honoring those restrictions," Skemer says, "is an obligation—what lawyers call 'donor covenant.' Scottie knew full well that her father wrote on paper of poor quality—paper that would not hold up to heavy use."[49] Scottie also required that Princeton make surrogates of the manuscripts available; by the early 1950s, Princeton did so in the form of microfilm, which was supplemented in the 1970s by a published facsimile edition and is now being replaced by digitization and online access. A visit to Princeton's campus, even in the slower summer months, helps me to understand the library's concerns about the impact of literary tourism on the fragile *Gatsby* manuscript. All day long, buses rumble through the quaint main drag of Nassau Street disgorging tourists, a good number of them college-age kids visiting from Europe and Asia. Many of them want to see *The Great Gatsby* manuscript. To my surprise, I learn from another Princeton librarian, Gabriel Swift, who assists researchers in rare books and special collections, that the manuscript comes in second on the Firestone Library most-requested list. That's because the item in the number one spot can be read only at Princeton. It's an unpublished short story by J. D. Salinger called "The Ocean Full of Bowling Balls" that was scheduled to appear in *Harper's* before Salinger pulled it. The story is a prequel to *The Catcher in the Rye* in that it deals with the death of Kenneth Caulfield (later Allie), Holden's brother. Salinger's will prohibits publication (or copying or digitization) until fifty years after his death (2060), although some pirated copies have begun surfacing recently on the Internet. Swift tells me that he fields e-mails from people all over the world who are planning to visit the United States and are set on coming to Princeton for that one Salinger story, which they're permitted to read in a preservation photocopy, not the original typescript. Of course, the requests for Salinger's elusive, unpublished story are of a different order than the requests to view the manuscript of what may be our most widely read Great American Novel.

Don C. Skemer emphasizes that *The Great Gatsby* is the university's single most important modern literary manuscript.

The vision of an unending stream of holidaymakers wearing Princeton Tiger T-shirts and snapping cell-phone shots of the manuscript of *The Great Gatsby* is nightmarish, but there's also something wrong about the manuscript's current if-a-tree-falls-in-a-forest situation. The 302 now-brittle pages of the autograph manuscript lie in state in a big walk-in storage room in Princeton's Firestone Library. The room is fireproof; the temperature is set at 67 degrees and the humidity at 45 percent. "It's our best vault," Skemer commented in an interview with *Princeton Alumni Weekly* (the very same publication that Fitzgerald was reading when he died). It's also a vault very few mortals ever get to enter, even those with plausible scholarly reasons. Of course, I tried. I couldn't even talk my way onto the elevator to look at the vault from the outside. Princeton's crucial mission is to safeguard one of the most cherished manuscripts in American culture, but doing so means sealing up *The Great Gatsby* in the dark. Something like the National Archives Rotunda or the British Library's display room is needed as a site for our national *literary* treasures. Princeton's Firestone Library is in the midst of a total renovation, and Skemer is hopeful that some sort of rotating display of highlights of the library's collection may be possible in the planned state-of-the-art exhibition gallery.

I want to turn away from the vault now and go back to the grubby, pencil-smudged gestation of *Gatsby*. In his detailed letter of November 20, 1924, Perkins responded to the typescript Fitzgerald sent him, and Fitzgerald went into overdrive making changes. In the introduction to the Cambridge edition of *Trimalchio,* editor and scholar James L. W. West III says that reading *Trimalchio* "is like listening to a well-known musical composition, but played in a different key and with an alternate bridge passage."[50] It's a reading experience I find frustrating; I'm itching for Fitzgerald to hurry up and find his way to realizing *The Great Gatsby.*

To do so, Fitzgerald took the manuscript he was calling "Trimalchio" down to its skeleton, then he redesigned the structure, ripped out dull patches, and trimmed superfluous words and passages. A stark indication of how intensely and continuously Fitzgerald was rewriting *Gatsby* is seen in the scribbling on the set of galleys that Max Perkins sent to Fitzgerald in the winter of 1924–1925. Conventionally, when a novel is in galleys, it's all but done. Fitzgerald, however, revised that set of galleys so extensively that Perkins had to have the galleys reset.

F. Scott Fitzgerald's eraser. Though Fitzgerald didn't type, Scottie claimed this eraser belonged to her father. (MATTHEW J. & ARLYN BRUCCOLI COLLECTION OF F. SCOTT FITZGERALD, UNIVERSITY OF SOUTH CAROLINA LIBRARIES)

That second set of galleys incorporated Fitzgerald's changes and, subsequently, picked up still more changes.

Some of the alterations were large scale: The relationship between Nick and Jordan faded in prominence, and Jordan, in particular, receded as a character. Originally, Gatsby's life story was presented in what was a big flat stretch of retrospection in chapter 8. Taking Perkins's advice, Fitzgerald broke up that long biographical section and scattered it throughout the earlier chapters of the novel. Chapter 3 (Gatsby's first party) was originally chapter 2; Fitzgerald pushed it back to make readers wait longer to finally meet Gatsby. That change also makes the first three chapters of the novel more symmetrical, in that we readers are treated to a three-tiered tour of the American class system: East Egg's old money in chapter 1, the valley of ashes in chapter 2, and West Egg's gaudy new-money revels in chapter 3. Fitzgerald originally set the big Plaza Hotel confrontation scene between Tom and Gatsby and Daisy at a baseball game at the Polo Grounds, and then in Central Park. (New York City offered Fitzgerald an endless array of choices.)

It's startling to realize that the novel's landmark symbol—the green light at the end of Daisy's dock—was an eleventh-hour addition, but that addition makes more sense when you learn that Nick's incantatory meditation on Dutch sailors and the "fresh, green breast of the new world" originally appeared at the end of chapter 1. Wisely, Fitzgerald transferred that passage to the final page of the novel, so Daisy's green light was inserted at the beginning of the novel to visually tie her romantic "promise" to America's. On the final page of his novel, Fitzgerald wrote a word that Perkins queried, one that still throws my students when I ask them to read the end of *Gatsby* out loud. Perkins wondered whether *orgastic* was a mistake. Fitzgerald responded that "'orgastic' is the adjective from 'orgasm' and it expresses exactly the intended ecstasy."[51]

There are many, many, more changes, macro and micro. I'm delighted but puzzled by Fitzgerald's decision to cross out what looks like the *Heyers* in that over-the-top party list in chapter four and write in the *Corrigans*. (Is it funnier? More ethnic? More melodious?) The "short halt" that Nick takes in chapter 6 doesn't appear in the autograph manuscript; instead, chapter 6 begins abruptly with the intrusion of Tom and his riding friends into Gatsby's mansion. And first time round, Fitzgerald wrote his immortal line differently: "So we beat on, a boat against the current, borne back ceaselessly with the past." Changing that lone boat to boats sounds, to my ears, more collectively American.

In her sharp and entertaining book on rewriting, *The Artful Edit*, Susan Bell devotes two chapters to Fitzgerald's revisions of *The Great Gatsby*. (She begins the first chapter by admitting that she hadn't read *Gatsby* since high school; when she read it again in 2002 at the age of forty-three, she says, "I was floored. Every sentence and event felt necessary."[52]) Bell demonstrates, among other things, how essential the quality of restraint—a quality many critics don't associate with the symbol-heavy *Gatsby*—is to its final achievement. Here's just one example: In "Trimalchio," Fitzgerald went overboard in stressing the bright white beauty of Daisy and Jordan in the Buchanans' living room. The "Trimalchio" version reads: "They were both in white, and their dresses were rippling and fluttering as if they had just blown in after a short flight around the house. I must have stood for a few moments on the threshold, dazzled by the alabaster light, listening to the whip and snap of the curtains and the groan of a picture on the wall."

In the final less-is-more version, Fitzgerald trusts in his language — and his readers — and doesn't belabor the image:

"They were both in white, and their dresses were rippling and fluttering as if they had just been blown back in after a short flight around the house. I must have stood for a few moments listening to the whip and snap of the curtains and the groan of a picture on the wall."

Fitzgerald made hundreds of such excisions and small shavings of a word or a phrase here and there. In addition to the personal editorial input Fitzgerald received from Zelda, he also responded to suggestions from other editors at Scribner's and from Ring Lardner and his brother. Rex Lardner was an editor at *Liberty* magazine and had read *The Great Gatsby* in proof when it was being considered for serialization. *Liberty* declined the novel in December 1924, and the rejection letter explains why: "It is too ripe for us.... We could not publish this story with as many mistresses and as much adultery as there is in it."[53]

These changes work to clarify the design of *Gatsby*, highlight the class theme, and render Nick more contemplative and likable. Perhaps this is an instance where someone like me, who's read the novel so many times, may not be the best person to judge. I see — and hear — Fitzgerald's changes as better because they accord with the rhythms I've become habituated to, rereading after rereading.

Well, that's not quite true. There is one particular part of *Gatsby* that Fitzgerald kept playing with: Fitzgerald never found what he considered the right title for his third novel. The working title for *Gatsby* during the spring and summer of 1924 had been "Among Ash Heaps and Millionaires," which I think is pretty good in that it captures the novel's class concerns (although it does nothing for the central theme of lost illusion). When Fitzgerald sent the typescript of the book to Perkins, the title, at first, was "The Great Gatsby" (the preference of Perkins and Zelda). By the time the novel was in galleys, Fitzgerald was calling it "Trimalchio," after a character in the first-century Roman work *Satyricon*, by Petronius. (As Sarah Churchwell points out, a new edition of *Satyricon* was all the rage in the early 1920s, and T. S. Eliot prefaced *The Waste Land* with a headnote from the play.) In the original play, Trimalchio is a freed slave who's climbed up the ladder of Roman society through hard work. He's known for throwing extravagant parties with grotesque gourmet dishes like live birds sewn up in a roasted pig. Need I say that the title "Trimalchio" was a bad idea? Gatsby is not a bombastic type; his parties—which he doesn't seem to enjoy—are a lure for Daisy, the one person he wants to impress. Wise Max Perkins tactfully nixed "Trimalchio," and so Fitzgerald brainstormed a slew of other feeble to awful titles: "Trimalchio in West Egg," "Gold-Hatted Gatsby," "Gatsby," "The High-Bouncing Lover," "On the Road to West Egg," and "Under the Red, White, and Blue." Fitzgerald wasn't fond of "The Great Gatsby" because he said that Gatsby wasn't really great (although Nick thinks he is, and such illusions are what the novel is about). Fitzgerald also felt that "Gatsby" sounded too much like Sinclair Lewis's 1922 novel *Babbitt*. (Lewis, by the way, is another one of Fitzgerald's contemporaries who won the Nobel Prize—in his case, in 1930.)

The moral here is that everyone, even F. Scott Fitzgerald,

needs a good editor, and Fitzgerald had the best. Max Perkins reinforced Fitzgerald's best impulses, bucked him up when he was flooded with self-doubt, and wasn't afraid to tell him when his ideas were weak. On March 7, 1925, Fitzgerald cabled Perkins to ask if it was too late to change the title of *The Great Gatsby* back to "Gold-Hatted Gatsby" or "Trimalchio." Happily, it was.

All through these long months of shepherding *Gatsby* through revisions, Perkins was at his desk at Scribner's in New York while Fitzgerald and his family were on the move. Maybe jumping from place to place helped Fitzgerald manage his nervous energy; maybe the moves also helped distract Scott and Zelda from their marital troubles. They left the Riviera in early November to spend the winter in Rome, but Italy was a bust: since they couldn't find an apartment to rent, they wound up staying at a damp and expensive hotel. In response to Harold Ober's suggestion that he write about his Italian sojourn, Fitzgerald proposed an article called "Pope Siphilis the Sixth and His Morons." (Fitzgerald had come a long way since that 1921 request for an audience with the pope.) At Ober's tactful urging, that article eventually morphed into "The High Cost of Macaroni"—which Ober was still unable to sell.[54] In February, the Fitzgeralds moved to a hotel on Capri, and Fitzgerald began work on the *Gatsby*-cluster story "The Rich Boy." Then, after a couple of months, they packed up again and left for Paris. That spring was probably the most momentous spring of Fitzgerald's life: *The Great Gatsby* came out on April 10, and sometime before the first of May, on a mission as a self-appointed talent scout for Scribner's, Fitzgerald arranged to meet and then charmed a promising writer—Ernest Hemingway—at the

Dingo American Bar in Montparnasse. For Fitzgerald, both events would turn out to be disappointments.

I've been a book reviewer for three decades. Perhaps delusionally, I think I'm right roughly 95 percent of the time in my opinion about the books I review. Still, I look at the reviews that *The Great Gatsby* got in the spring of 1925 and what I mostly feel is queasiness about my profession and self-doubt that, maybe, had I been a reviewer then, *Gatsby* might have been one of those rare novels that I got wrong. Perhaps even worse, I wonder if I would have reviewed it in the first place. I get upwards of two hundred books a week delivered to my front porch, sent by publishers hoping for a review on *Fresh Air*. If I take a mental time capsule back and imagine a roughly equivalent situation in 1925 (when a lot fewer books were published each year), I honestly think that my first reaction upon ripping open the Scribner's mailer and seeing a slim novel called *The Great Gatsby* might have been: *Oh, another Fitzgerald.* Like most other reviewers, I would have had Fitzgerald pegged as a "topical" Jazz Age writer, and I think I would have been a little weary of his "flappers and philosophers." I might well have passed on novel number three. *After all,* I could have reasoned, *it looks a little thin, and the title is kind of blah.* But then there's that arresting Francis Cugat dust jacket. I've never judged a book by its cover, but I have lifted books out of the slush pile *because* of their covers—Frank McCourt's *Angela's Ashes* was one such visually induced pick. I think I would have lingered over that review copy of *The Great Gatsby* because of Cugat's offbeat dust-jacket illustration, which suggests that the story inside also might be something original. I would have dipped into chapter 1. Usually, I give a novel fifty pages. If something authentic about the story doesn't grab me by then—its setting or characters or story or *voice*—I move on to another review candidate. By page 50 in *Gatsby*, I know I would have been hooked by Nick's voice. (This is the adult book-reviewer "me" I'm talking about, not the jaded high-school girl who thought the book was boring.) At least, I'd like to think so, but who knows? The assigning of literary merit is highly contingent.

Plenty of *Gatsby*'s very first reviewers and adult readers, however, were not hooked. Most of *Gatsby*'s reviews fall into the gray zone of mixed, with outright praise from notable elites and many pans from the proletarian newspaper reviewers. Self-flagellating Fitzgerald always kept a clipping in his scrapbook of that dreadful unsigned review that ran in the *New York World* on April 12: "F. Scott Fitzgerald's Latest a Dud." Three days later, Ruth Snyder in the *New York Evening World* concluded her plot-summary-heavy review with this definitive verdict: "We are quite convinced after reading 'The Great Gatsby' that Mr. Fitzgerald is not one of the great American writers of to-day." Another female reviewer (there seem to have been a preponderance of them in the 1920s, unlike today), Ruth Hale in the *Brooklyn Daily Eagle*, was clearly fed up with reading Fitzgerald. Her lede reads: "F. Scott Fitzgerald is a strange little bird." From there, her estimation plummets: "Why he should be called an author, or why any of us should behave as if he were, has never been explained satisfactorily to me." At the end of May, an unsigned review in *America* called *Gatsby* "an inferior novel" and, a day later, the *Times-Picayune* review bore the headline: "Literature—and Less."[55]

Those are some of the worst of the worst; then there are the raves from the highbrows. I think that even those readers who find Gertrude Stein indigestible have to relent a little after taking a look at her letter of May 22, 1925, about *Gatsby:*

> *My dear Fitzgerald*
> *Here we are and have read your book and it is a good book. I like the melody of your dedication it shows that you have a background of beauty and tenderness and that is a comfort. The next good thing is that you write naturally in sentences and that too is a comfort.*[56]

T. S. Eliot may have been the very first person to reread and reread *The Great Gatsby* for pleasure. In a much-quoted verdict, he said that *Gatsby* was "the first step that American fiction has taken since Henry James."[57] Eliot also said, in his letter to Fitzgerald of December 31, 1925, that he had read the novel three times. More publicly influential was critic Gilbert Seldes's glowing review in the *Dial,* the modernist literary magazine that first published *The Waste Land* in America. Seldes is the prominent contemporary critic who came closest to getting *Gatsby* the first time. His long review, which came out in August 1925, deserves to be read in full, but here are some telling snippets:

> The concentration of the book is so intense that the principal characters exist almost as essences, as biting acids that find themselves in the same golden cup and have no choice but to act upon each other....
> [Gatsby] had dedicated himself to the accomplishment of a supreme object, to restore to himself an illusion he

had lost; he set about it, in a pathetic American way, by becoming incredibly rich.[58]

The Seldes review clearly made Fitzgerald's new friend Hemingway jealous. So Hemingway turned around and did something that in today's Internet lingo is known as "pity trolling." He told Fitzgerald that Seldes's laudatory review was bad for him psychologically, because such a tribute set the bar too high for his future writing. There are many reasons why Fitzgerald struggled for nine years to write a novel after *Gatsby*, but the seed of self-doubt that Hemingway watered certainly may have contributed to the blight.

The reviews were one thing, but also missing the mark were the letters about *Gatsby* that Fitzgerald received from some of his closest literary friends. Almost all are in agreement that it's his best work yet, and...they're looking forward to something even better. Occasionally, the long knives come out. Maybe tough criticism by colleagues is a sign that the 1920s enjoyed a more serious literary culture than our own; maybe, too, there was something in Fitzgerald's character—an openness, a vulnerability—that encouraged the bluntness. Most of the letters from Fitzgerald's writer friends are dated in the summer of 1925. In two quite long letters Fitzgerald's Princeton friend and literary mentor John Peale Bishop objects to the brevity of the book and the vagueness of Gatsby. In a short note, Paul Rosenfeld calls Gatsby "extraordinarily American, like ice cream soda with arsenic flavoring," and then lights into Nick's passivity as a narrator and the by now oft-repeated charge of vagueness: "Not that I doubt the reality of his passion; but there was not quite enough of it to make me feel at home in it."[59] Fitzgerald answered all of the *Gatsby*-related letters—both enthusiastic and critical—with the humility of an author whose novel isn't selling very well. Responding to a kind, if imprecise, note he received from novelist James Branch Cabell ("You have here written a solidly and sharply excellent book"[60]), Fitzgerald wrote to him in early May: "Thank you for writing me such a nice letter about my novel....I'm afraid the book isn't a popular success but two or three letters, of which yours is one, have made it a success for me."[61]

The Great Gatsby's first printing of 20,870 hard covers were sold at two dollars a copy, earning Fitzgerald, at a 15 percent royalty, $6,261.[62] A second printing of three thousand copies was ordered in August; a portion of this second printing still remained in the Scribner's warehouse upon Fitzgerald's death. (In January 1925, an ebullient Fitzgerald had predicted to Perkins that the sales for his third novel would reach eighty thousand copies, the total first-year sales of his two previous novels.) Because of this second printing, *Gatsby* was never technically out of print; however, in the way of the vast majority of literary novels, it soon vanished from bookstore shelves. If anyone, including Fitzgerald, wanted to buy *Gatsby,* he or she had to order a copy from Scribner's.

By mid-May 1925, Fitzgerald was referring in letters to *Gatsby*'s "flop" and to "the wearying fact that it isn't going to sell."[63] By the fall of that year, the book was dead. There were no paperbacks back then, of course, and no author tours or audiobooks. In the only recordings we have of Fitzgerald's voice—recordings that he made on a whim one day in Hollywood, reciting poems by Keats ("Ode to a Nightingale"), John Masefield ("On Growing Old"), and Shakespeare (lines from

Othello)—his hammy overarticulation makes him sound like he belongs to the Edwardian rather than the Jazz Age.

The following year saw some reappearances of *The Great Gatsby* in altered form. The novel was serialized in five issues of the *Famous Story Magazine*, from April to August, at twenty-five cents an issue. Some poor writer had the grubby task of trying to come up with short headnotes in order to jog readers' memories of the plot from issue to issue. Thus, in the May issue, we're reminded, "As the story began: Jay Gatsby was waiting patiently in his mammoth, ivy-wreathed castle on a fashionable point of Long Island Sound, for the realization of a dream." I noted that an edition of *Gatsby* was published in 1926 in England by Chatto and Windus after Fitzgerald's usual British publisher, Collins, passed. The British edition was swiftly remaindered. By 2003, however, the Brits had changed their minds. During that year, the BBC conducted a massive survey of the British public's reading tastes. Called the Big Read (not to be confused with the NEA program of the same name), it asked over three-quarters of a million people about their best-loved novel of all time. The winner was J.R.R. Tolkien's *The Lord of the Rings* (in general, the list skewed heavily to fantasy fiction and British authors). *The Great Gatsby,* however, came in at a very respectable number 43, admittedly trailing *The Catcher in the Rye* (number 15) and Fitzgerald's old nemesis *Gone with the Wind* (number 21).

In 1926, the novel was translated into French as *Gatsby le magnifique.* In 1928, *Gatsby* was also translated into German (*Der grosse Gatsby*) without anyone taking much notice. More of an event was the play of *The Great Gatsby* that opened in New York's Ambassador Theatre on February 2, 1926, directed by the young George Cukor. *New York Times* drama critic Brooks Atkinson generally liked it but made a point of saying that Owen Davis's script "loses some of the perfect nuances of the novel's comedy and character that cannot be translated in terms of the theatre."[64] There, we have Atkinson not only remarking on the humor of *Gatsby*, but also originating the now critical commonplace that *Gatsby* is "untranslatable" to stage and screen. Alexander Woollcott, whose own writing was always good for a laugh, reviewed the play favorably for the *New York World* and particularly praised James Rennie as Gatsby, "this made-while-you-wait gentleman of Fitzgerald's imagining."[65] (Rennie, by the way, was married to Dorothy Gish, sister of Lillian. When the Gish sisters' mother became seriously ill in England in May of 1926, the successful play closed abruptly so that Rennie could sail off to be at his wife's side. It ran for 113 performances.)

A major way in which the play streamlined the novel was to turn George Wilson into the Buchanans' chauffeur. The silent movie, which came out in November of 1926, followed Davis's script. This time round, "chauffeur" George Wilson was played by William Powell — he who later went on to star in the suave Thin Man movies. The astute reviewer for the *New York Times* noted that Powell was "not quite in his element."[66] Luminous actress Lois Wilson still holds the title as the movies' only dark-haired Daisy. Apart from the rollicking trailer, complete with a cavalcade of Busby Berkeley dancing girls, no prints have ever been found of this silent film; it's assumed the nitrate film decomposed into dust, as the novel might have done. What remains are tantalizing references in the reviews to "swimming pool orgies" and "a regular movie deluge of rain" in the Daisy-Gatsby reunion scene. Both the play and the film conjured up a "happy" ending. Gatsby, Christ-like, dies so that others may live more fully: his murder brings Tom and Daisy together again, and they resolve to become better people. It would take the Alan Ladd noir version of *Gatsby* in 1949 to chisel that whitewash off the ending.

Fitzgerald made a quite tidy $25,000 from the sale of the rights to *Gatsby* to Broadway and to Famous Players for the 1926 film. Like the tides, the money ran out almost as soon as it came in. In 1934, after *Tender Is the Night* was published to mixed reviews and disappointing sales (although, as scholars have pointed out, three printings and roughly fifteen thousand copies was no mean accomplishment in the darkest days of the Great Depression), Bennett Cerf invited Fitzgerald to write the introduction for a Modern Library reprint of *The Great Gatsby*. Fitzgerald was paid fifty dollars for the introduction to the edition, which would sell for ninety-five cents. Fitzgerald was unhappy with his introduction (where he sounds exhausted and self-pitying) and asked Cerf for the chance to rewrite it— at his own expense—for future reprintings of *Gatsby* in the Modern Library series. That opportunity never came. Sales were meager; five thousand copies were printed—and languished. Cerf admired the novel and kept hoping that sales would pick up, but *Gatsby* ultimately earned the distinction of being one of the poorest-selling titles in Modern Library history. The novel was discontinued as a Modern Library title in 1939. Almost sixty years later, in 1998, the editorial board of the Modern Library issued a list of its top one hundred novels of the twentieth century. *The Great Gatsby* landed in second place, right under James Joyce's *Ulysses*.

There were two more resurrections of *The Great Gatsby* before Fitzgerald's death. The novel appeared on May 23, 1937, in the Sunday supplements of newspapers such as the *Philadelphia Inquirer* and the *Chicago Herald-Examiner*. Last summer I sat down with a well-preserved copy of the *Herald-Examiner*'s *Gatsby* in the rare-book room of the Ernest F. Hollings Special Collections Library on the campus of the University of South Carolina. The first page of the supplement features a striking color illustration of a Gatsby (with a Clark Gable mustache) staring hungrily at a dark-haired Daisy with a peony in her hair (the flower Zelda liked to wear). Although the supplement claimed that *Gatsby* was "Complete in this Issue," I found it to be more a case of "all the novel that's fit to print." This *Gatsby* was bowdlerized, probably to accord with a Sunday-supplement preference for sweetness and light. Tom's racist rant was omitted; a hungover Nick doesn't wake near McKee's bed at the end of chapter 2; African Americans and Eastern European immigrants have been swept off the Queensboro Bridge; and Wolfshiem—no longer identified as Jewish!—speaks the king's English and has ditched the molar cuff links. All mentions of breasts—both the dangling breast of the newly deceased Myrtle Wilson and the "fresh, green breast of the new world"—have been expunged. At the end of the supplement, right under Fitzgerald's immortal final lines, the ad for the following Sunday's novel appears: "Next Week: *Of Lena Geyer*," a 1936 operatic melodrama by Marcia Davenport.

Also in 1937, the British pulp magazine the *Argosy* reprinted *The Great Gatsby* on its smeary pages. Neither this nor the Sunday-supplement appearances could have offered much comfort to Fitzgerald. These days, many Great Books comics—or "sequential-art narratives," as some cartoonists call them—are expensive artistic creations in their own right; many are also garbage. The Sunday-supplement and *Argosy* editions of *Gatsby* were pretty wretched, although not as bad as a homemade graphic version of *Gatsby* that's floating around on the web. A sampling of the dialogue goes like this:

Gatsby: "I'm in love with Daisy."

Nick: "Yeah, I guess she is hot and rich."

At least Fitzgerald was spared seeing that.

In short, *The Great Gatsby*'s afterlife in the late 1920s through the 1930s was faint. The literary crowd remembered the novel as a sign of Fitzgerald's growing promise as a writer; when that promise failed to materialize in *Tender Is the Night*, Fitzgerald— and his greatest creation—were forgotten, except as once-racy holdovers from the Jazz Age. When a lone fan wrote Fitzgerald in the late 1930s asking for an author photograph, he was told that none were available and that Fitzgerald was holding off "until it's time for a death mask."[67]

This "premature-burial" horror tale is not unique to *Gatsby* or Fitzgerald. So many of our greatest books—*Moby-Dick*, the collected works of both Poe and Dickinson—were rediscovered years after their authors' deaths. I mostly believe in a meritocracy when it comes to literature; I think the cream does eventually rise to the top. But the key word there is *eventually*; the meritocracy doesn't pay attention to deadlines. What distinguishes Fitzgerald's life story from that of other now-famous authors' is that his initial rise, then fall, then postmortem rise happened so rapidly and in such extremes.

Fitzgerald kept working; after all, he had Scottie and Zelda to support. But more than that, he continued to take himself seriously as a writer even when Hollywood treated him as little better than a hack, putting him to work for a few weeks on one picture and then pulling him off that and assigning him to another one. There's a story about those Hollywood years that I can't get out of my head. Shortly after he met Sheilah Graham in 1937, Fitzgerald read in the paper that the Pasadena Playhouse was presenting a stage adaptation of his short story "The Diamond as Big as the Ritz." Fitzgerald decided to put on the dog. He called the playhouse, announced that he was the author, and reserved two seats. He also reserved a chauffeured limousine and took Sheilah, in evening clothes, out to dinner and on to the theater. When they arrived, no one was in the lobby. It turned out that some students were performing the play in an upstairs hall. The upstairs hall was pretty empty too, just about a dozen or so casually dressed people — mostly the players' mothers, it seemed — in the audience. Afterward, Fitzgerald went backstage to congratulate the student players, later telling Sheilah they were "nice kids — I told them they'd done a good job."[68]

Anyone who loves Fitzgerald can't help but wish that he could have had a glimpse into the future. Just a couple of decades beyond his own death, he would have seen crowds of students, much like those Pasadena amateur actors, reading *The Great Gatsby* in college and high-school classrooms across America. Further on, he would have seen several more *Gatsby* films, the operas, the ballet, and *Gatz*. He would have seen volumes of criticism and biographies towering in piles "as big as the Ritz." And he would have seen the money. How he would have reveled in the money.

But Fitzgerald saw none of that. In the late 1930s, he drew

up a three-page list for Sheilah Graham of "Possibly Valuable Books" in his library. The list included a first edition of *The Waste Land* and "notes" on his personal copies of his own books. At the end of page 3, he writes: "Probable value of library at Forced Sale $300.00."[69] Fitzgerald's last royalty check was for $13.13, and, as his young secretary Frances Kroll Ring remembered, when that final royalty statement came through from Scribner's, "the handful of sales proved that the author, himself, was the only purchaser. He told me about it, laughing bitterly."[70] No wonder parents want their children to become doctors and lawyers.

In May 1940, Fitzgerald wrote a letter to Max Perkins in which he abruptly detoured from updates about his work in Hollywood to talk for two paragraphs about *Gatsby*. I think it's one of the saddest literary letters ever written. As often happens with Fitzgerald, though, there's also that eerie quality of prescience:

> I wish I was in print. It will be odd a year or so from now when Scottie assures her friends I was an author and finds that no book is procurable....
>
> Would the 25 cent press keep *Gatsby* in the public eye—*or is the book unpopular.* Has it *had* its chance? Would a popular reissue in that series with a preface *not* by me but by one of its admirers—I can maybe pick one—make it a favorite with class rooms, profs, lovers of English prose—anybody. But to die, so completely and unjustly after having given so much. Even now there is little published in American fiction that doesn't slightly bare my stamp—in a *small* way I was an original.[71]

5

"Here Lies One Whose Name Was Writ in Water"*

I live in Washington, DC, a city riddled with places that are off-limits to average citizens: restricted corridors of power, hidden tunnels and bunkers. My chief entrée into these places is through suspense fiction, but once in a while, I get a taste of what it's like to be an insider. So it was that on a bright October morning in 2012, I was led onto an elevator in the Library of Congress and taken down, down, down, to the underground stacks, a staff-only zone. It's very cold down there and dim—a subterranean library with none of the grandeur of the public rooms above. A worker wearing earbuds and pushing a squeaky metal cart full of books occasionally walks by; otherwise, it's silent as the proverbial tomb. I felt like Nicholas Cage in those National Treasure movies, poking around far beneath official historic sites in order to ferret out clues to mysteries of national importance.

---

* Epitaph composed by the poet John Keats for his own gravestone.

The particular mystery I was trying to solve that day was this: How did *The Great Gatsby*, all but dead itself after Fitzgerald's death, come roaring back to life so forcefully that within two decades it infiltrated the syllabi and textbooks of high schools and colleges across the land and was embraced as one of our Great American Novels? I thought the Library of Congress should be able to provide some answers since, after all, it is the nation's premier research library. It's also a tough place to navigate alone. Luckily, since the day I first stepped into the cathedral-like main reading room, outfitted with my preferred old-school tools of number 2 pencils and legal pads, I've had a top-notch guide. Abby Yochelson is a reference librarian at the Library of Congress who specializes in literary research. She's about my age and elegant, with salt-and-pepper hair and a stylish wardrobe of shawls and sweaters she wears against the library's chill. With her calm approach to research, Abby neutralizes my terror of what I've come to think of as the Blob—the spreading ooze of Fitzgerald books, articles, films, and artifacts that expand exponentially with each passing year. (Maybe, as Abby eventually confesses to me, the fact that she just doesn't get the magic of *The Great Gatsby* inoculates her against feeling overwhelmed by the novel itself and the sheer volume of criticism and other material it's generated.) After our first meeting, in the fall of 2011, Abby carried out a targeted search in the Library of Congress's online catalog. The results listed more than fifty-five works—primarily books—on the subject of F. Scott Fitzgerald's life alone; another seventy-one under the subheading "criticism and interpretation"; and another sixty-plus exclusively on *The Great Gatsby*. She helped me put together a dense list of reference works on the 1920s, a compendium of contemporary book reviews, a catalog of news-papers and popular magazines of Fitzgerald's time, and a sum-mary of the TV, radio, and motion-picture adaptations of *Gatsby* as well as of Fitzgerald's other novels and stories. These tallies don't take into account all the thousands upon thousands of scholarly articles on Fitzgerald nor the various editions of the primary works themselves. The big kahuna of the latter is the Cambridge Edition of the Works of F. Scott Fitzgerald series, which began to appear in 1991—starting with *The Great Gatsby*. It will ultimately number seventeen volumes. Abby also recommended that I log on to the WorldCat online site, which itemizes the collections of seventy thousand libraries world-wide. Just doing a targeted search for books with the subject line "*The Great Gatsby*," I came up with 250 titles. Had I but world enough, and time.

Critics began taking second looks at Fitzgerald's work even before his coffin was lowered into the ground (for the first time). The *New York Times* obituary set the patronizing tone for the first wave of Fitzgerald reevaluations, which saw him as an author defined by the Jazz Age: "Mr. Fitzgerald in his life and writings epitomized 'all the sad young men' of the post-war generation.... Roughly, his own career began and ended with the Nineteen Twenties.... The promise of his brilliant career was never fulfilled."[1] As Arnold Gingrich, Fitzgerald's editor at *Esquire,* complained to Sheilah Graham, most of the obituaries, respectful as they were, barely mentioned *The Great Gatsby.*[2] The one exception to the general tone of polite wistfulness was the story filed by the ultraconservative Hearst columnist Westbrook Pegler on December 26, the day before Fitzgerald was buried. Pegler's ranting lede, decrying the hedonism of the 1920s, anticipates the kind of criticisms the silent majority would level against those darn hippies during the 1960s: "The death of Scott Fitzgerald recalls memories of a queer brand of undisciplined and self-indulgent brats who were determined not to pull their weight in the boat and wanted the world to drop everything and sit down and bawl with them."[3] Posthumously, at least, Fitzgerald found himself in good company: Pegler made a career out of damning Franklin and Eleanor Roosevelt, the Supreme Court, the New Deal, and (big surprise) labor unions.

Spurred on in part by Pegler's nastiness, critics such as Malcolm Cowley, Stephen Vincent Benét, Paul Rosenfeld, and Glenway Wescott wrote evocative reconsiderations of Fitzgerald over the next few years and published them in the general-interest literary magazines that flourished in mid-twentieth-century America. Thirty of those essays would reappear in the first essay collection devoted to Fitzgerald: *F. Scott Fitzgerald: The Man and His Work,* edited by Alfred Kazin. (Curiously, the publisher of this 1951 essay collection, the World Publishing Company, otherwise specialized in dictionaries and Bibles.)

To this day, I think Fitzgerald brings out some of the best critical writing in his sympathetic readers. Here, for instance, is Lionel Trilling on Fitzgerald: "Fitzgerald lacked prudence, as his heroes did, lacked that blind instinct for self-protection which the writer needs and the American writer needs in double measure. But that is all he lacked—and it is the generous fault, even the heroic fault."[4] I also think Fitzgerald infiltrated some of his admirers' writing in less direct ways. In 1951, Alfred Kazin published his book *A Walker in the City,* one of the great memoirs about twentieth-century New York. Throughout, Kazin, who grew up the child of immigrants in Brownsville, Brooklyn, looks over the East River to what he repeatedly calls "Beyond." "Beyond" is Manhattan, the land of success and completely acculturated Americans. You can't tell me Kazin wasn't thinking of *Gatsby* when he wrote those passages suffused with yearning for something across the water, out of reach.

In addition to the supportive critics, Fitzgerald's close friends rallied round after his death, concerned that his name, like Keats's, was also "writ in water." Edmund Wilson, acting at the behest of Maxwell Perkins and Howard Ober, labored over the unfinished draft of *The Love of the Last Tycoon*. In 1941 Scribner's brought out Wilson's edition of the fragment under the title *The Last Tycoon*. That volume also included *The Great Gatsby* and some of Fitzgerald's most famous short stories. In 1945, against Perkins's wishes, Wilson's edition of *The Crack-Up* came out. *The Crack-Up* essays clearly resonated with at least one segment of readers in the 1930s: the clinically depressed. The Fitzgerald Papers at Princeton University yield up a number of fan letters from readers battling their own demons— some of them are, in fact, writing from sanitariums. Many of these fellow sufferers had read the *Crack-Up* essays in *Esquire;* others, the awful Michel Mok 1936 birthday interview in the *New York Post*. Uniformly, these letters are poignant in their generous desire to "buck up" Fitzgerald and assure him that "your best years are ahead of you."[5]

Another old friend of Fitzgerald's youth, Dorothy Parker, selected the writings—including *The Great Gatsby*—that would be in *The Viking Portable Library: F. Scott Fitzgerald*, which came out in 1945. That edition included a beautiful tribute to Fitzgerald by his buddy John O'Hara. Another (sometime) buddy, John Dos Passos, contributed to a 1946 book called *I Wish I'd Written That* an excerpt from the beginning of chapter 3 of *The Great Gatsby*.

In 1950, screenwriter Budd Schulberg wrote a bestselling novel about Fitzgerald, *The Disenchanted*. (Schulberg had accompanied Fitzgerald on a disastrous trip to Dartmouth in 1939 to work on the script for a college movie called *Winter Carnival*. Fitzgerald drank so heavily during that trip that he was fired by his studio bosses at United Artists.) *The Disenchanted* fixed in the public's mind the popular image of Fitzgerald as a tragic drunk; in 1958, it was turned into a Broadway play with Jason Robards as the Fitzgerald character. In 1951, another literary compatriot, Malcolm Cowley, introduced a collection called *The Stories of F. Scott Fitzgerald*, and also in that year, the first biography of Fitzgerald appeared: Arthur Mizener's *The Far Side of Paradise*.

There's a pattern to this reconstruction of Fitzgerald's literary reputation: Fellow writers, most of whom knew Fitzgerald pretty well and who still had influence within the literary culture, keep writing about him and his work. Curiosity and reconsiderations of Fitzgerald then spread throughout the larger culture. The years 1950 and 1951 seem critical. Schulberg, Mizener, the Kazin essay collection, and the Cowley short-story volume all appear during this period. What else is going on in America then that might have triggered this Fitzgerald Revival? Here's one hypothesis: This is a time of Cold War calcification, when intellectuals are being asked whether they are on the side of America or its Soviet foe. Might the American qualities of *The Great Gatsby* and even Fitzgerald's lesser work have somehow resonated again at this point?

Sheilah Graham entered the arena somewhat belatedly in 1958 with her bestselling memoir *Beloved Infidel*, made into a movie that same year with Deborah Kerr as Graham and a wooden Gregory Peck as Fitzgerald. A few years later, in 1964, Ernest Hemingway's posthumously published memoir *A Moveable Feast* painted a devastating picture of Fitzgerald as a weakling, in thrall to a jealous and insane wife. In addition to tweaking the "rich are different from you and me" anecdote so that he got to deliver the triumphant punch line, Hemingway also told a humiliating tale about taking Fitzgerald on a museum expedition to look at nude classical statues in order to allay his alleged anxiety over the size of his penis. That gossipy swipe at Fitzgerald sparked a startling colloquium, of sorts, on the pages of *Esquire* magazine: the subject wasn't Fitzgerald's fiction but his anatomy. Sheilah Graham and *Esquire* editor Arnold Gingrich contributed their expert opinions.[6]

These are some of the first stirrings of what the stalwart Frances Kroll Ring derisively called the "Fitzorama."[7] Undeniably, these books, articles, and films were crucial to kickstarting the Fitzgerald Revival, although, as Fitzgerald scholar Ruth Prigozy points out, there wasn't much to "revive," since Fitzgerald had never gotten his proper critical due the first time round. In the basement of the Library of Congress that fall morning, however, I'm trying to trace something wider and more elusive. I want to get a sense of how appreciation for Fitzgerald rippled out of this relatively closed circle of journalists and writers, critics and scholars. How did *The Great Gatsby*, in particular, come to be embraced not just by "the smarties" (to use the poet Stevie Smith's mocking term) but also by civilian readers? Hence my expedition down into the bowels of the Library of Congress with the intrepid Abby.

In the subbasement of the Thomas Jefferson Building that October morning, Abby and I are carrying out a search that will no longer be possible just a few months from now. We're combing through the metal stacks that hold the Library of Congress's extensive collection of American literature anthologies—organized by series and date—trying to figure out when Fitzgerald's writings first began to seep into high-school and college textbooks. Because of the crunch for space that bedevils the Library of Congress and so many other research libraries around the world, these musty literature anthologies are about to be shipped to an off-site storage facility where they'll be shelved, not by subject, but by size. While we still can, Abby and I are doing something akin to prospecting for gold: we're rifling through all of the volumes in chronological order, looking for a Fitzgerald "strike." In the future, researchers who want to see these anthologies will have to request them from off-site, and, unless they're willing to fill out hundreds of library call slips in the hopes of discovering the right volumes, they'll have to know beforehand where the gold is located.

This search is making me sentimental for lost illusions. The American canon as presented in these mid-twentieth-century anthologies seems so stately and self-evident. Increase Mather begets Cotton Mather; Edgar Allan Poe spawns Edgar Lee Masters; the hellish visions of Jonathan Edwards bloom anew in Nathaniel Hawthorne. All through my college years, as an

English major, I accepted without question this pale priestly procession of American literary genius. (It took groundbreaking literary feminists like Ellen Moers and Sandra Gilbert and Susan Gubar to knock some epiphanies into me in graduate school.) Except for a few outliers like Emily Dickinson and Louisa May Alcott—who couldn't be considered geniuses because they were too "simple" (Dickinson) or wrote for children (Alcott)—everyone in the anthologies' great-writers category was a white male. Things are so much simpler when everyone belongs to the same privileged club, even if, as *The Great Gatsby* reminds us, some white males are born members and others can't even buy their way in.

Like its literature, America itself seems more "graspable" in these anthologies. Some of the volumes display quaint regional maps on the insides of their covers. If you're of a certain age, you'll remember these chamber of commerce fantasies in which Iowa is represented by a giant ear of corn, Texas by cattle, California by oranges, and New York by the Empire State Building (HOME AGAIN). I could get lost in this Lotus-Eaters' Land of Literary Anthologies, but we're pressed for time and it is seriously freezing down here. Abby and I are alternating crouching near the floor and stretching up to the tallest shelves, calling out dates—1950! 1961!—every time we find a Fitzgerald hit. I don't remember who first shouted that particular "Eureka!" but, as it turns out, the earliest sighting of F. Scott Fitzgerald will be in an anthology that came out the year after his death. The 1941 edition of the decades-long-running *Adventures in American Literature* contains picturesque swatches of Americana cowboy songs and speeches by Robert E. Lee and "Negro" spirituals. In a summary essay introducing selections from contemporary literature, the Omniscient Voice of this volume declares: "A group who were in the heyday of youth during the twenties — Ernest Hemingway, F. Scott Fitzgerald, and John Dos Passos — represent rebellion against the manners and standards of conservative society. With the coming of the depression, the cynics of the 'jazz age' have given way."[8] Fitzgerald a cynic? Did the Omniscient Voice ever read *Gatsby*, not to mention almost everything else Fitzgerald ever wrote? My nostalgia for the simpler wisdom of the olden days is souring, fast.

Other than this single entry of his name, Fitzgerald simply doesn't exist within the anthologies on the Library of Congress's shelves from the 1940s. Hemingway, Faulkner, Dreiser, and O'Neill are all over the place, but no Fitzgerald. About nine months after this search, I'll come upon an anthology from 1945 in Ernest F. Hollings Special Collections Library at the University of South Carolina. *North, East, South, West* bills itself as "a regional anthology of American writing" and mentions Fitzgerald as a regionalist: "F. Scott Fitzgerald was born in Minnesota in 1896, but almost everything he wrote...established him as an Easterner. He was the best of our writers of death and disenchantment in the twenties."[9] That odd labeling of Fitzgerald as a regionalist also pops up in the 1958 edition of *Adventures in American Literature;* once again, though, the anthology doesn't bother to include an excerpt of Fitzgerald's writing. To add insult to injury, that wedging of Fitzgerald into the regionalist subcategory follows a breathless paragraph applauding the work of the four Americans "who have won the coveted Nobel prize."[10] At that time, the fab four were Sinclair Lewis, Pearl Buck, William Faulkner, and Fitzgerald's old "frenemy" Ernest Hemingway.

During the hours Abby and I spend underground mining the anthologies, our hands will become coated with a substance used by the Library of Congress in its "mass deacidification" process: the attempt to stabilize the poor-quality paper that makes so many nineteenth- and twentieth-century books crumble. But it's worth a morning's exposure to unknown chemicals to trace, however stumblingly, America's dawning awareness of Fitzgerald. As I would have guessed, Fitzgerald gets included more frequently in the anthologies of the 1950s, while the 1960s volumes are so rich in mentions that they constitute a veritable Treasure of the Sierra Madre. "Winter Dreams" and "The Rich Boy" are Fitzgerald's most anthologized short stories during those two decades, and, as a measure of how literary tastes change, the now diminished *Beautiful and Damned* is mentioned in a few anthologies as one of Fitzgerald's best novels, while *Tender Is the Night* is frequently passed over in silence. What's genuinely thrilling, though, is to catch the earliest glints of recognition that Fitzgerald—and *The Great Gatsby*—may be the genuine article: a great writer and his masterpiece.

The 1955 revised edition of *The College Anthology of American Literature* includes one of the earliest excerpts from *Gatsby* (the first party at Gatsby's house, where he and Nick meet). The 1961 anthology *American Literature: A College Survey* senses something is a-stirring out there in the culture but doesn't want to commit to the Fitzgerald Revival just yet. That anthology's introduction to "Winter Dreams" impartially observes that Fitzgerald's reputation "has undergone an extraordinary rehabilitation"[11] during the past decade. The 1964 edition of *American Literature* also featured "Winter Dreams" and these restrained words of approval: "Within the past few years

Fitzgerald's novels and short stories have been rediscovered and he is again highly regarded as an outstanding American writer.... *The Great Gatsby* is Fitzgerald's best novel."[12]

One of Fitzgerald's most brilliant advocates, the critic Alfred Kazin, served on an all-star editorial committee for the 1962 anthology *Major Writers of America;* not surprisingly, that anthology contained a generous and varied sampling of Fitzgerald ("The Rich Boy," "Echoes of the Jazz Age," "Ring," "The Crack-Up"), as well as the verdict that *The Great Gatsby* was "probably Fitzgerald's most flawless novel."[13] By 1968, our irrepressible old friend *Adventures in American Literature* declares that "*The Great Gatsby* is a novel some critics consider one of the best written in the twentieth century."[14] In academic-speak, that constitutes a rave.

The literature anthologies are a mineshaft down into the lost world of high-school and college classrooms of the 1940s, 1950s, and 1960s. The other passageway would be through a wide sampling of the syllabi for English courses of those decades, but the Library of Congress doesn't keep any collections of those. In fact, as Abby comments to me, even high schools and university departments that once maintained archives of course descriptions have switched over to online versions, so that any traces of what American students are reading in their English courses today are dispersed into the netherworld of the Internet. Everywhere I travel on my Fitzgerald investigations—physically and virtually—I ask about old syllabi and come up empty. A librarian at Teachers College, Columbia University, suggests that Fitzgerald may be mentioned in various old reading lists recommended by state and city school boards but says that I'd have to search for them hid-

den within the mammoth catalog listings for each individual
school board. "This would be a rather onerous task!" she cheerily
cautions.[15] A kind curator at the New York City Municipal
Archives does manage to exhume a set of guidelines, circa 1967,
for curriculum development in "English Language Arts, Grades
5–12" in the New York City public-school system. The guidelines recommend *The Great Gatsby* as a promising title for a unit
on "American man's desire for success."

I want to conclude this backward glance at how Fitzgerald
became swiftly transformed from has-been to required reading
by looking at two brief recollections by a significant mother-
daughter pair. Sheilah Graham first read *The Great Gatsby*
when F. Scott Fitzgerald gave her a copy during their Hollywood years together in the late 1930s; to do so, he had to special-
order the novel from Scribner's, since bookstores no longer had
any of his works in stock. In the epilogue to her 1958 memoir,
Beloved Infidel, Graham ruminates on a great shift in opinion
on Fitzgerald that's already happened:

> If Scott were sitting beside me in my study on this Sep-
> tember day, what would he think, how would he feel, to
> know his high estate in the world of letters today? That he
> has been the subject of critical studies, of a biography, a
> novel and a play; that his own stories have been drama-
> tized for audiences of millions; that college students read
> him today not only because he is required reading in the
> universities but because they love his writing.[16]

One of the college literature professors who's been teaching
Fitzgerald to her students since the 1970s is Graham's own

daughter Wendy Fairey, an English professor at Brooklyn College. In her afterword to a new edition of *College of One*, another of her mother's Fitzgerald memoirs, Fairey drolly comments:

> Whenever I teach *The Great Gatsby*, as I have so many times in my forty years in the college classroom, I always wonder if I will tell the students my story.... Perhaps there's been a little sag in the classroom energy and I turn to the story to reinvigorate us.... Interest at this point increases, usually mixed with a bit of understandable anxiety that an aging female professor, talking about her mother's lover, has become unpredictable.[17]

There's the Fitzgerald Revival in the classroom within the span of one generation as encapsulated in the experiences of Sheilah Graham and her English professor daughter. Were Fairey to rely only on family anecdotes to augment her interpretations of *Gatsby*, she'd be considered not only "unpredictable," but quaint. (I doubt that she's doing so; she's identified as having served as director of Women's Studies at Brooklyn College, which means she must be steeped in feminist theory, at least.) *The Great Gatsby* has been interrogated, deconstructed, diced, and spliced by academic critics with such gusto that a collection of all the scholarly articles ever published on just the novel could reconstitute the lost Bering land bridge between Alaska and Siberia. (The first dissertation on Fitzgerald that I've found was written in 1945. It's called "The Development of the Fitzgerald Hero" and was written by a PhD candidate at Louisiana State University; by 1966, a scholar named Virginia Hallam submitted what looks like the first dissertation on the

Fitzgerald Revival itself, "The Critical and Popular Reception of F. Scott Fitzgerald," to the University of Pennsylvania, my alma mater. That dissertation lists the books and articles that constitute some of Fitzgerald's academic revival without making any larger interpretations of why the revival happened in the first place.) In contemporary college literature classrooms, one popular textbook, *Critical Theory: A User-Friendly Guide,* uses *The Great Gatsby* as the bull's-eye target against which to hurl all variant of contemporary critical theory: there's postcolonialist *Gatsby,* structuralist *Gatsby,* queer theory *Gatsby,* semiotic *Gatsby,* cultural studies *Gatsby,* and on and on and on.

The full story of Fitzgerald's "second act" in American life, however, is not confined to the clean, well-lighted spaces of bookstores, libraries, and classrooms. In fact, this part of that story doesn't even take place in the United States but in American army bases, convoys, military hospitals, and even POW camps in Europe and the Far East. In a posthumous twist of fate he might have appreciated, former Second Lieutenant F. Scott Fitzgerald's greatest novel, along with some of his best short stories, were sent into service overseas during World War II.

When I was growing up, I remember my father, who served on a destroyer escort during World War II, telling me about these "funny paperbacks" that were around back then. Like so many men of his generation, my dad didn't talk a lot about his service, so anything he said about those war years stayed with me. It wasn't until a few weeks after my descent into the Library of Congress stacks with Abby that I finally saw what my father meant by *funny paperbacks.*

On this chilly morning a week before Thanksgiving, Abby and I have ascended to a Platonic readers' heaven. The Rare

Book and Special Collections reading room at the Library of Congress is a beautiful, wood-paneled space, modeled on Independence Hall in Philadelphia. I'm there to read two of the paperbacks in the library's collection of Armed Services Editions, ASEs, the funny paperbacks that were distributed to the army and navy during World War II. The Library of Congress has the only complete set of ASEs in the world, all 1,322 titles.

The ASE program is often referred to as "the biggest book giveaway in world history." Between the time it was launched, in 1943, to its end, in 1947, nearly 123 million books were distributed to U.S. troops overseas, everything from *Hopalong Cassidy's Protégé* to Margaret Mead's *Coming of Age in Samoa;* Homer's *Odyssey* to *Webster's New Handy Dictionary;* Mary O'Hara's *My Friend Flicka* to Melville's *Moby-Dick.* The program was the brainchild of the Council on Books in Wartime, a group of publishers, librarians, and booksellers whose aim was to do their part for the war effort. Because boredom was an ever-present problem for America's men in uniform when they weren't fighting, the military brass was always looking for ways to keep up morale. The council hit on the idea of distributing inexpensive paperbacks to servicemen overseas, in military hospitals, and even in POW camps in Germany and Japan through an arrangement with the International YMCA.

The council, whose motto was Books Are Weapons in the War of Ideas, decided that in order to generate the hundreds of thousands of books needed—and to ensure that good books would be sent to the troops—it had to get involved in the actual production of paperbacks. (Earlier in the war, civilians had been urged to send books to the troops; thus, GIs and sailors got bombarded with duds from many an attic and basement.) Agencies from the army and navy, the War Production Board, seventy publishing companies, and more than a dozen printing houses, composition firms, and paper suppliers rallied to the cause. Portability was key: the books had to fit into servicemen's pockets. The solution was to print the books on inexpensive paper on presses otherwise used to print the *Reader's Digest* or pulp magazines. The smaller books would measure 5½ inches by 3⅞ inches; longer books would be 6½ inches by 4½ inches. Margins were practically nonexistent, and the text inside was printed in side-by-side columns on every page. (Ninety of the ASEs would eventually have to be condensed, Wilkie Collins's *The Moonstone*, Kathleen Winsor's *Forever Amber*, and *Moby-Dick* among them.)

The design of the books was uniform: the rear cover featured sparkling copy about the story and the author; the front usually displayed a miniature of the book's original cover. Since the ASEs weren't meant to last for more than six or seven readings and since they were sent overseas, they wouldn't flood the civilian market after the war. In the patriotic spirit of the war effort, authors and publishers each received a royalty of half a cent a copy, and five printing firms agreed to produce the books at less than half their normal percentage of profit. The cost of printing was six cents a copy. The very first ASE to roll off the presses in 1943 was *The Education of Hyman Kaplan* by Leo Rosten, a humorous send-up of a newly arrived immigrant's experiences in English class at night school.

The semi-forgotten existence of the World War II ASE program is a feel-good revelation for those of us solitary bookworms who occasionally wonder if reading serves any larger societal purpose. Never before and never since in American history has love of country dovetailed so practically with love of books. The launch of the ASE program was heralded throughout 1943 on the pages of *Publishers' Weekly*. Sometimes, the bookish enthusiasm of individual reporters verged on the delusional. A long article about the ASEs that appeared in September of that year talked about World War II as though it were the ideal opportunity for citizen soldiers to sit around and catch up on their reading:

> Even after shipping overseas the soldier may have plenty of time on his hands. As the war has developed so far, comparatively few are engaged on actual battle fronts. Thousands find themselves on tropical isles— without Dotty Lamour—...Under these circumstances men become voracious readers. For subject matter, a letter from home takes first place; after that, almost anything but a missionary tract is acceptable.[18]

Hyperbolic literary fantasies aside, the simple testimony from servicemen of what those funny paperbacks meant to them is powerful. At a conference in honor of the fortieth anniversary of the ASEs, held at the Library of Congress in 1983, a World War II veteran named Arnold Gates recalled how during the Battle of Saipan he carried a copy of Carl Sandburg's *Storm Over the Land* in his helmet: "During the lulls in the battle I would read what he wrote about another war and found a great deal of comfort and reassurance."[19] Years later, Sandburg inscribed the book for Gates. Some ASEs even reached the front lines: The task forces heading to the Marshall

Islands, the Marianas, and Okinawa were given books as they departed from Hawaii.

The most mind-boggling mass distribution of ASEs occurred as American invasion forces were marshaling in southern England before crossing the English Channel on D-day. As Stephen Ambrose describes it in his sweeping history of the invasion, the camps where the troops were assembling were equipped with improvised movie theaters, great food (steak and pork chops, fresh eggs, even ice cream on an all-you-can-eat basis), and paperback libraries full of ASEs. General Eisenhower's staff approved the distribution of a "copy of an Armed Services Edition...to each soldier as he boarded the invasion barge."[20] Soldiers reportedly discarded all nonessentials before crossing the Channel—spare blankets and souvenirs—but not a single book was left behind. The descendants of any D-day veterans who managed to hold on to their ASEs through Normandy Beach and beyond would now own a valuable collectible. Referred to as D-day books, those titles included *The Grapes of Wrath, The Adventures of Tom Sawyer, The Adventures of Huckleberry Finn, The Short Stories of Stephen Vincent Benét, Death Comes for the Archbishop, Cross Creek,* and one of the most popular ASEs of them all, *A Tree Grows in Brooklyn.*[21]

I'd love to know where the ASEs stored in archival boxes in the Library of Congress's rare-book room have come from and under what circumstances they were read some seventy years ago. I've read accounts of ASE sets being dropped by parachute to remote islands in the Pacific and even brought up to front lines where battle-weary men would crawl on their bellies to get the books. Two thousand copies of each ASE title were set aside for distribution in prison camps in Germany and Japan.

The two ASEs I've come to the Library of Congress to hold and read probably didn't see action, but they may well have fueled a revolution. In 1945, after the surrenders of Germany and Japan, the Armed Services Editions printed and distributed 155,000 copies of *The Great Gatsby* and 90,000 copies of what was known as a "made edition" of *The Diamond as Big as the Ritz and Other Stories*. (Made editions were specially composed for the ASE program.) *The Great Gatsby*'s entry into World War II was—like Jay Gatsby's entry into his own story—a bit belated and quiet. But, again like Jay Gatsby himself, the ASE seems to have made a lasting impression. Maybe the post-surrender distribution of *Gatsby* and Fitzgerald's stories was fortuitous: in 1945, the millions of American servicemen stationed abroad might have had more time to read. Those servicemen would constitute an undreamed-of vast new audience for *Gatsby*. Recall that Fitzgerald, even in his most ambitious moments in 1925, fantasized about selling only around 70,000 copies of the novel. Let's do the math: 155,000 ASE copies of *Gatsby*—designed to be read about seven times—is over a million readings of the novel, as compared to Scribner's sales of, tops, about 23,000 copies of the novel in 1925. Even if those ASE estimated readings are inflated, one of the things some of these World War II servicemen carried with them back home was an awakened interest in F. Scott Fitzgerald.

When I exhume it from its archival box, ASE #862 of *The Great Gatsby* looks to me like a thicker version of a child's flip book. (*The Diamond as Big as the Ritz*, ASE #1043, will turn out to be bigger, more the size of a book of postcards.) *The Great Gatsby* is printed in yellow letters against a green background; a

The Armed Services Edition of The Great Gatsby. (ERIC FRAZIER, REPRINTED COURTESY OF THE LIBRARY OF CONGRESS RARE BOOK AND SPECIAL COLLECTIONS DIVISION)

red band running across the bottom of the ASE assures readers that "This Is the Complete Book—Not a Digest." Inside, the full text of *Gatsby* is printed on double columns with the thinnest of margins. At the end of the novel, there's a little essay about Fitzgerald and his career that gives the wrong date for his death, 1941, but ends on a rousing (if grammatically confused) note: "Today, people are discovering Jay Gatsby and critics still shouting about it." I check and see that *orgastic* on the final page has been misprinted, as it was in some other later editions of the novel, as the more salacious *orgiastic*. The real thrill to be found in this edition of *Gatsby*, however, lies on its back cover. There, some anonymous blurbist began a mission that would be carried on by millions of English teachers in classrooms around the world unto this very day: he (or she) enthusiastically assures the prospective readers of this ASE edition of *The Great Gatsby* that they won't be bored. Instead, in the hands of the ASE blurbist, *Gatsby* becomes an action-packed crime story:

> Just as Scott Fitzgerald's *This Side of Paradise* immortalized college life in the America of the 1920s, so *The Great Gatsby* presented a deathless figure in the person of Jay Gatsby, one of the first, and certainly one of the greatest, of the "racketeers" in American fiction. Gatsby is a great and mysterious figure. The story of his life among the Long Island bootleggers and society people of well-remembered years is unequalled.[22]

I wonder how many GIs and sailors stuck with *Gatsby* after that pitch, redolent of bullets and booze? Nick's elegiac opening words must have baffled more than a few of these guys. Then again, those overseas readers in uniform were something of a captive audience for *Gatsby;* as compared to your average over-scheduled high-school student, I'd bet that, given the lack of alternatives, most of the soldiers who picked up *Gatsby* read the entire novel, cover to flimsy ASE cover.

The troops probably didn't need any prodding to read the numerous mystery titles available as ASEs—everything from classic British tales of Sherlock Holmes and Dorothy Sayers to the courtroom dramas of Erle Stanley Gardner and the hard-boiled fiction of Raymond Chandler. I could use a Holmes or Perry Mason right now to help me figure out the lingering riddle of the ASE *Gatsby:* Why was Fitzgerald's novel lifted out of its near-two-decades-old remaindered pile and chosen for the ASE program in the first place? According to the various accounts I've read, an unpaid advisory committee met twice a month to select the books, which came "from many sources."[23] Approximately thirty new titles were added each month. Consensus had to be reached about each selection, which was then presented to the army and navy for approval. (Censorship occasionally came into play when books were thought to be "political" or otherwise scandalous. Zane Grey's *Riders of the Purple Sage*, for instance, was vetoed because it contained an attack on Mormons.)

In hopes of solving this whodunit, I'll spend hours in the main reading room of the Library of Congress poring through old articles about the ASE program contained in musty copies of *Publishers' Weekly* from the mid-1940s. Black-and-white photographs accompanying a 1943 article heralding the ASEs depict publishing eminences sitting around a gleaming wooden table on which stacks of paper are squarely aligned. Aside from one woman, all the participants are straight out of central casting: white men who look like they're thinking serious thoughts about Literature. This was a time when publishing and academia were still waspy, inbred preserves. (I imagine the mangy Beat writers — Ginsberg, Kerouac, Corso — gathering in the shadows under similar tables in a few years' time, overthrowing those neat piles of paper, the politeness of it all.) Another section of this extensive *Publishers' Weekly* profile of the program lists the names of the members of the ASE selection committee: Mark Van Doren; Harry Hansen, literary editor of the *New York World-Telegram;* Amy Loveman of the Book-of-the-Month Club and the *Saturday Review;* Edward C. Aswell of Harper, Russell Doubleday; Jennie Flexner of the New York Public Library; and then, the only name that suggests a direct link to F. Scott Fitzgerald: Nicholas Wreden, president of the American Booksellers Association and manager of the Scribner's bookstore on 597 Fifth Avenue.

Scribner's. Max Perkins was still plugging away there in 1943. (In fact, he worked up until his sudden death in 1947 from an advanced case of pneumonia that he'd ignored.) Perkins had very reluctantly consented to be interviewed by Malcolm Cowley for a *New Yorker* profile that ran in two successive issues in April 1944. Entitled "Unshaken Friend," it introduced the wider literary public to the role that this unassuming man who always "dressed in shabby and inconspicuous grays"[24] had played in shaping the American literature of the twentieth century through Fitzgerald, Hemingway, and Thomas Wolfe, among others. Scribner's—through Perkins and, perhaps, through the intervention of bookstore manager Nicholas Wreden on the ASE selection committee—would forever remain F. Scott Fitzgerald's "unshaken friend."

Thinking of Perkins alive and working throughout the war years makes me wonder about Zelda. Would she have been aware of the reclamation efforts by Fitzgerald's friends and admirers in the early years of the 1940s? Would she have known about the ASEs of *The Great Gatsby* and *Diamond as Big as the Ritz*? Zelda was living in Montgomery, Alabama, with her mother when Scott died. Apart from Scottie, of course, and Scott's Princeton friend John Biggs, who became the executor of his estate, Zelda also had contact with Harold Ober, Max Perkins, and Edmund Wilson, as well as other longtime friends, like Gerald and Sara Murphy. She lived through World War II, going in and out of Highland Hospital in Asheville, North Carolina. It's an indicator of how shaky the Fitzgerald family finances were that Zelda sometimes bussed tables for money at the Richmond Hill Inn in West Asheville between stays at the hospital. In 1948, Zelda, housed in an upper room of the hospital awaiting the next day's electroshock treatment, died in a fire set by a night supervisor who was said to be a recovered mental patient.[25] The same Episcopalian minister, Raymond P. Black, who had so dismissively performed Scott's funeral officiated at the burial of Zelda's ashes at the Rockville Union Cemetery.

Rooting around for information about Zelda during World War II, I come across a reference to a letter she wrote in February of 1943. It's preserved in something called the Noel F. Parrish papers at the Library of Congress, some fifty-eight containers of material. I'd never heard of Parrish, but it turns out that he was the white commander of the Tuskegee Army Airfield, responsible for training the Tuskegee Airmen. Parrish, according to testimonies I read, was hailed for his progressive racial views: he worked to improve life on the base, defusing tensions with local whites and arranging visits by celebrities like Lena Horne and Langston Hughes. Tuskegee was about thirty-five miles from Zelda's parents' home at 322 Sayre Street in Montgomery, and Parrish and Zelda somehow met. Judging by her letter, they shared a love of literature. Zelda starts off thanking Parrish for the loan of a book but quickly segues into a grand estimation of Scott's writing against the backdrop of World Wars I and II:

The significance of social machination which colour Scott's work always offer promise of another good time— as if just living might once again become a relevant estate.

Scott's generation—and mine—made the adjustment from the Victorian age to the bitter gallantries of the last war, found a philosophy of tragic truncate exaltation to tide it over the heart-broken memories of men frozen in box cars and drowned in mud on the lost frontier of foreign countries. Now that age is tired resigned but not too philosophic. We await the end with a list too full of suicides and too fraught with tragedy to bring much hope to the current debacle.[26]

Zelda's language is so interior, she might as well be talking to herself, though the phrase *tragic truncate exaltation* stays with me. She sounds exhausted and, sadly, beyond whatever lift the news of a burgeoning Fitzgerald Revival could give to her. As Scott wrote in a letter to Scottie the week before he died: "The insane are always mere guests on earth, eternal strangers carrying around broken decalogues that they cannot read."[27]

Though they weren't the very first paperbacks, the ASEs helped usher in the paperback revolution of the late 1940s and 1950s, so crucial to resurrecting and broadly repackaging Fitzgerald's writing. (Cheap paper editions of books, such as the penny dreadfuls and railway-edition reprints of Victorian novels, had been around since the nineteenth century, but their quality—inside and out—was low.) In 1935, Penguin Books launched a line of mystery and literature titles in paper and sold them in Woolworth's stores throughout Great Britain. As its name suggests, Pocket Books brought out the first pocket-size paperback books in the United States, in 1939, inaugurating its imprint with ten titles at twenty-five cents each; Avon Books came along in 1941, quickly followed by Popular Library and

Dell.[28] In 1946, Bantam chose *The Great Gatsby* as one of its
first ten titles when it entered into the book market with paper-
bound editions. When the 1949 Alan Ladd movie of *The Great
Gatsby* came out, Bantam added a beefcake dust jacket to this
paperback, showing a bare-chested Alan Ladd standing by
his swimming pool as Howard Da Silva's Wilson points a gun
at his back. Penguin, which had kicked off the paperback
revolution, chose *The Great Gatsby* in 1950 as the first of its
Fitzgerald titles.

Just how helpful were paperbacks to *Gatsby*'s fortunes? Bantam reprinted *Gatsby* five times between 1946 and 1954. A
1951 edition of the Bantam paperback includes this advice to
readers on the first page: "You will understand, when you read
this novel, why a great wave of popularity for Fitzgerald's books
is sweeping the entire country."[29] A Charles Scribner's Sons
royalty report to Scottie dated February 1, 1952, shows that
from merely July to December of that year, Bantam sold
140,701 copies of *The Great Gatsby*.[30]

Of course, paperbacks weren't the only new cultural com-
modities on the block in the late 1940s and 1950s: early television scavenged popular novels and plays for story material.[31]
Many of Fitzgerald's novels and short stories got a new life on
the small screen, among them *The Last Tycoon* (1949), "The
Rich Boy" (1952), and *The Great Gatsby* (1958), all of which
were produced for the *Philco Television Playhouse* series. *The Last
Tycoon* (1951) and *The Great Gatsby* (1955) were part of the
lineup of *Robert Montgomery Presents*, and *CBS's Playhouse 90*
aired dramatic adaptations of those two novels in 1957 and
1958, respectively. DuMont Television produced "Babylon
Revisited" in 1953.

Works of fiction began invoking *Gatsby* at least as early as 1930 with Nathanael West's classic anti-Hollywood novel *The Day of the Locust*. West and Fitzgerald were mutual admirers. In his introduction to the 1934 Modern Library edition of *The Great Gatsby*, Fitzgerald generously mentioned West's *Miss Lonelyhearts* as an example of a first-rate novel by a promising younger writer; Fitzgerald also wrote a letter of recommendation for West, who had applied for a Guggenheim Fellowship. (He didn't get it.) In one of those grotesque turns of literary history, the two men died within twenty-four hours of each other: West and his wife, Eileen McKenney (the inspiration for the Broadway play *My Sister Eileen*), were driving back from a Mexican vacation on December 22, 1940, when he ran a stop sign. The ensuing collision was fatal for them both. Most accounts of the accident say that West was upset upon hearing of the death of Fitzgerald the previous day. Fitzgerald had praised *The Day of the Locust*, which came out in 1939, but apparently didn't see the darkly parodic echoes of *Gatsby* that I think are pretty apparent: the siren in *Locust* is named Faye Greener (Daisy *Fay*, *green* light, get it?); the "dreamer" in West's novel also ends up drowning, this time around in a "sea" of fans at a Hollywood premiere.

Charles Jackson, author of the 1944 novel *The Lost Weekend*— about an alcoholic writer modeled, in part, on Fitzgerald—also fed the Fitzgerald Revival. Jackson worshipped Fitzgerald, to the point that he had had Fitzgerald's nine books expensively bound in Moroccan leather and even impulsively called up Fitzgerald (whom he didn't know) after reading *Tender Is the Night*. "Why don't you write me a letter about it?" Fitzgerald reportedly said in an effort to cut the conversation short. "I think you're a little tight right now."[32] In an arresting scene in *The Lost Weekend*, the main character, Don Birnam, presents a booze-fueled lecture to a room of imaginary students:

"He took down *The Great Gatsby* and ran his finger over the fine green binding. 'There is no such thing,' he said aloud, 'as a flawless novel. But if there is, this is it.' "[33]

When Billy Wilder made *The Lost Weekend* into an Academy Award–winning film, in 1945, he said he had yet another alcoholic writer, Raymond Chandler, in mind as the model for Don Birnam. (Wilder and Chandler had worked together on the 1944 film *Double Indemnity*.) I like to think of Fitzgerald and Chandler "meeting" in *The Lost Weekend*, since it's not clear whether they ever actually met in Hollywood.

Those are some of the highlights of the Fitzgerald Revival from the top down (the critics and academics) and bottom up (legions of soldiers reading their ASEs, the transfixed masses of new television viewers). In the decade before he died, Fitzgerald was forgotten by the general reader, written off by many of his peers. He was in the situation he imagined for Nick in *The Great Gatsby:* living beyond the golden moment in his own life. Now another such golden moment was happening for Fitzgerald, posthumously.

One sure confirmation that the revival was gathering force was the snorts of derision from the contrarians—a band alive and thriving today. In 1946, Robert Frost was in residence at Bread Loaf, the famed summer writers' colony in Vermont. An interviewer asked Frost about the renewed interest in *Gatsby* and the poet shrugged: "Now they're reviving F. Scott Fitzgerald. I finally got around to reading *The Great Gatsby* and I was disappointed....We are ever so much nastier now than even

Fitzgerald was then."[34] Five years later, the maverick literary critic Leslie Fiedler objected to all the Fitzgerald fuss in an essay with the deceptively dull title of "Some Notes on F. Scott Fitzgerald." To Fiedler, Fitzgerald was a "fictionist with a 'second-rate sensitive mind'":

> We are likely to overestimate his books in excessive repentance of the critical errors of the 'thirties — for having preferred Steinbeck or James T. Farrell for reasons we would no longer defend. Fitzgerald has come to seem more and more poignantly the girl we left behind — dead, to boot, before we returned to the old homestead, and therefore particularly amenable to sentimental idealization.[35]

The contrarians remind us that not everyone was (or is) smitten by his reading (or subsequent rereadings) of Fitzgerald. In advance of the premiere of the Baz Luhrmann film of *The Great Gatsby* in May 2013, *New York* magazine book critic Kathryn Schultz made a splash with her essay "Why I Despise *The Great Gatsby*." Schultz declared: "I find *Gatsby* aesthetically overrated, psychologically vacant, and morally complacent; I think we kid ourselves about the lessons it contains. None of this would matter much to me if *Gatsby* were not also sacrosanct." Schultz's pan went viral because, these days, saying you "despise" *Gatsby* — the novel that is now so much part of the fabric of our American life — is like saying you "despise" cotton. (Despise, *really?* I understand when people tell me they were underwhelmed or even bored by *Gatsby*, especially on first reading, but hatred seems an extreme response to such a subtle novel.)

As the Fitzgerald Revival of the late 1940s and beyond was

barreling through American classrooms, bookstores, libraries, and popular culture, some of Fitzgerald's own descendants were a little slow to catch the fever. Eleanor Lanahan, the elder of Scottie's two daughters, was born in 1947. In the illuminating biography that she later wrote about her mother, *Scottie*, Eleanor recalls her embarrassment when a guest at a dinner party addressed a remark to her about *The Great Gatsby*, which the eighteen-year-old had never read. Eleanor resolved to "sneak to the book stacks at Sarah Lawrence College"[36] the following semester. Eleanor elaborated in an e-mail to me, written in the summer of 2013 during the Baz Luhrmann *Gatsby* madness:

> My mother was always very low-key about her father, her heritage, his books....She told me nothing about my grandparents until I was about eleven years old....She didn't say much about Gatsby as literature. Once my mother told me she thought Gatsby was popular on college curriculums because of its brevity....Nobody in my family ever spoke of Gatsby as "The Great American Novel"—and "only" 20 years ago my father, who was a trustee of the Fitzgerald literary trusts—although my parents were long divorced, expressed his surprise that the book continued to be read, and turned into films, plays and ballets. Interest was sure to peak, he felt, and would soon.

Scottie Fitzgerald was crucial to fostering her father's posthumous entry into the American canon. By refusing executor John Biggs's advice that she sell off her father's papers piecemeal and insisting instead that his manuscripts and letters be

kept together, she preserved a treasure trove open to generations of scholars and interested general readers. Scottie seems
to me, from afar, to be one of literary history's most likable
"daughters of." Despite the fact that during the latter part of
her childhood and throughout her adolescence her mother was
emotionally erratic and frequently institutionalized and her
father depressed and drinking, I've come across only one or two
negative comments that she made about her parents. To be
such a resolute "glass-half-full" kind of person, Scottie had to
be adept at seeing only what she wanted to see, but one thing
she never seems to have been in denial about was her father's
talent. In that low-key way her daughter Eleanor describes it,
Scottie, even as a teenager, knew that her father's writing was
special. I say this because of the evidence of the letters: Scottie
saved her father's letters to her, even though they were often
dictatorial and chiding.

But despite Scottie's good instincts about her father's writing, she didn't know much of anything about his books or short
stories as she was growing up. Fitzgerald himself seems
responsible for this blackout. In a conversation with scholar
Matthew J. Bruccoli that was recorded in Montgomery, Alabama, in 1977, Scottie recalled that she didn't read her father's
work—with the possible exception of the short story "The
Curious Case of Benjamin Button"—"until the summer I
graduated from high school" (circa 1939). Scottie told Bruccoli
that she thought her father "didn't want me not to like them."
Instead, he read Dickens and Kipling aloud to her. Scottie told
Bruccoli that her father also enthusiastically recommended
Vanity Fair, the Oz books, the works of Jules Verne, and *The
Three Musketeers* to her.

Bruccoli, Bruccoli, Bruccoli. This funny vegetable of a name pops up all over the place in Fitzgerald Land. (References to Bruccoli have already been liberally scattered through the earlier chapters of this book.) I was familiar with the name from my Scribner's authorized edition of *The Great Gatsby*, which Matthew J. Bruccoli edited, as well as from my critical readings in American literature over the past few decades. In addition to Fitzgerald, his first love, Bruccoli was an authority on, among others, Hemingway, John O'Hara, Thomas Wolfe, Joseph Heller, and Ross Macdonald (who venerated *The Great Gatsby* and in 1966 wrote an excellent Lew Archer mystery novel based on it, *Black Money*). But it wasn't until I began doing serious research on *Gatsby* that I grasped the scope of Matthew J. Bruccoli's magnificent obsession with F. Scott Fitzgerald.

Every great writer deserves an ardent acolyte, a super-reader who will dedicate a career to generating biographies, critical editions, articles, and monographs. For Henry James, there was Leon Edel; Jane Austen, F. R. Leavis; James Joyce, Richard Ellmann. The Fitzgerald Revival, as I've said, was sparked by a determined reclamation effort on the part of Fitzgerald's well-placed literary friends and admirers; it was given a timely boost by the intervention of the ASE editions and the paperback revolution. Scottie Fitzgerald also played a central role as the steward of her parents'—and particularly her father's—literary and cultural memory. But the Fitzgerald Revival kicks it up a notch when the Bronx-born scholar with the difficult-to-pronounce last name enters the arena. (Bruccoli is pronounced "*Brook*-uhly.") Though he always appeared in photographs dressed in jacket and tie, Bruccoli looked more like a gumshoe or a bouncer than a professor. His trademark crew cut and scowl, as well as his fondness for flashy sports cars, added to the tough-guy aura. Improbably, Bruccoli became Scottie Fitzgerald's scholarly soul mate and F. Scott Fitzgerald's most ardent champion.

Not everyone in the Fitzgerald community is a fan of the late Matthew J. Bruccoli (he died in 2008). As you'd expect with such a larger-than-life and, sometimes, abrasive character, he had his detractors. There are folks who say Bruccoli thought he *was* F. Scott Fitzgerald and who maintain that he made it difficult for other scholars to gain access to some Fitzgerald material. Bruccoli edited *The Cambridge Edition of "The Great Gatsby,"* which was published in 1991—the first volume in that series of the works of F. Scott Fitzgerald. But Bruccoli fell out with the Fitzgerald estate because, among other things, he wanted to change some of the language of *Gatsby* to accord with Fitzgerald's later thoughts. Again, depending on whom you talk to, Bruccoli was either trying to be true to Fitzgerald's intentions or trying to play Fitzgerald himself. Admire or disparage him, everyone who had dealings with Bruccoli agrees that he was a force to be reckoned with. That's why I think I've "met" Matthew J. Bruccoli in the best possible way: through his writing.

When I entered graduate school in the late 1970s, there were more than a few characters like him around, people who lived and breathed their chosen subjects. As annoying, even offensive, as some of them could be, they did more than just adopt theoretical positions toward literature; they actually *knew* things. Bruccoli had an encyclopedic knowledge of all things Fitzgerald; more than for that, though, I admire him (at a safe distance) for the enthusiasm of his writing. Bruccoli—like Alfred

Kazin, Edmund Wilson, and their fellow public intellectuals of the mid-twentieth century—wasn't afraid to be subjective, to put his opinions and feelings into his criticism. I find one statement in particular that Bruccoli made about Fitzgerald endearing. He said that Fitzgerald knew he had created a masterpiece in *The Great Gatsby* because "geniuses know what they are doing or trying to do."[37] It's no longer considered intellectually sophisticated to use words like *masterpiece* and *genius*. Sometimes, though, a work like *Gatsby* demands the risk of ridicule.

Bruccoli was interviewed many times about his love for Fitzgerald. He was good copy: a gravel-voiced professor who knew how to tell a story and didn't pull his punches when it came to rating other writers and critics.[38] The story Bruccoli told about how he came to fall in love with Fitzgerald is directly tied to Fitzgerald's early infiltration into American popular culture. Bruccoli said he first discovered Fitzgerald in 1949, when he was a teenager riding in the back of his parents' Dodge on a Sunday afternoon and listening to a radio dramatization of "The Diamond as Big as the Ritz." Smitten, he went to his high-school library the next day to take out Fitzgerald's short stories, only to be met by bewilderment from the school librarian. The Fitzgerald Revival hadn't yet reached Bruccoli's corner of the Bronx.

Undeterred, Bruccoli ferreted out Fitzgerald in other New York City libraries. (One later newspaper profile appropriately dubbed him "Bruccoli the Bulldog."[39]) Some years later, he and his wife, Arlyn, would pay thirty-five dollars—in five-dollar installments—for a dust-jacketed first edition of *The Great Gatsby*. That volume, and the many, many other valuable

Fitzgerald editions to follow, would become jewels in the crown of the Ernest F. Hollings Special Collections Library at the University of South Carolina, where Bruccoli was a distinguished member of the faculty from 1969 until his death, in 2008. That collection now has three first-edition *Gatsbys*, each worth well over a hundred thousand dollars. In 1994 (the last time anyone attempted an estimate), the Matthew J. and Arlyn Bruccoli Collection as a whole was valued conservatively at $1.2 million.

I think even his detractors would grant that Bruccoli's story, like Gatsby's, is primarily about love, not money. Bruccoli met and bonded with Scottie Fitzgerald at a charity auction in 1964, where he was trying to buy two Fitzgerald books. When he missed out on both, Scottie Fitzgerald—who'd donated the books and who observed his disappointment—bought a third Fitzgerald volume someone else had donated and presented it to Bruccoli. Years later, when she was dying, Scottie arranged for some of her father's books to be sent to Bruccoli after her death. Bruccoli said, "She felt that she was letting me down by leaving."[40]

That memory conveys a sense of the relationship that the scholar and the "daughter of" had. Their partnership stretched over two decades, during which time they collaborated on several books. When the shooting script for the 1974 film of *The Great Gatsby* was delivered to Scottie for approval, she and Bruccoli sat up together all night with a pot of coffee, reading it at her Georgetown home. Film enthusiasts will recall that Francis Ford Coppola wrote that script after an earlier script by Truman Capote was deemed, in Coppola's words, "too loopy."[41] Coppola remembers that he had two or three weeks to write the script and that, though he had read *Gatsby,* he didn't remember much of it. When he reread it for his assignment, Coppola was "shocked to find almost no dialogue between Gatsby and Daisy in the book."[42] (Coppola improvised dialogue drawn from Fitzgerald's many rich girl–poor boy short stories.) For the premiere of that film in New York on March 27, 1974, Scottie invited the Bruccolis—as well as ninety cousins and friends, including the steadfast Judge John Biggs and his wife—to stay at the Waldorf-Astoria as her guests. After the screening, Paramount further whipped up *Gatsby* fever by hosting a banquet for two thousand guests in the Waldorf's ballroom, decorated with three thousand white roses and two hundred and fifty potted plants.[43]

That lavish *Gatsby* adventure was preceded by a more curious excursion that Scottie and Matthew Bruccoli took together into one of the byways of the extended Fitzgerald Revival. In 1969, the bandleader Artie Shaw contacted Scottie about making a Broadway musical out of *The Great Gatsby.* Bruccoli accompanied Scottie to several meetings in hotels and restaurants. Bruccoli recalled that "at one of the restaurants...[Artie Shaw] decided to sing us the musical score. It was fairly cringe-making."[44] The musical was never made, but, oh, to have been a fly on that restaurant wall.

On his own, Bruccoli wrote or edited some sixty scholarly books, many of them on Fitzgerald or his Jazz Age compatriots like Ring Lardner, John O'Hara, and, of course, Hemingway. In 1981, he published *Some Sort of Epic Grandeur,* recognized by many scholars as the gold-standard biography of F. Scott Fitzgerald, although there's a faction who think Arthur Mizener's 1951 book *The Far Side of Paradise* is still the best. (If I had to choose only one, I'd vote for Bruccoli's biography, because Mizener's feels dated and a bit censored. For instance, presumably because Edouard Jozan was still alive, his name was changed in that section of the biography.) Bruccoli wielded so much weight at the University of South Carolina that whenever any significant Fitzgeraldiana came up for sale, he was usually able to convince the administration to raise the money for him to make a serious bid. In 1994, Bruccoli and Arlyn, a collector and scholar in her own right, partly donated, partly sold their own vast archive of Fitzgerald's papers and belongings to the University of South Carolina.

That archive is what brings me to the home of the Gamecocks in the steamy midsummer of 2013. Maybe Bruccoli had restricted access to some Fitzgerald material in the past, but the archive doesn't reflect any tendencies toward territoriality. Bruccoli said that anyone was welcome to use his collection as long as that person wasn't wearing a baseball hat and his or her hands were clean. I show up bareheaded and scrubbed.

And wet. It's raining in Columbia when I arrive. Indeed, it will rain so torrentially every afternoon for the next four days that, on my final morning on campus, my visit to the library will have to be canceled because the university loses power due to "weather." The University of South Carolina was founded in 1801 and there are some lovely antebellum buildings around, but the daily monsoon creates "muddy swamps" and "prehistoric marshes" in the grass and pathways, rendering them as impassable as Nick's "irregular lawn" on the fateful afternoon that Gatsby and Daisy are reunited. The fungal gloom of the campus is enhanced by the fact that I arrive between summer sessions, so the place is pretty deserted. All in all, ideal weather conditions for a few days' deep immersion in the Bruccoli Collection.

Jeffrey Makala, the friendly and astute rare-books and special collections librarian who will be my guide, confirms my opinion that librarians, along with independent-bookstore owners and dedicated middle- and high-school teachers, are the most selfless guardians of literature on earth. I introduce myself with a lame joke about making sure that I didn't wear a baseball hat. Jeffrey smiles politely and says that, in Bruccoli's day, researchers also had to make sure they didn't mention they were working on trendy topics like "theorizing Fitzgerald" or "Fitzgerald and gender." Within five minutes of my arrival, Jeffrey leads me downstairs to the vault where the Fitzgerald treasures are kept. There, yet another by-product of my Catholic upbringing quickly surfaces: my excessive reverence for relics. I'm soon so overwhelmed by what Jeffrey is placing in my (clean) hands, that my most oft-repeated comment is "Wow!" (Professor Bruccoli, doubtless, would not have been impressed.) I hold, in succession, the collection's three first editions, with dust jackets, of *The Great Gatsby*. Beautiful. The night sky on their dust jackets is a deeper greenish blue than paperback reproductions suggest. Jeffrey lifts more treasures off the immaculate shelving in the vault and begins handing them to me: the inscribed silver flask that Zelda gave to Scott in 1919; Fitzgerald's walking stick; the copy of *For Whom the Bell Tolls* that Hemingway inscribed to Fitzgerald; Fitzgerald's (unsigned!) copy of the Scribner's contract for *The Great Gatsby*. Wow! Wow! Wow! I'm behaving like one of those notorious literary tourists, but there's an undeniable thrill to holding the real thing in your hands. Besides, why should I feel self-conscious when Fitzgerald himself behaved like the consummately uncool culture vulture, forever kneeling before those writers and artists—Edith Wharton, James Joyce, Isadora Duncan—he worshipped?

Granted, there are also some lesser specimens of Fitzgeraldiana in the collection, examples of what Meyer Wolfshiem would have called tchotchkes stored elsewhere in the lower regions of the library. The following day, Jeffrey will lead me into another pristine storage area that houses the almost-complete collection of Armed Services Editions that Bruccoli began buying in 1959. (Ever on the lookout for a find in a secondhand bookstore, Jeffrey keeps a scribbled list in his wallet of the ASE titles the collection lacks.) High atop some beige metal shelves are two rattan end tables from Fitzgerald's Baltimore days. On another nearby shelf sits a neatly boxed porcelain Gatsby Dollhouse from the 1970s, complete with figures of Daisy and Gatsby, as well as a Gatsby light-up roadster. "Pool not included," Jeffrey quips.

On my second damp day in Columbia, after my initial dazzlement has gotten under control, Jeffrey and I have lunch together to talk some more about Professor Bruccoli and the collection. Jeffrey tells me about a Fitzgerald family sofa from the 1930s that Scottie Fitzgerald gave to Bruccoli. At the time, the Hollings Special Collections Library declined to accept the couch, so Professor Bruccoli ended up giving it to the residential college within the university. Jeffrey says the students there call the couch Zelda. On the way back from lunch, we walk over to that college to take a look at the new, reupholstered Zelda—the handiwork of prisoners at the state penitentiary—but that building is being renovated and the couch must be in storage somewhere. I miss out on sitting on Zelda, but I get a great consolation prize. When we arrive back at the library, Jeffrey unlocks an exhibition case. First, he hands me Fitzgerald's typewriter eraser. (I'm a bit confused by this relic since Fitzgerald didn't type, but Jeffrey tells me the eraser was a gift from Scottie, so her father must have used it.) Much more poignant is the second object Jeffrey takes out of the exhibition case: a battered brown leather briefcase that Fitzgerald used in Hollywood. Fitzgerald's name is engraved in gold letters on the front of the briefcase, as is his address: 597 Fifth Avenue. That's the address of the Charles Scribner's Sons Building, Fitzgerald's only permanent home.

The excitement of these unexpected hands-on encounters aside, I've come prepared for this research trip with my own wish list of things I want to study, and near the top is Sylvia Plath's copy of *The Great Gatsby* that she read—and marked up—as an undergrad at Smith College. The young Plath read the 1949 Grosset and Dunlap edition, which looks a lot like my cherished antique blue editions of the Nancy Drew books. (Fittingly, given their common love of fast roadsters, Gatsby and Nancy briefly shared a publisher.) How did the undergraduate Plath read Fitzgerald? The answer is *studiously*. Plath underlines words and sentences on practically every page of her *Gatsby*. Most of the underlinings have something to do with color symbolism. (Plath's professor must have been of the breed of scholarly symbol hunters.) There are lines under Myrtle's sister's "sticky bob of red hair," George Wilson's "light blue eyes," and Myrtle's "brown figured dress." Indeed, a lot of the comments and underlinings convey the impression of a good student taking down a professor's lecture notes. In the margin

F. Scott Fitzgerald's briefcase. (MATTHEW J. & ARLYN BRUCCOLI COLLECTION OF F. SCOTT FITZGERALD, UNIVERSITY OF SOUTH CAROLINA LIBRARIES)

of that scene in the final chapter where Tom and Nick meet again, Plath has written in blocky ink letters: TOM RESPONSIBLE FOR GATSBY'S DEATH. Other notes fall into the category of commentary that a student makes when she or he is trying to be sophisticated: Plath writes *l'ennui* next to the paragraph in chapter 1 where Daisy tosses off her "beautiful fool" speech. But a few of the comments have the feel of a sensitive reader—a poet in the making—savoring the language. On page 103 of her edition, Plath underlines this description of Daisy: "A damp streak of hair lay like a dash of blue paint across her cheek." And earlier in the novel, when Jordan declares that she likes "big parties because they're so intimate," Plath prints *good* next to the passage. Just as you'd expect, Plath underlines the last line of *The Great Gatsby*.

As I said, I came to the Hollings Special Collections Library with a list of must-see items, but on that first trip down into the vault, Jeffrey generously shows me a treasure that I didn't even know existed. Many serious readers of *The Great Gatsby* are also unaware of this find, even though, like Poe's purloined letter, it's lying out in the open, prominently listed on the library's website for the Bruccoli Collection and mentioned by Bruccoli in an afterword he wrote accompanying the library's publication of a facsimile edition of the *Trimalchio* galleys in 2000.

This treasure in plain sight, like the prize in Poe's story, is a letter. It's written in Fitzgerald's hand and the heading on the top right corner reads *Great Neck, L.I.* It's addressed to a Mr. Baldwin, who Jeffrey tells me was Charles Crittenden Baldwin, a journalist who wrote a book called *The Men Who Make Our Novels*, published in 1924. Fitzgerald's letter, folded in three places and marked by cigarette burns on the right margin, seems to be a response to the general questionnaire that Baldwin sent out to novelists when he was working on that book.

The letter was tipped into a first edition of *Tales of the Jazz Age* that the Hollings Special Collections Library bought in the 1990s. (*Tipped in* is book collectors' lingo for an object, almost always a piece of paper, that's attached, usually by glue, to a page of a book by its corners.) By the 1990s, exhaustive collections of Fitzgerald's letters had already been published, so this letter was left out in the cold. In it, Fitzgerald is begging off writing "very full" answers to interview questions because "I'm sailing for Europe in two days and at my wit's end for time." That internal reference puts the date of this letter sometime in late April of 1924.

After Fitzgerald, ever the people pleaser, goes ahead and gives Baldwin some basic biographical facts of his life and recommends that Baldwin read a *Smart Set* profile of him that was published that spring, the revelation here comes in the third paragraph of the letter:

"My third novel (unpublished) is just finished."

Just finished? Did I read that right? It's never been clear how much of *The Great Gatsby* Fitzgerald wrote in that unheated room above the garage on Gateway Drive. If he's telling the truth here (and why would he be lying?), then a completed draft of *Gatsby* sailed over to Europe with Scott, Zelda, and Scottie on the SS *Minnewaska* in the spring of 1924. That version of *Gatsby*, Bruccoli logically speculates, would be the first version, the one with the omniscient narrator whom Fitzgerald wisely rejected in favor of Nick. What's exciting about this letter is that it takes the writing of the first draft of *Gatsby* back to the spring, rather than the summer, of 1924. This might not be breaking news to most of the world, but since the composition history of Fitzgerald's masterpiece is so convoluted and fragmentary (recall that missing typescript of the first draft), any information is precious. But what's even more remarkable is that, as the opening sentence of that third paragraph in his letter to Mr. Baldwin goes on, Fitzgerald tries to define his new novel. The sentence reads: "My third novel (unpublished) is just finished + quite different from my other two in that it is an attempt at . . ." *Agh! What is that word?*

The mystery word that Fitzgerald wrote in fountain pen in his mostly legible script falls on one of the letter folds. The word starts with an *f* and it could be *form* or *force* or *farce.* So, here we have F. Scott Fitzgerald defining in one word the essence of what may be the greatest American novel of all time, and the word is indecipherable. Terrific—a postmodern nonending to this treasure hunt. I call upon Jeffrey for help and he obligingly comes from his office to peer at the letter in the rare-books reading room. Jeffrey votes for *farce,* which I like, because the comic nature of *The Great Gatsby* is so often overlooked. In his afterword to the *Trimalchio* facsimile, Bruccoli printed a typescript of the letter and used the word *form.* Weeks later, when I take a photocopy of the letter to Princeton, Don C. Skemer, who hadn't seen it before, also votes for *form. Form* is the most logical choice given what we know about Fitzgerald's focus on *Gatsby*'s structure. Still later, I e-mail a scanned copy of the letter to Scott Shepherd, the brilliant actor who played Nick Carraway—and memorized the entire text of *The Great Gatsby*—in the Elevator Repair Service's production of *Gatz.* Shepherd, who's thoroughly immersed in *Gatsby* and Fitzgerald—votes for *form* as well. *Farce, form, force*—you decide for yourself. Here's a facsimile of the letter, which goes on to talk about the novel that will become *The Great Gatsby* in the context of modern American fiction.

On my last day at the Hollings Special Collections Library, the day before the power outage, I request to see something

An uncollected letter in which Fitzgerald is writing to "Mr. Baldwin" about The Great Gatsby. (MATTHEW J. & ARLYN BRUCCOLI COLLECTION OF F. SCOTT FITZGERALD, UNIVERSITY OF SOUTH CAROLINA LIBRARIES) precious and personal. Forget literary tourism, I'm way over the line now and into literary voyeurism. The rare-book staffer brings out three photo albums, the kind with the black paper where, in olden days, people pasted in their black-and-white photos. Scott and Zelda put together these three albums; they span the years 1924 to 1931. Some of these photos I've seen before in a wonderful book that Scottie Fitzgerald and Matthew J. Bruccoli, along with editor Joan P. Kerr, first published in 1974, called *The Romantic Egoists,* which is also the title written on the third album: "The Romantic Egoists: Our Fourth Trip Abroad 3/1929–9/1931 Europe, Africa, etc." The paper in these fragile albums is crumbling, but the images are alive because they're out of focus, silly, and sometimes even unflattering. (Zelda and Scottie look fat in a few that are shot at bad angles.) On the first page of the first album is the most vibrant picture I've ever seen of Zelda; it's blurry because she's moving, mugging for the camera with her pointed fingers holding up her chin. Zelda, to me, often looks uncomfortable in photos, but this one is charming. By the third album, there are snapshots of "A Costume Ball" at Prangins, the Swiss mental clinic where Zelda was treated: Zelda is dressed as a lampshade and her psychiatrist, Dr. Forel, poses as a caveman. In between, the Fitzgeralds commit the forgivable crime of most new parents with a camera: they take way too many photos of baby Scottie. True to form, right before a picture of Scott holding Scottie over waves breaking on a beach, Scott has written (and misspelled) *Rivierra.* It's the Riviera in 1924, the summer of *The Great Gatsby.* These three albums restore messy humanity back to the legendary Fitzgeralds. Scott is a playful dad and Zelda has been

A photograph of Zelda from Fitzgerald's personal album. (MATTHEW J. & ARLYN BRUCCOLI COLLECTION OF F. SCOTT FITZGERALD, UNIVERSITY OF SOUTH CAROLINA LIBRARIES)

transformed from the jokey-if-affectionate name of a couch that art students sit on to an all-too-human person.

There's one more item on my must-see list: a typed note that seems minor compared to all the Fitzgerald treasures tucked away here in South Carolina. Still, it's a note that speaks volumes about the speed and force (*farce? form?*) with which the Fitzgerald Revival took hold in American literary culture. The note, from the fall of 1971, is on Kent State University Press letterhead and it's from the director of the press, C. Howard Allen, to Edmund Wilson. Allen is writing to Wilson to ask him to blurb a new book about Fitzgerald by scholar Jackson R.

Bryer and—who else?—Matthew J. Bruccoli. The book is called *F. Scott Fitzgerald in His Own Time* and it's an interesting miscellany of mostly minor pieces by Fitzgerald (short stories written for the school newspaper, book reviews) along with reviews of his own work. Wilson, who by all reports was not a nice man, couldn't be bothered to write a note on a separate piece of paper. He scrawled this handwritten response at the bottom of Allen's letter and then must have stuffed the letter into an envelope and sent it back. Wilson's response, in full, reads:

> I am tired to the point of nausea of books on Scott Fitzgerald. Do tell Bruccoli to get interested in some other writer.
>
> Edmund Wilson.[45]

Edmund Wilson, who'd kick-started the Fitzgerald Revival back in the 1940s with his editions of *The Last Tycoon* and *The Crack-Up*, came to realize that he'd created a Frankenstein's monster. His friend Scott Fitzgerald—whom Wilson had supported but also condescended to during Fitzgerald's lifetime—had become such a posthumous sensation by the early 1970s that it seemed clear Wilson would forever be in his shadow, instead of the other way round. Wilson may have been "tired to the point of nausea" of books on Fitzgerald, but America—and the world—wanted more editions of Fitzgerald's work, more biographies, more movies, even more criticism. Everything Fitzgerald wrote was roaring back into print and selling. Fitzgerald was inspiring a new generation of writers who loved his language. Writers as seemingly far removed from Fitzgerald as Norman Mailer, Margaret Atwood, Paul Auster, Don DeLillo, Annie Dillard, John le Carré, and fellow St. Paulite *Peanuts* cartoonist Charles Schulz were reading and being bowled over by him.[46] While working at *Time* magazine in the 1950s, gonzo journalist Hunter S. Thompson typed out every word of *The Great Gatsby* and *A Farewell to Arms* to get a visceral feel for Fitzgerald's and Hemingway's style. Another famous, albeit fictional, character who read those two novels in tandem was Holden Caulfield. In *The Catcher in the Rye,* Holden Caulfield tells us that his older brother, D.B., makes him read *A Farewell to Arms* (a "phony book" in Holden's estimation) and *The Great Gatsby.* "I was crazy about *The Great Gatsby,*" says Holden. "Old Gatsby. Old sport. That killed me."[47] Holden's laudatory outburst first occurs in the crucial Fitzgerald Revival year of 1951.

By 1960, *The Great Gatsby* became the first volume in the paperback Scribner's Library. In 1961, it was reprinted in a Scribner School Edition intended for high schools, and the *Gatsby* invasion force was launched. Ever since the 1960s, Scribner's has continued to repackage *Gatsby* in textbook series and collections. In classrooms across America and, verily, the world, paperbacks bearing Cugat's *Celestial Eyes* (or, more recently, Leonardo DiCaprio's hooded ones) are marked up with yellow highlighters and scribbled lecture notes: *green light = money, Nick = unreliable,* and *Eckleburg = eyes of God. The Great Gatsby* is thrown into lockers along with sweaty gym clothes and hairbrushes; it rides home in backpacks filled with lip gloss and Doritos crumbs and cell phones. It's downloaded on electronic reading devices, sometimes from illegal websites.

(The copyright for *The Great Gatsby* runs out in 2020.) Students fall asleep over it in their beds, are mildly bored by it in their English classes, and, every once in a while, fall in love with it on first read. Far from disappearing, this odd little novel from 1925 has turned out to be unsinkable.

6

"I Didn't Get It the First Time"

Chapter 4 of *The Great Gatsby* begins with that kooky list of names of Gatsby's party guests during the summer of 1922. Nick introduces the list by saying:

> Once I wrote down on the empty spaces of a time-table the names of those who came to Gatsby's house that summer. I can still read the grey names and they will give you a better impression than my generalities of those who accepted Gatsby's hospitality and paid him the subtle tribute of knowing nothing whatever about him.[1]

Fitzgerald's novel, like Gatsby's house, has also hosted plenty of guests, many of them also paying "the subtle tribute" of learning only the most superficial details about the story. I've already referred to some of these guests in the course of this book, but here—in homage to Fitzgerald's list—is a very short roll call of still more of the knockoffs, tributes, kitschy products, and outright atrocities that *The Great Gatsby* has inspired:

From the online marketplace comes a gray T-shirt emblazoned with the logo "I Party with Jay Gatsby"; a plastic computer cover decorated with the eyes of Dr. T. J. Eckleburg; Gatsby Facial Clear Japanese Oil Blotting Papers; and Classic Adventures: *The Great Gatsby,* a computer game, updated for iPad users in 2012, in which Nick searches for Gatsby through various levels (a party scene, the valley of ashes), all the while dodging wacky waiters and the ray-gun eyes of Dr. T. J. Eckleburg. At the successful end of this quest, Gatsby cries: "You found me, old sport!" And speaking of the computer world, the Internet site Seattle.curbed.com reports that Microsoft mogul Bill Gates has a quote from *Gatsby* engraved on the ceiling of the library in his mansion near Seattle. The quote reads: "He had come a long way to this blue lawn, and his dream must have seemed so close that he could hardly fail to grasp it."

From the world of movies and TV comes *G,* a 2002 film starring Blair Underwood in which Gatsby is reimagined as a hip-hop mogul who visits the Hamptons in order to win back the love of his life. Woody Allen's *Midnight in Paris* (2011) features Owen Wilson as a modern-day writer who lives every fan's Lost Generation fantasy by hanging out with the Fitzgeralds and Hemingways in the City of Light, circa 1926. *Last Call,* a Showtime movie made in 2002, showcases Jeremy Irons as Fitzgerald and Neve Campbell as his modest-but-spunky secretary Frances Kroll Ring. *Gatsby* allusions or story lines inform episodes of *Modern Family, South Park, Mad Men, How I Met Your Mother, Californication, Pan Am, Entourage,* and *Seinfeld.* (In the last, Elaine's eccentric boss Mr. Peterman orders her to create a "Gatsby Swing Top." Here's how he explains his vision of that garment: "I saw a woman in our hallway wearing one of these as a top. What exquisite beauty. I ran down the hallway to talk to her, but the elevator door closed. It was not to be. Perhaps our paths will cross again someday.") During an episode of *The Wire*, *The Great Gatsby* is discussed in a prison English class. D'Angelo Barksdale, a character described as a "middle manager" in a drug-dealing empire, nails the pessimistic interpretation of Gatsby's final lines:

"Where we come from, what we go through, how we go through it—all that shit matters. Like, at the end of the book? Boats and tides and all? It's like, you can change up. You can say you somebody new. You can give yourself a whole new story. But what came first is who you really are."

From the world of music and literature comes a Seattle-based indie rock band named Gatsby's American Dream and a young-adult novel about teenage socialites called *Great* by comedian Sara Benincasa. Other novels riff on the Fitzgeralds' life together, including four fictional histories in 2013 alone that delved into Zelda's troubled consciousness: *Z*, by Therese Anne French; *Superzelda*, a graphic novelization of Zelda's life, by Tiziana Lo Porto; *Call Me Zelda*, by Erika Robuck; and *Beautiful Fools* by R. Clifton Spargo. Still other novels have followed in *Gatsby*'s distinctive tire tracks, including Chris Bohjalian's *The Double Bind*, which imagines an aging Daisy and Tom, out of shape and still bickering; *Banana Republic*, by Eric Rauchway, in which a humbled Tom Buchanan travels down to Nicaragua to bolster his sagging finances; and Tom Carson's *Daisy Buchanan's Daughter*, which follows little Pammy as she grows up in the American century. (That novel opens on an arresting vision of Pammy as an eighty-year-old woman waiting to talk to George W. Bush, after which she plans to blow her brains out to protest the Iraq War.) The best *Gatsby* updating I've read yet is *Netherland*, Joseph O'Neill's post-9/11 novel about New York City. In it, a "Dutch sailor" named Hans van den Broek meets a charismatic con man from Trinidad who dreams of building a cricket stadium where immigrants of all nations can come together. Chuck Ramkissoon, this contemporary Gatsby, doesn't have a driver's license, so he makes use of Hans to chauffeur him back and forth through the glittering streets and the waste places of Manhattan and the outer boroughs. In the end, Hans, on the Staten Island Ferry, surveys the skyline of Manhattan, and O'Neill credibly tips his hat to Fitzgerald's matchless final paragraphs in *Gatsby*.

In addition to all these, I randomly take note of the existence of a Gatsby Charitable Foundation in London named after the novel, the Great Gatsby Dining Room on the Royal Caribbean ocean liner the *Grandeur of the Seas* (What? No Moby-Dick Whale-of-a-Buffet?), and the Daisy Buchanan engagement ring copied by jewelers around the country in the wake of the Baz Luhrmann film. One day, when I was clumsily texting a message and misspelled *Gatsby*, I discovered that my iPhone autocorrects the name. In New York City, the Plaza Hotel offers a luxury art deco stay in the Fitzgerald Suite and *Gatsby*-themed cocktails in its bar. Governors Island hosts an annual Jazz Age lawn party in which guests dress like Gatsby's hangers-on, and the New York Yankees fan store offers a retro Gatsby cap stamped with the Yankees logo. Finally, there's the accounting, kept by *Daily Howler* blogger Bob Somerby, of the number of times *New York Times* columnist Maureen Dowd compares Bill and Hillary Clinton to Tom and Daisy Buchanan; it's currently at five.

All these pilgrims and pretenders have come to Fitzgerald's novel in recent years.

In turn, *The Great Gatsby* has gone a-roving all over the world as a literary ambassador of the American Dream. Frequently, when I visit my own university's library looking for a critical work on *Gatsby*, I'm informed via computer that the desired book is in the stacks...in Qatar. *Gatsby* is a strong presence in the library offerings and classrooms of Education City in Doha, the capital of Qatar, where Georgetown and other American, Canadian, and European colleges and universities have established desert outposts. Given that the average summer temperature in Qatar is over 100 degrees, the Qataris must snicker at *Gatsby*'s complaint about the New York summer heat in chapter 7 ("Hot!...Hot!...Hot!...Is it hot enough for you? Is it hot? Is it...?"[2]). Azar Nafisi, in her 2003 blockbuster memoir, read not only *Lolita* but also *Gatsby* in Tehran with her students. So fierce were the arguments about *Gatsby* as the literary stand-in for America, the Great Satan, that Nafisi was inspired to put the novel on trial. The prosecutors were those students who saw the novel as an exaltation of everything decadent about the United States; Nafisi, acting as a lawyer for the defense, spoke powerfully about the purity of Gatsby's vision: "The dream is not about money but what [Gatsby] imagines he can become. It is not a comment on America as a materialistic country but as an *idealistic* one, one that has turned money into a means of retrieving a dream. There is nothing crass here, or the crassness is so mingled with the dream that it becomes very difficult to differentiate between the two."[3]

The Great Gatsby's newest and largest foreign market of readers are those students and teachers of English living in the People's Republic of China. Fitzgerald's novel resonates in a country that recently has discovered the thrills of entrepreneurial self-invention and conspicuous consumption (and where many people, out of necessity, are closemouthed about their pasts). The Baz Luhrmann film was one of only thirty-four foreign films given the green light to be shown in China in 2013. In a *New Yorker* blog, an American teacher of English observed that, in advance of that film showing, *Gatsby* fever was in the air—and in advertisements—in Beijing: "The ad copy for the colorful men's dress shirts sold by the Chinese fashion label Masa Maso invites the shopper to recall the lesson of 'The Amazing Gai-Ci-Bi'—or, as it's known in the West, 'The Great Gatsby.' 'Don't forget,' the ads warn, 'that as soon as the protagonist, Gatsby, obtained fame and fortune, he went out and bought beautiful, brightly colored shirts that transformed his image in Daisy's eyes. It's true: put on a flower-print shirt, and it will show you the door to a whole new world!'"[4]

For firsthand information about *Gatsby*'s reception in the People's Republic of China, I turn to an expert at my graduate-school alma mater. Peter Conn is the Vartan Gregorian Chair in English at the University of Pennsylvania and the author of the acclaimed 1998 book *Pearl S. Buck: A Cultural Biography.* In the summer of 2013, under the auspices of the Ford Foundation, he convened a seminar for a group of Chinese teachers of American literature at Guangxi Normal University in Guilin. Conn described the participants as "mostly younger scholars, all with doctorates from universities in West China." *The Great*

Gatsby was among the dozen or so American texts of the 1920s and 1930s on his syllabus. Conn recalls:

> Responses to *Gatsby* varied, but divided almost equally on the issue of Gatsby's "greatness." Quite a number quoted Nick's early comment on Gatsby's "extraordinary gift for hope," but they construed this in different ways. For some, this signaled an admirable talent for self-invention—a talent they connected with the fluidity of American society, compared to the more rigid constraints of China. Even in 2013, in the midst of explosive change, several of them argued that no one born and reared in China could emerge from "his Platonic conception of himself."
>
> For others, Gatsby's optimism bespoke American overreach: the US has too often exhibited a tendency to re-make much of the world in its Platonic conception of how everyone ought to behave. A couple of these readers also drew a line between Gatsby's criminal career and America's buccaneering behavior both in the Old West (for them, the Hopalong Cassidy reference is rather sinister).
>
> A couple of teachers admitted that they would really like to have attended one of Gatsby's parties. To this I replied: "me, too."[5]

Another segment of *The Great Gatsby*'s international readership first encounters the novel after immigration to the United States. A 2008 article in the *New York Times* headlined "Gatsby's Green Light Beckons a New Set of Strivers" reported on how first- and second-generation Americans respond to their required reading of *Gatsby* in high school. Jinzho Wang, then a fourteen-year-old sophomore at the Boston Latin School who arrived in America with her family in 2006, told the *Times* reporter that her "green light" was Harvard. "But if I don't get into Harvard, I will not die, right? The journey toward the dream is the most important thing." Another student, Vimin To, a fifteen-year-old sophomore whose Vietnamese father immigrated to America, said, "It's a very inspiring tale, especially when you're from a background such as Mr. Gatsby."[6]

In twenty-first-century American lit classrooms all around the world, *The Great Gatsby* rules! Except, that is, in the classrooms that mattered most to F. Scott Fitzgerald. "No one has taught a seminar on Fitzgerald at Princeton for at least a decade," Don C. Skemer tells me during my visit to the Fitzgerald Papers at Firestone Library. "Elaine Showalter was the last," he adds, referring to the well-known feminist literary scholar. I'm saddened, thinking of how Fitzgerald died in the act of reading the *Princeton Alumni Weekly* and making penciled notes—I've seen them!—in the margins of an article about Princeton football. I follow up with Showalter, who retired early from Princeton in 2003. She tells me that she offered that seminar on the work of both Scott and Zelda Fitzgerald, as well as Hemingway, in the late 1990s and recalls, "Fitzgerald was regarded as somewhat passé although I'm sure *Gatsby* was taught in the American lit surveys." Checking the 2013–2014 English courses at Princeton, I see that James Joyce rates a seminar and that there are seminars devoted to *Moby-Dick* and James and Faulkner, but none on Fitzgerald. I'd be completely embittered on Fitzgerald's behalf were it not for one upper-level course, Modernism and Ornament, that mentions Fitzgerald, among other writers, in its description.

The relative cold shoulder of Fitzgerald by his beloved Old Nassau makes me think about the reaction I've gotten from colleagues at my own university when I mention that I'm working on a book about *The Great Gatsby*. Some of them have been clearly underwhelmed, even a little patronizing, as though I'd unwrapped an American cheese sandwich on Wonder Bread at a faculty meeting. ("Oh, Fitzgerald? I haven't read him in a long time.") *Gatsby* and its author are too ubiquitous to be intellectually sexy. I decide to see what the other Ivy League universities think of Fitzgerald.

Spending a couple of hours reading English Department course descriptions for the 2013–2014 academic year would turn even Edmund Wilson into a business major. There's an air of aggressive absurdity around many of these syllabi so heavily inflected with jargon about postcolonialism and culture theory; it's as though John Cleese's Basil Fawlty drew up these reading lists the same way he would draw up odd menus of prawns, pickles, and organ meats and shove them at intimidated hotel guests. We've come a long strange way from those undisputed Great Books lists that Fitzgerald loved to compose for Sheilah Graham and others; nothing in English departments is taken for granted anymore, not even the "human-ness" of human beings. One peculiar new trend my survey reveals is that "problematizing the human" is a popular pedagogical topic.

Let's start at Jinzho Wang's green light: Harvard. A whopper of a course called Fictions of America claims to stretch from the sixteenth to the twenty-first centuries and features modernists such as Stein and Cather, but no Fitzgerald. He does turn up in a course description for American Modernism, but only Thomas Hardy and James Joyce's *Ulysses* merit their own seminars. Dartmouth, where Fitzgerald's screenwriting career came to a crashing end during that awful research trip with Budd Schulberg for *Winter Carnival,* seems to have shut him out entirely. Once again, Joyce commands his own seminar, as does Faulkner.

Yale, as far as I can tell, is the most defiantly traditional of the Ivies, featuring an upper-level course in the major works of Hemingway, Fitzgerald, and Faulkner. Columbia, near where Fitzgerald lived in upper Upper Manhattan for a time in 1919, apparently has no use for him at all: a course called Modernist Texts gives us Yeats, Eliot, and Auden. The Modern Novel consists of Joyce, Woolf, and James. The unkindest cut of all: a course at Columbia called, simply, Modernism features Yeats, Joyce, Stein, and Hemingway, but not Fitzgerald.

True to my frustrating graduate-school memories of the place, the University of Pennsylvania's English Department listings are difficult to access, but after repeated tries I finally gain entry. One course, the Twentieth Century, cites *The Great Gatsby* as a guiding text for the rest of the syllabus! I'm proud that Penn has come through for Fitzgerald. Cornell offers a course in Literary and Civic Fictions where Fitzgerald rubs shoulders with Cather, Hemingway, Stein, West, and Faulkner. Brown, however, trumps the rest of the Ivies: Fitzgerald is listed in four English courses there, including one that's devoted entirely to the Roaring Twenties. So things aren't as bleak as I feared: Fitzgerald doesn't have the status to rate a seminar (Faulkner is the clear winner in that category), but his name pops up often enough in chronologically themed courses. Before I quit this excursion, I log in to one more English department's course listings for 2013–2014. St. Olaf's, in

Northfield, Minnesota, is the "small Lutheran college" that James Gatz attended, working his way through as a janitor for all of two weeks. Gatz, Nick tells us, was "dismayed by [St. Olaf's] ferocious indifference to the drums of his destiny."[7] The college is still indifferent: There's nary a trace of *The Great Gatsby* in St. Olaf's English Department, unless it's buried within the reading lists of catchy-named courses like Romanticism and Rock Music and Sex, Madness, and Marriage.

The Great Gatsby's erratic presence in college curricula is surely a consequence of its unrivaled high-school popularity: the novel trails in the college bowls but wins the high-school English tournaments. *The Catcher in the Rye* and *To Kill a Mockingbird* are worthy runners-up, but *Gatsby* is the novel that comes closest to being a literary sure thing on American high-school syllabi. Very, very rarely do I encounter first-year students in my college classes who haven't already read the novel. I don't remember a lot about my own first reading of *The Great Gatsby*, which in itself tells me something. Other high-school novels (especially *Jane Eyre* and *A Tale of Two Cities*) made vivid impressions. I wonder what young first-time readers see in the novel these days? It's one thing to read or hear reports about what high-school students think of *Gatsby*, but I want to sit in a classroom and hear those discussions as they happen. So I decide to do something I haven't felt the urge to do in almost forty years: return to my old high school. *Can't repeat the past? Why of course you can!* In my case, all you have to do is e-mail your old English teacher and ask.

A few months after that e-mail, I'm riding in a cab on the Queensboro Bridge, going the wrong way. When Nick effuses that "the city seen from the Queensboro Bridge is always the city seen for the first time, in its first wild promise of all the mystery and the beauty in the world," he and Gatsby are riding in Gatsby's "gorgeous" car driving *into* New York. I'm heading into Long Island City—which Fitzgerald apparently paid so little attention to when he himself drove through it on those trips from Great Neck that he misidentifies it as Astoria in the novel. And, anyway, what does it matter? Queens is just the place Fitzgerald's characters have to drive through to get to someplace better, either into Manhattan or out to the Eggs.

Of course, it's changed a lot since I was a kid. Gentrification has arrived in Long Island City, and condos are rising up on the Queens side of the East River, taking over streets that used to be crowded with factories, body shops, and, in the residential sections, three-story walk-up apartment houses like the one I grew up in. You can still see a spectacular view of the Empire State Building from Forty-Third Avenue in Sunnyside (a block away from my family's old apartment), but the Manhattan skyline is rapidly being blotted out by one graceless high-rise after another. My lost city.

The cab crosses over the bridge and turns left onto Twenty-First Street to drive into Astoria. That's when I see a new sign that declares the Queensboro Bridge has been renamed the Ed Koch Queensboro Bridge. Good luck with that. At the rededication ceremony in 2011, Koch gamely read aloud the Queensboro Bridge passage from *Gatsby*. Ever since my cabbie picked me up at Penn Station, he's been complaining nonstop about another New York City mayor: Michael Bloomberg. The cabbie thinks that New York under Bloomberg targets working people for fines and taxes. The rant began when he spotted a cop ticketing another cab on Park Avenue and Forty-Third Street. I can't make out everything the cabbie says—eventually I find out he's from Vietnam—but *money* and *Bloomberg* are his most oft-repeated words. As we rode over the bridge, he pointed out the ugly new skyscrapers (Bloomberg!), and, in a voice that approached a shout, he sputtered that "foreigners" favored by Bloomberg were profiting from the construction. I think I can see where this is going. Sure enough, as we bump through the pitted streets of Astoria, I make out the word *Jew*. Because I'm a student of *The Great Gatsby*, my exasperation with this guy's anti-Semitism is leavened with fascination for how life just keeps on mirroring art. When he and Gatsby cross the bridge, Nick notices the presence of immigrants from "south-eastern Europe" and African Americans ("two bucks and a girl"); here I am on the same bridge ninety-one years later with a guy—an immigrant himself—who's expressing the same kind of fears about "others" elbowing in on and getting too big a piece of the American pie. Before I get out at my destination—St. John's Prep on Crescent Street in Astoria—I ask the cabbie what he thinks of President Obama. "Obama good, he's real American," the cabbie asserts. The dividing line between "real American" and "other" in twenty-first-century New York seems murkier than it was in Tom Buchanan's paranoid worldview.

Here's another congruity between life and art that didn't hit me until I was in that cab and heard—between snorts of "Bloomberg!" and "Money!"—the all-news station on the radio announce the date, along with the time and weather: April 10, eighty-eight years to the day since *The Great Gatsby* first appeared on the shelves of bookstores across America.

This is the portentous date I've blindly chosen for a visit back to my old high school, where I'm going to sit in on an honors English class reading *The Great Gatsby* for the first time. The fact that my old high school is located in Astoria and, thus, stands within the geography of the novel is a bonus. What's it like to read one of our Great American Novels for the first time as you're sitting in a classroom in a neighborhood that that novel (briefly and unflatteringly) describes? I can't remember, but maybe these kids can tell me.

Back in my day, it was called Mater Christi Diocesan High School, and there was a boys' side and a girls' side whose Berlin Wall perimeters were patrolled by the Christian Brothers and the Sisters of Mercy, respectively. The beige brick building (which I'm saddened to see is now surrounded by a chain-link fence topped with barbed wire) is shaped roughly like an *M* topped in the middle with a tall silver cross. When I was a student, the rumor was that the place had been built as a sanitarium and the *M* signified *Mental.* "There's some truth lurking beneath that rumor," says Jason Booth, the young teacher whose class I'm visiting. When he meets me at the front entrance and hears my reminiscence (the first of many that he'll graciously listen to over the next day and a half), he surprises me by saying: "The school was built on the site of some kind of a rest home or sanitarium and the word is that Dylan Thomas's wife, Caitlin, was treated here after he died and she broke down." Yet another hard-drinking male artist and his tormented wife.

The school merged with St. John's Prep in 1980; that's when the partitions came tumbling down and classes became co-ed. As Mr. Booth leads me into the hallway, I see that, as I expected, the population of my old school has changed in other ways, too, reflecting the presence of kids of color and newer waves of immigrants who now make Queens one of the most ethnically and racially diverse places on earth. Lots of teenage black, Latino, Indian, Asian, and Central European faces glance curiously at me as we walk by. Mater Christi, back then, was largely Tom Buchanan's vision of how America should be. (Well, not quite: given Buchanan's biases and the pervasive anti-Catholic hostility of white Protestants in the twenties, he probably had little use for parochial schools.) Coming toward us now is a miracle. Mrs. Maureen Flood was my sophomore English teacher at Mater Christi in 1970. I remember her as blond and peppy, always smiling. She was a new mother back then, married to Mr. Edward Flood, the boys' phys ed coach. At a nostalgic moment a few years ago, I'd joined the school's online alumni association and made a small contribution to the scholarship fund. Incredibly, Mrs. Flood—who is now the school's vice principal—e-mailed me to thank me and congratulate me on my newly published memoir. I was floored. I was a shy teenager, and my strategy for survival at such a big school (Mater Christi had about two thousand students back then) was to fade into the woodwork. In my senior year, I was editor in chief of the school newspaper, the *Crescent Tower,* but that was a behind-the-scenes position, not high-profile like student council or cheerleader. I never thought that anybody at the school would remember me.

But Mrs. Flood is the sort of dedicated teacher who seems to remember every student she's ever taught. She tells me several times that she can still see me sitting in her English class, circa 1970, a girl with long brown hair and an "intense" expression on my face. My long hair got chopped decades ago, and the intense expression has left me with what my mother calls "crowbars" around my eyes; in contrast, time has been incredibly kind to this kindest of teachers. Now a grandmother, she's remained trim and energetic; her hair (still blond!) brushes her shoulders in a layered suggestion of the flip I once knew. Mrs. Flood's first name, like mine, is Maureen, and I silently congratulate myself on the ease with which the grown-up me addresses her by it, but still, there are psychological slippages throughout this visit when my teenage self resurfaces. I feel myself stiffen when, during our first conversation in her office, Mrs. Flood and I reminisce about the senior trip to Rocking Horse Ranch in upstate New York. As Mrs. Flood reminds me, she and her husband chaperoned that overnight trip, during which some girls were caught with liquor bottles in their room. The ringleader Mrs. Flood now names was a friend of a friend of mine. Given that I was on the outer fringes of that crowd, I probably downed some of the Southern Comfort or vodka or whatever was being passing around. My only solid memory of that class trip was that two girlfriends and I performed as the Supremes in the talent show we put on in the hotel hallway. It was 1973 and we wore Afro wigs we'd made out of Brillo pads. F. Scott Fitzgerald is not alone in having done or said or written stupid things about race in his youth.

Mrs. Flood and I will have a lot more time for conversation because she's insisted that I stay with her and her husband, Ed, now director of athletics, at their home in Forest Hills. Now, though, it's time for her to escort me to Mr. Booth's last-period honors English class. Walking through the hallways, still lined with beige metal lockers, I experience Freud's theory of the uncanny writ large. Familiar things are strangely off; there's the alien presence of boys in the halls, and some of the girls have on a lot of makeup and they aren't waiting, as we once did, till they get off the school grounds to roll their uniform skirts up short. During this first afternoon and throughout the next day, I'll see the kids reach out and touch their teachers' arms and shoulders to get their attention; sometimes, they'll even make jokes. Things are much more relaxed. And then there's me: *Aiyee!* I'm middle-aged! Walking through these familiar halls, I feel like the Crypt Keeper. When I'm introduced in class after class as a graduate of Mater Christi, class of 1973, and a former student of Mrs. Flood, there are audible gasps along with good-natured hoots and applause—*1973?* If Nick were ever to return to West Egg, this is how he would feel, like a crinkled ghost. I remember how we used to laugh at those teachers we thought were impossibly old and odd, like our biology nun who was gaga over African violets. Now, in the eyes of these kids, I'm the elderly eccentric, gaga over *Gatsby*.

Fortunately for me, the students in Mr. Booth's honors English class in American literature are nice as well as smart. The students are plowing their way through an ambitious syllabus; they've already read *Moby-Dick* and they're set to tackle *The Grapes of Wrath* after reading some of Timothy Egan's great book about the Dustbowl, *The Worst Hard Time*. Sandwiched in there is *The Great Gatsby*. Unwittingly intensifying my feeling of being the Ghost of High School Past, Mr. Booth has put a projection of my NPR black-and-white headshot on the whiteboard in front of the class. I hover ectoplasmically on the screen. He turns things over to me and I start to talk a little bit about why I love *Gatsby*. Wrong move. This is the last class period of the day, so the kids are tired, and my lecture is a snooze-athon. Time to stir up some class participation. I ask for a show of hands: Who liked the novel? Who didn't? I assure the students that Mr. Booth isn't looking (he obligingly covers his eyes). About six students really liked it, another six say it was okay, and one or two brave souls say they didn't like it at all. One girl with an earnest look on her round face raises her hand and asks me, "Why did he write it?" I launch into some biographical patter about Fitzgerald coming from an insecure economic background that left him feeling like an outsider/insider, but after class, I'll kick myself. Although it often feels like a cheap teaching trick, I should have turned the question back on her: Why do *you* think he wrote it? What do *you* think Fitzgerald needed to tell us? That's what I'm here to find out.

After raising a few other discussion topics that fizzle, I decide to show a clip of the preview of the upcoming Baz Luhrmann movie. The room erupts! Kids start dancing around in their seats to the heavy bass sound track. They smile at the glitz, the 3-D visions of familiar places like the Queensboro Bridge and what looks like the el train that runs over Thirty-First Street in Astoria. (That el, or elevated subway train, mentioned in the novel began running in 1917, so it was new when Fitzgerald would have driven under it on his road trips back and forth between Great Neck and Manhattan.) The kids softly say "Yeah!" whenever Leonardo DiCaprio appears on-screen—they think Leo is cool—and tell me they can't wait to see the movie. The preview clip gets the same electric reaction in every classroom at the Prep—all five of them—that I visit the next day. The kids' excitement has an effect on me. I've been dreading this latest film version of *Gatsby;* it's such a subtle novel, and Luhrmann is about as subtle as that Southern Comfort my friends and I used to drink, but the students make me see that *Gatsby* has enough glitz in it to justify Luhrmann's over-the-top treatment. I try to impress the kids with the perks of being a book reviewer by whipping out my advance review copy of the Scribner's edition of *Gatsby* with DiCaprio and other cast members on the cover. (What it gains in glamour, this new edition loses in substance: the excellent introduction by Matthew J. Bruccoli has been dropped.) We rate the other actors: Tobey Maguire as Nick is okay (Spider-Man!), but the students don't know Carey Mulligan. The boys, in particular, want someone hotter for the part of Daisy. Scarlett Johansson is mentioned, as is Jessica Alba.

I seize on the Alba suggestion to point out that Daisy is described as dark-haired in the novel and I tell them about Fitzgerald's first, also dark-haired, love, Ginevra King. When they fell in love, Ginevra, at sixteen, and Scott, at eighteen, were the same ages as many of the kids sitting before me in this classroom. I tell them the story about Ginevra's wealthy father supposedly saying within Scott's earshot: "Poor boys shouldn't think of marrying rich girls." Again, the classroom comes alive. The kids are one with the humiliated young Fitzgerald: they're still in that tender time of life where they might meet and try to please the parents of their girlfriends or boyfriends. A few short years later, Fitzgerald wouldn't have cared so much about whether Ginevra's father thought he was good enough for his daughter. Some of the students make a great connection between Mr. King's dissing of young Fitzgerald and the way Tom Buchanan shows his contempt for a defeated Gatsby by letting him and Daisy drive back alone together from the Plaza to Long Island. "He disrespected Gatsby," some of the boys say about Tom, like they know firsthand what it means to be disrespected.

After class, Mr. Booth—Jason—and I leave St. John's and walk down the block to grab an after-school pick-me-up at Fatty's, a neighborhood hangout for some of the teachers. I already like Jason a lot. He's a good teacher, demanding but funny, and not condescending at all. The students obviously love him. A beanpole of a guy, Jason has kids of his own—two little boys, two and nine months—and he commutes hours each day on the Long Island Expressway between the Prep and Huntington, Long Island, where he and his wife have bought a house. (House prices in Astoria these days are prohibitive. I'm told that modest two-family brick "mother-daughter" houses— grandma on the ground floor; daughter and family on the second—are now going for over a million.) Over beers and a chicken sandwich that we split (teaching is draining work), Jason explains that he began working at the Prep a few years ago. A philosophy major in college, he didn't feel the pull of literature until grad school (the essays of David Foster Wallace—a philosophy major turned writer of fiction—are a special love), so he empathizes with those students who don't like to read.

I tell Jason that his class's enthusiasm for the wildness of the movie clip has started to make me rethink one of my grounding assumptions about *Gatsby*: that the first time we read it, we're too young. When I was traveling around the country as a *Great Gatsby* troubadour for the Big Read project, I was forever telling the mostly middle-aged and elderly folks gathered at the local bookstores and libraries that, although it's fine to read

Gatsby in high school, we can't know enough about regret and loss to really appreciate the novel. My gray-headed audiences would always nod energetically at that judgment. But the kids in Jason's honors class have shown me something different: there's another layer of the novel that's all about obsession, insatiability, and "too-muchness." Certainly Gatsby's zoomed-in focus on Daisy and the all-or-nothing demand that she love him back sounds more like the consuming passions of adolescence than the tempered desires of middle age or even today's twenty-somethings. ("He's like a stalker," sniffed a blasé female student about Gatsby in one of my own upper-level lit classes at Georgetown a few years ago.) Looking back on his friend's rise from James Gatz to Jay Gatsby, Nick says midway through the novel: "He invented just the sort of Jay Gatsby that a seventeen-year-old boy would be likely to invent, and to this conception he was faithful to the end."[8] There's a *Gatsby* for when you're older and more rueful, but there's also a *Gatsby* for the young and reckless. Maybe that's the dimension of the novel that melts into the shadows for us older rereaders of the novel, who naturally gravitate toward Nick's more measured and mournful voice.

Jason's students, by the way, didn't much care for Nick, and not many of the students I meet in other classes on the following day will have a good word to say about him. Generally speaking, they think Nick is passive, something of a sellout. They don't like the scene at the end where he relents and shakes the odious Tom Buchanan's hand. They say they want someone who "acts," not just "talks." Gatsby is okay, he's "pure"; Nick is wishy-washy. No matter how·hard I work to demonstrate Nick's deep love for Gatsby, the kids are unimpressed. At a certain point in my standard rap on Nick's overwhelming love for Gatsby, I rein myself in. These days, in college classes, academic criticism, and adult reading groups, there's a lot of speculation about the homoerotic bond between Nick and Gatsby. No one at St. John's Prep, however, questions Nick's masculinity or the nature of his love for Gatsby. Maybe the kids are too young to feel comfortable with me, a stranger, discussing sexuality in the classroom. The Catholic identity of the Prep may also dampen classroom discussions of homosexuality. It was another, much more blinkered age, but I don't remember even knowing that lesbian and gay people existed until I got to college.

At Fatty's, I tell Jason about my fascination with *Gatsby*'s drowning imagery and he's all ears, even more so as another round of beers appears on the table. (It will later turn out that Mr. Booth and I have been unintentionally AWOL! When we return to the Prep after about an hour and a half at Fatty's, Mrs. Flood greets us in the lobby and says she's been calling to find out where we are. My cell phone and Jason's were turned off during his class. Mrs. Flood is laughing about our disappearance, but I feel like I'm about to get a demerit.) Jason brings up a famous drowning disaster in Astoria's past that I now hazily remember. A few blocks from where we're sitting is Astoria Park, which borders the East River. When I was very little, my mother used to take me there to swim in Astoria Pool, one of the giant municipal pools built by Robert Moses in the 1930s. I still have nightmares about Astoria Pool because it was always so crowded and over it looms the Triborough Bridge and an old railroad bridge called the Hell Gate that connects Astoria with Randalls and Wards Islands and the Bronx.

The Hell Gate spans a section of the East River notorious for its dangerous currents. On June 15, 1904, that section of the river was the site of the greatest one-day loss of life in New York City before September 11. A steamboat called the *General Slocum* was taking German American parishioners from St. Mark's Lutheran Church in what was then Little Germany on Manhattan's Lower East Side to picnic grounds on the North Shore of Long Island (in the vicinity of *Gatsby*'s Eggs). The ship caught fire in the East River and began sinking. The life preservers on board turned out to be rotted, and, like most Americans of the time, the passengers—almost all of them women and children—couldn't swim. Eyewitness accounts of the tragedy include awful testimony about mothers shoving their children into the available life preservers and tossing them off the burning ship into the river, only to watch them drown. The final official tally of victims was 1,301. Jason tells me that one of the apartments he and his then fiancée first looked at in Astoria had a nice view of Astoria Park. Walking around the park, he noticed a plaque by the East River memorializing the spot as the site where the *General Slocum* sank. It wasn't a deal-breaker, but Jason passed on the apartment.

The *General Slocum* disaster, it turns out, will be mentioned by other teachers during my pilgrimage back to Astoria and I'll later be reminded that James Joyce, in *Ulysses*, mentions the *Slocum* disaster often because Bloomsday (June 16, 1904) is set on the following day.[9] I'll also hear about another vanished piece of nearby New York history: an old amusement park and swimming hole called North Beach, built in 1886 on the shores of Flushing Bay and now buried under the runways of LaGuardia Airport. As an outer-borough "resort" destination,

North Beach rivaled *Gatsby's* Coney Island. North Beach comes up because I talk in almost all the classes about the adjacent Corona Ash Dumps, which appears in *Gatsby* as the valley of ashes. After I spend the night at the Floods' house in Forest Hills, the three of us drive back into Astoria on the Grand Central Parkway, and Mrs. Flood points at the spot where North Beach would have been and waves at the former site of the Corona Ash Dumps, leveled to create the 1939 World's Fair grounds, which were then leveled to create the 1964 World's Fair grounds.

For a while, I'm excited to think that North Beach might have been the site where John Dos Passos and Zelda Fitzgerald shared that scary Ferris wheel ride, but the dates don't quite work. The Fitzgeralds and Dos Passos became friends in the fall of 1922, when Scott and Zelda were about to embark on their Great Neck period that would feed so directly into the creation of *Gatsby*. North Beach was closed by then, shuttered by Prohibition a year earlier…although maybe a lone Ferris wheel was still operating?

The Great Gatsby itself is sensitive to the living presence of New York City's vanished past, most evocatively at the end when Nick tells us that "the inessential houses began to melt away" and he "became aware of the old island here that flowered once for Dutch sailors' eyes."[10] On my second morning at the Prep, I'm experiencing some strong tidal pulls back into the past myself. When we reach her office around seven thirty, Mrs. Flood tells me that she usually attends morning Mass in the chapel. She asks if I'd like to go with her. To my own lapsed Catholic surprise, I answer, "I'd love to!" We walk the stairs up to the wood-paneled chapel, still a quiet sanctuary in the swirling scrum of high school. I'm cheered to see a Catholic feminist touch I'd forgotten about: a statue of the Virgin Mary, rather than the usual crucifix, hanging above the altar. (The old name of my high school, Mater Christi, is Latin for "Mother of Christ.") The young priest saying Mass that morning for a small group of faculty is Indian, another sign of changing times. It's a beautiful start to the day, yet, of course, I also feel like Nick Carraway—both inside and outside the action; participating in the Mass but also standing apart and wondering— as I've done since my late teens—about what I really believe. I take communion, but my prayer afterward is more of just a secular awareness of gratitude: for this school; for such a welcome-back embrace from Mrs. Flood, her husband, and the other teachers; for the amused kindness of the students.

Half an hour later, I'm sitting with Mrs. Flood in her office talking about *Gatsby* while waiting for morning classes to begin. The school intercom comes alive, startling me with the priest's voice. (I'd forgotten about intercoms.) The priest preaches a morning lesson about three wealthy men who were offered coffee by their host. Some of the cups were beautiful, some old and cracked. Predictably, all the men helped themselves to the best cups. The moral of the story turns out to be that the vessels that contain the coffee (or our souls) don't count for much; it's what's inside the vessels (the coffee; our souls) that matters. As Mrs. Flood and I listen to this intercom sermon, she smiles. Father has just confirmed an interpretation of *The Great Gatsby* that she's been proposing. "I always thought the novel was about the fact that Gatsby was looking for the wrong things to fill him up," she says to me. "Am I wrong? What do you think? Gatsby wants money and clothes and

Daisy, but if you're not fulfilled within yourself, you won't really be happy in the end."

I hesitate. It's not that Mrs. Flood is off base, it's just that her reading seems to diminish the part of Gatsby that I love the most: his identity as a go-for-broke Promethean overreacher—for better or worse, an American. I don't even care much what he's striving for; it's that he throws his whole being into the effort. I think of Gatsby's and Daisy's reunion in chapter 5 of the novel and of the passage where Nick comments that "there must have been moments even that afternoon when Daisy tumbled short of his dreams—not through her own fault but because of the colossal vitality of his illusion."[11] I can't summon up that quote from memory so I stumble: "Daisy and his house, the car and all those shirts—Gatsby doesn't want them, per se, or he does, but they're just material things that embody some grander yearning that he has and can't fulfill." But I'm not eloquent enough to be convincing, and the intercom interruption by Father's parable of the coffee cups is like a disembodied seal of approval for Mrs. Flood's reading. "See?" She laughs in happy triumph when the intercom crackles off.

I keep turning Mrs. Flood's take on the novel over in my mind throughout the next few weeks. It bothers me, but I'd choose it over the misreading of *Gatsby,* now amplified a million-fold by the looming Luhrmann *Gatsby* premiere, that the novel is the literary equivalent of a luxury spending spree. Ask the average American adult what he or she remembers about *Gatsby*—as I have, courtesy of my Big Read travels—and you'll hear first about Gatsby's doomed romance with Daisy and second about all the things he buys when he makes it big: his car or the mansion and those shirts. How ironic that our greatest Great American Novel about class and the ultimate emptiness of "getting and spending" is commonly (and mistakenly) recalled as a celebration of the consumer society that was taking shape in the 1920s. This reading of *Gatsby* is the culture's way of taming its disconcerting questions about the price of American success. Yes, our most American and un-American novel, all at once.

Mrs. Flood is locked into meetings that morning, so she hands me a class schedule and sends me out into the crowded hallways of the Prep all on my own. The sheet of yellow legal paper lists classes, times, room numbers—all I need to feel completely fourteen years old again is a combination lock and a bad case of acne. Throughout the day, I'll self-consciously use the girls' bathroom (was that a whiff of cigarette smoke from 1972?) and, during a free period, step into the teachers' lounge to help myself to coffee. Never once during that day do I shake off the sense of needing to ask permission. As bells ring me from class to class, I'm the interloper fumbling my way into once-familiar classrooms. In Mr. Peter Vanderberg's journalism class (12:30 to 1:05), I'll meet an African American kid with a big personality who says he wants to be a sportswriter, and an unguarded young woman who could be Italian or Hispanic who's genuinely puzzled by my patter about some of the symbolism in the novel. She asks me: "How do you learn to read like that? Do they teach you that in college?" Not always, I want to tell her.

In Mr. Booth's two back-to-back sections of introductory English, another girl will ask the kind of question that, by college, you learn not to ask because it's considered uncool: "Do you think Nick and Jordan will get back together again?" I love that question because it suggests that Fitzgerald's characters are so alive to her, she wants to take them beyond the end of the novel (as the 1949 film of *The Great Gatsby* did). In Mr. Booth's second section, I ask the students why they think Daisy cries when she sees Gatsby's stockpile of rainbow-hued shirts. I often ask classes that question because I'm never sure what that scene means. A dark-haired girl raises her hand and says something I've never thought of: "She cries because she sees that Gatsby is just like Tom now. The poor boy she loved is gone. He's rich like Tom, so he's changed." Her comment stops class discussion dead in its tracks for a few minutes because it feels so emotionally smart. I've never thought of Gatsby "becoming" like Tom. I'm not sure if she's right but I love that this novel, like all great novels, spawns seemingly endless sharp interpretation.

Two tall guys stay after class to talk to me some more about the last page of the novel and the eyes of Dr. T. J. Eckleburg, that perennial favorite. At 11:50 (my stomach is rumbling) I visit a New York literature class—a version of the very same class I teach at Georgetown. Mr. Michael Matthews, the teacher, is one of those dynamic characters kids adore. He's older, with the build of a prizefighter, an impression that's intensified by his rat-a-tat speaking style. I've been given a heads-up about Mr. Matthews by some of the other teachers, who've told me he has a serious obsession with the Kennedys. Sure enough, his classroom is jam-packed with magazine pictures, books, bobble heads, and other memorabilia of John and Bobby, Rose and Jackie. Mr. Matthews usually starts class with a slide show about the Meaning of Life, things he wants the kids to know. Today, it's Sacher torte and Bob Dylan. Because it's April—National Poetry Month—there's also a slide of the inside of Edna

293

St. Vincent Millay's famous house in Greenwich Village, which, at nine and a half feet wide, is the narrowest house in New York City. Millay was sometimes a genius of a poet, a sexually and professionally bold woman in the man's world of literature. But you wouldn't exactly call her empathic. Edmund Wilson quotes her as cattily saying about Fitzgerald that:

> To meet F. Scott Fitzgerald is to think of a stupid old woman with whom someone has left a diamond; she is extremely proud of the diamond and shows it to everyone who comes by, and everyone is surprised that such an ignorant old woman should possess so valuable a jewel; for in nothing does she appear so inept as in the remarks she makes about the diamond.[12]

The Millay tribute ends with a recording of "Recuerdo" and Mr. Matthews talks about the Staten Island Ferry and how it's such a better deal (free!) than the touristy Circle Line. Segueing into *Gatsby*, Mr. Matthews claims to have read the novel over one hundred times (he's got me beat) and talks about the figure of Owl Eyes and the theme of seeing in *Gatsby*. He asks the girls in the class: "Would any of you marry Tom?" Boos and shouts of *"No!"* Then one handsome boy who, I later learn, is Bangladeshi turns directly to me and says: "I think Fitzgerald is too hard on New Yorkers." I prick up my ears because I've been curious about how these kids feel about the way Fitzgerald describes Astoria and the surrounding locale, but this boy means something more sweeping: "He overexaggerates the callousness of New Yorkers." Mr. Matthews points out that everyone in the novel is from somewhere else, but that doesn't stop other students from piling on and taking righteous offense. They decide that precisely because Tom and Daisy and Jordan are not native New Yorkers, they try extra-hard to be tough and unfeeling. Could be. Converts are almost always more zealous than those born into the fold.

My second day at the Prep closes with a return visit to Mr. Booth's last-period honors English. The class is more talkative now that I'm a familiar presence. Today, I hear more explicit strands of what I'm now thinking of as the Catholic reading of *Gatsby*. The kids mention Gatsby worshipping false gods and how he's restless because he's not content with himself as he is. I can see why, Catholicism aside, this reading would appeal to high-school students, especially those reared on the self-affirming PBS children's programming of the past forty years or so. "Love yourself." "Be yourself." "Be proud of who you are." Gatsby is none of this. He runs counter to those doctrines of self-esteem and, instead, reaches back to an older America—a Ben Franklin–Horatio Alger America—where striving was the reigning doctrine. When I was in Catholic grammar school, we were taught a jingle by the nuns: "Good, better, best/Never let it rest/Until your good is better/and your better, best." Gatsby embodies this restless reaching for perfection. Nick refers to Gatsby's "incorruptible dream,"[13] and, over the past two days, the students, like we readers always do, have contradicted themselves by also expressing admiration for Gatsby's obsessive singleness of purpose.

At the end of this last class of the day, I'm introduced to a graduating senior I've been hearing about since I walked into the Prep yesterday. She's the daughter of immigrants from Albania and she's just been accepted to Harvard on scholarship.

Mrs. Flood has told me about how much this girl loves to read and how she would always request extra reading to take home, beyond what was required for her English courses. She is lovely, with a gentle round face and dark hair. We talk for a while about books and I tell her how thrilled I am for her. As we're saying our good-byes, I find myself saying: "Don't let them psyche you out at Harvard. You and the other good students in this honors class could hold your own with the students in my literature classes at Georgetown. You're as good as they are. Don't let them psyche you out."

She smiles and thanks me and leaves the room. I have to laugh because I realize that I'm so far gone, I've just unconsciously bombarded this Harvard-bound young woman with a gentler paraphrase of Nick's last words to his friend: "They're a rotten crowd.... You're worth the whole damn bunch put together."[14]

How real is the American Dream? What kind of price do you have to pay for trying to achieve it? *Gatsby* mulls over those and other questions in some of the most gorgeous language ever written, language that never gets old. The kids at St. John's Prep can't know this yet about *The Great Gatsby;* they're just at the start of their journey with the novel. For many of them, high school will be the only time they ever read *Gatsby,* but others will go back to it, either because *Gatsby* is assigned in another class or because they've become teachers themselves or because something, like a new movie, prompts them to reread it. And, without a doubt, some of those St. John's students will fall in love with *The Great Gatsby* and they'll want to reread it more than once, like novelist Jonathan Franzen has said he does every year or two: "[Fitzgerald] tells the central fable of America, and yet you feel like you're eating whipped cream."[15]

During that visit back to my old high school, I quoted a few passages from *Gatsby* from memory. It's a feat that never fails to impress students because memorization is a lost art, rendered obsolete in an age where a click of your cell phone can give you the entire text of *The Odyssey*. But if you love a work of literature, you want to absorb it, make it part of you. "I'd like to tattoo the entire text of *The Great Gatsby* all over my body," the novelist Michael Cunningham told me a few years ago.

Scott Shepherd has pretty much done just that—tattooed Gatsby on his brain, if not his body. Shepherd has read the novel more times than anyone else, living or dead. Even F. Scott Fitzgerald himself didn't read *The Great Gatsby* as many times as Scott Shepherd has. That's because Shepherd is the actor who stars as Nick Carraway in the Elevator Repair Service's seven-hour production of *Gatz,* which I saw twice at the Public Theater in New York. Shepherd, as Nick, was onstage almost the entire time and he's committed the entire book to memory, every sentence of it. He's performed *Gatz* hundreds of times around the world, from Minneapolis to London, Princeton to Brisbane.

Because Shepherd is *The Great Gatsby*'s champion rereader—and because seeing *Gatz* on that Thanksgiving Eve in 2010 is what made me think about writing a book about *The Great Gatsby* in the first place—I wanted to talk to him. I wanted to know whether Shepherd continued to find something new in the novel on his fiftieth, seventy-fifth, and two hundredth rereadings. I wanted to know what those discoveries were and whether or not *Gatsby* is really inexhaustible to someone who's taken reading it to the limit. Shepherd graciously agreed to talk to me over the phone one Saturday afternoon in August, just after he'd finished an extreme workout and was, uncharacteristically, out of breath for a while. Talking to Scott Shepherd is a thrilling experience for anyone who loves *The Great Gatsby*, because whenever we'd start to discuss specific passages in the novel, Shepherd would pause and then recite the passage. At one point we were talking about Fitzgerald's relentless need to rewrite and Shepherd mentioned the party list that opens chapter 4. He described how, on the manuscript pages, you could see Fitzgerald revising, changing some names "for no other reason than to work on the music" of that list. Of course, I goofily told Shepherd how my own last name was a late addition to that roster; Shepherd paused and then said, "Oh, yes, the Corrigans." Then he continued: "And the Kellehers and the Dewars and the Scullys and S. W. Belcher and the Smirkes..."

Shepherd told me that he's never gotten tired of *Gatsby* exactly but that there were times when he'd "get stuck in a pattern and have to push through it to see other possibilities. But that's the nature of theater." I asked him if he thought there was any part of the novel that wasn't perfect. Shepherd said he found patches where the novel might have benefited from a touch more rewriting: "The beginning of chapter six was sometimes tough," he told me, referring to the four-and-a-half-page summary of Gatsby's early background. "That's when the audience [for *Gatz*] would just be back from the dinner break and they'd be logy with food. There's something about that section that feels *deliberate*." Shepherd, of course, knows *The Great Gatsby*'s history and he noted that Max Perkins had trouble with the original, longer version of Gatsby's biography, advising Fitzgerald to break it up more. "In my mind, I see Fitzgerald inventing more specifics in the backstory because Perkins told him to, while at the same time dealing with his strong impulse to leave most of the questions unanswered. The result is, to my ear, a slightly obligatory and vaguely evasive quality that's artificial in comparison to the rest of the book."

As far as discovering things about the novel during his marathon rereadings, Shepherd said he grew more aware of the almost geometrical patterning of *Gatsby* as time went by, more conscious of the way a certain scene would comment on another: "One thing I started to get interested in later [in the performances of *Gatz*] was how Nick's romantic thread paralleled with Gatsby's." Shepherd cited the first kiss that Nick and Jordan exchange in Central Park at the end of chapter 4 and how much more cynical, in retrospect, that encounter feels once we hear about Gatsby's transcendent first kiss with Daisy at the end of chapter 6: "He knew that when he kissed this girl, and forever wed his unutterable visions to her perishable breath, his mind would never romp again like the mind of God."[16] Shepherd recalled that during the performances of *Gatz* he began to catch smaller moments that speak to the tight design of the book, like in chapter 3 when a wife, weary of her husband's flirtation, keeps appearing at his side "like an angry diamond" and how that quick moment flows into the next scene where "highly indignant wives" are "lifted kicking into the night" by husbands whose patience has run out at party's end.

Because Shepherd recited *Gatsby* out loud every night during *Gatz*'s runs, he's particularly sensitive to how the novel sounds. One thing Shepherd told me made me appreciate something that I think I was only semiconscious of before. Shepherd said that Nick "sneaks in a couple of other narrative voices" at certain times in the story. As an example, Shepherd again referred to that section where Nick describes Gatsby's first kiss with Daisy. Nick's diction there is more sentimental and elevated than his usual speaking voice. That's because Nick is paraphrasing Gatsby's voice. "I don't know how he accomplished it, how it goes down so easy," Shepherd said. "It's telling that the book works so well in performance. [Fitzgerald's] comic timing was excellent."[17]

One other thing Scott Shepherd mentioned stays with me: he said that, after all those performances of *Gatz*, there are still parts of the novel he hasn't figured out. "I don't know, still, if I can fully explain what's going on with Nick and Jordan at the end," he said, homing in on Nick's cryptic kiss-off line to Jordan: "I'm thirty....I'm five years too old to lie to myself and call it honor."[18]

There are still parts of *The Great Gatsby* that I haven't figured out either, but I want to. That, surely, is one of the aspects of the novel that makes it great: I know there's something in those passages that's important, and my failure to understand their meaning feels like my failure as a reader, not Fitzgerald's as a writer. I know, for instance, that I probably will never quite arrive at a completely satisfying reading of those last six and a half pages of *The Great Gatsby*, pages that the critic Jonathan Yardley, who says he's read the novel seven or eight times, calls "the most beautiful, compelling and *true* in all of American literature."[19] I understand some of what Fitzgerald is getting at, but I need to keep rereading to understand more.

Here's what I know so far: Fitzgerald was aiming for a big statement about America throughout *Gatsby* but especially in those final pages. Living in Great Neck and staring out into the waters of Manhasset Bay and, beyond them, Long Island Sound with Manhattan on the horizon must have inspired in him some thoughts about the origins of America and its promises. So many immigrants had poured into America via New York City by the early 1920s, re-creating the journey of those Dutch sailors. Fitzgerald was a man of his time; he was nervous about those alien hordes, but he also understood their yearning. Could America deliver on its promises? That's an open question in those last paragraphs that sound so mournful, like an elegy for a golden age now past. Listen as Nick, sitting on the sand among the darkened houses, tells us that "there were hardly any lights except the shadowy, moving glow of a ferryboat across the Sound." Whenever I read that description, I think of Walt Whitman's great 1856 poem about New York "Crossing Brooklyn Ferry" (originally called "Sun Down Poem"). I don't know if Fitzgerald, too, was thinking of that poem; nothing I've seen in Fitzgerald's letters, books, or papers indicates that he read Whitman. But, questions of influence aside, both Whitman and Fitzgerald are playing with the same image from classical mythology: the image of Charon's ferryboat crossing the river Styx carrying the souls of the dead into the underworld. Gatsby is on that ferry, taking the last leg of an American journey that starts with the Dutch explorers, continues through the boats that are carrying all those immigrants into America, and ends on a stately voyage to the land of the dead.

Water, water, everywhere. The University of South Carolina has the typescript of Fitzgerald's 1926 story "The Swimmers" in its collection. It's a powerful story about an American expatriate in France who wants to come home and eventually does when his marriage falls apart. On the last page of "The Swimmers," as he did in what are now those last paragraphs of *Gatsby*, Fitzgerald crosses out lines and pencils in words and phrases. Here, too, he's going for a big statement about America. The final sentences read:

> France was a land; England was a people; but America, *having about it still that quality of the idea, was harder to utter—it was* the graves at Shiloh and the tired, drawn nervous faces of its great men, and the country boys dying in the Argonne for a phrase that was empty before their bodies withered. It was a willingness of the heart.

I've italicized the biggest change Fitzgerald made to that last page of the typescript because "the idea of America" preoccupied Fitzgerald in his best writing: it's an idea he's trying so hard to nail in "The Swimmers" and at the end of *The Great Gatsby*.

As I've mentioned, those final paragraphs of *Gatsby* originally appeared at the end of chapter 1. You can see those "misplaced" paragraphs floating on the digitized manuscript copy of *The Great Gatsby* that Princeton University Library has put online. At some point, Fitzgerald realized that he needed to build up to that incantatory verdict on America, and so he went back and worked on Gatsby's story so that it would earn such an ending. After you read *The Great Gatsby* the first time, you reread it forevermore with the awareness that those last six and a half pages—and, especially, those final two paragraphs—are waiting for you. It's like what happens when you hear Beethoven's Ninth Symphony or "Hey, Jude" for the second

The final manuscript page of "The Swimmers." (MATTHEW J. & ARLYN BRUC-
COLI COLLECTION OF F. SCOTT FITZGERALD, UNIVERSITY OF SOUTH CAROLINA
LIBRARIES)

time: you know that something extraordinary lies at the end of the piece. I've quoted those lines throughout this book, but they deserve to be quoted in full one more time:

> Gatsby believed in the green light, the orgastic future that year by year recedes before us. It eluded us then, but that's no matter—tomorrow we will run faster, stretch out our arms farther.... And one fine morning——
>
> So we beat on, boats against the current, borne back ceaselessly into the past.

They never get old, those words. If they ever do, I'll know it's time to hang up my reading glasses. I read *The Maltese Falcon* some years after I first read *The Great Gatsby*, but there's a passage in Hammett's novel that comes closest to expressing for me what happens when a great work of art comes into your life and changes you. Hammett's detective Sam Spade is telling a story about a man named Flitcraft who has a near brush with death when a beam from a construction site almost falls on him. Spade says about Flitcraft: "He felt as though someone had lifted the lid off life and let him look at the works." That's how I feel when I read or hear or see any great work of art, but in particular, that's how I feel when I reread *The Great Gatsby* and reach those last paragraphs: I feel like Fitzgerald has taken the lid off life and let me look at the works.

And, because I still haven't learned enough, because I want to look harder, read smarter, I let a year or so go by and, inevitably, pick up *Gatsby* again.

Acknowledgments

Reading and rereading *The Great Gatsby* has been one of my life's chief pleasures, but reading is a largely solitary activity. In contrast, one of the unexpected benefits of writing this book was the opportunity it gave me to meet a vast community of readers, scholars, librarians, researchers, and students—many, many of them lovers of Fitzgerald's work.

Like F. Scott Fitzgerald, I, too, have been graced with the best of editors and agents. Reagan Arthur has been an enthusiastic proponent of this book from its very beginning, and her wise editorial guidance, terrific sense of humor, and openness to literary detours have encouraged me to take chances and, thus, become a better writer. My agent, Stuart Krichevsky, read three versions (at least) of my book proposal and kept pushing me to crystallize the idea for the kind of book about *Gatsby* he knew I wanted to write. I'm also thankful to Shana Cohen and Ross Harris of the Stuart Krichevsky Literary Agency for their help and good cheer.

At Little, Brown, I've been supported by an impressive group of talented and dedicated people. Jean Garnett shepherded my book through revisions and helped enormously in the daunting task of securing permissions; Jayne Yaffe Kemp guided the manuscript through production and put it in the hands of an outstanding copyeditor, Tracy Roe, to whom I owe a huge debt of gratitude. I also want to thank Carrie Neill for her skill in ushering my book out into the world.

So We Read On has greatly benefited from the close scrutiny of two eminent Fitzgerald scholars: Jackson R. Bryer and Morris Dickstein. I am very grateful to them both for taking time away from their own work to correct my errors and to share their deep knowledge of Fitzgerald. Any mistakes stubbornly remaining in this book are my own. Don C. Skemer, curator of manuscripts at Princeton University Library, generously introduced me to the F. Scott Fitzgerald Papers, discussed details of the library's extraordinary Fitzgerald holdings, and answered my many questions, particularly about the legal issues surrounding the display of the manuscript of *The Great Gatsby*. Also at Princeton, Gabriel Swift, reference librarian in rare books and special collections, was an enormous help in pointing me to crucial Fitzgerald material. At the Hollings Special Collections Library at the University of South Carolina, I was warmly welcomed and greatly enlightened by Jeffrey Makala, librarian for Special Collections and Instruction and Outreach. I am also grateful to Elizabeth Sudduth, director of the Irvin Department of Rare Books and Special Collections, and former director Patrick Scott for their kindness.

Without the expert guidance of Abby Yochelson, English and American literature reference specialist at the Library of Congress's main reading room, I would still be trying to find my way through the library's catalog. This book has benefited from her direction, and I personally have benefited from her friendship. John Cole, director of the Center for the Book at the Library of Congress, patiently shared his considerable knowledge of the history of the Armed Services Editions during and after World War II. The extensive holdings (including the Fitzgeralds' marriage license) of the New York City Municipal Archives were opened up to me by Eileen Flannelly, deputy commissioner of New York City Department of Records. I'm also indebted to Ken Cobb and Alexandra Hilton for unearthing Fitzgerald material for me in the archives.

Eleanor Lanahan, daughter of Scottie Fitzgerald and granddaughter of Scott and Zelda Fitzgerald, astonished me with her warmth and readiness to answer e-mail queries about her mother and grandparents. I can't imagine how many Fitzgerald researchers she's responded to over the years and I am very grateful for her generosity. Scott Shepherd's brilliant performance as Nick Carraway in *Gatz* was an impetus for this book. I am grateful for his talent and for the time he spent answering my questions and reading part of the manuscript. At Harold Ober Associates, Craig Tenney graciously responded to my time-sensitive requests for permission to quote from the Fitzgeralds' letters and other writings and to use some personal family photographs in this book. I am similarly indebted for permissions help from Yessenia Santos at Simon and Schuster, Keshida Layone of Condé Nast, and AnnaLee Pauls of Princeton University Library. Nan Graham, senior vice president and publisher of Scribner's, graciously answered my questions about the recent sales history of *The Great Gatsby*.

My work as book critic for the NPR program *Fresh Air* has given me not only a reader's dream job for over two decades but also an extended family (yes, it feels that way) of cherished friends and colleagues. I am especially grateful to Terry Gross,

Phyllis Myers, and Danny Miller for their personal and professional support. At NPR, I want to thank Kitty Eisele and Beth Novey, both of whom appear in this book.

David Kipen, who served as the NEA's director of literature, and Erika Koss, who helped spearhead the Big Read, invited me to go on the road for *The Great Gatsby* many years ago, and I'm thankful that they did. During two F. Scott Fitzgerald conferences, I was lucky enough to hear pianist Pamela York's renditions of songs from *Gatsby*, as well as her lectures on the music of the Jazz Age. Elaine Showalter generously shared her experiences in teaching Fitzgerald at Princeton, and Peter Conn, of the University of Pennsylvania, sent me accounts of his adventures teaching *Gatsby* in the People's Republic of China. J. Michael Lennon went out of his way to tell me about Norman Mailer's high estimation of *Gatsby* and to send me a hard-to-obtain booklet containing words of praise for *Gatsby* from other famous writers. (That booklet was published as part of the *F. Scott Fitzgerald Centenary Celebration* at the Thomas Cooper Library, University of South Carolina.) My two days spent sitting in on literature classes at my old high school, now called St. John's Prep, were a highlight of my research adventures for this book. Maureen Flood is my ideal of a compassionate and gifted teacher; Jason Booth welcomed me into his classroom and he and his students opened my eyes to another dimension of *Gatsby*. I also want to thank Michael Matthews, Kathleen Prager, Edward Flood, and Peter Vanderberg for their generosity and insights into *Gatsby* and Queens history and geography.

At Georgetown, I'm fortunate to have a wonderful group of friends, colleagues, and students. Special thanks go to intrepid graduate-student researcher Katie Collins, who discovered many of the contemporary sightings of *Gatsby* in popular culture mentioned in this book. I also want to thank Barbara Feinman Todd, Dennis Todd, Denise Brennan, Doug Reed, David Gewanter, Joy Young, Joseph Fruscione, Dinaw Mengestu, Donna Evan-Kesef, Elizabeth Velez, Artemis Kirk, Robert Billingsley, Jill Hollingsworth, Michael Kazin, Judd Spray, Annalisa Adams, and Maria Vrcek. Other good friends patiently listened to me talk about *Gatsby* and provided all manner of support. I'd like to especially thank Carol Kent, Mary Beth McMahon, Constance Casey, Aviva Kempner, Mary Ellen Maher Harkins, Eileen Floyd Frawley, Karen Pataky, Paige Trevor, Rick Bilski, Margaret Talbot, Dick Lipez, Joe Wheaton, Jessica Blake Hawke, Lori Milstein, David Sahr, Christine Hughes, Virginia Marra, Lois Rosen, Betty Miller, Willie Pataky, and Maddie Yeselson. A special shout-out goes to Kenneth Meyerson for his dogged attempts to identify the source of a cartoon from F. Scott Fitzgerald's *Gatsby* scrapbook.

This book began in the early hours of Thanksgiving Day 2010 when, after listening to me rattle on about the production of *Gatz* we had both just seen, my husband, Richard Yeselson, said: "*This* is the book you should write. You should write about *The Great Gatsby*. You love it." He is my most ardent champion, my best reader, and my loving ally. This book is dedicated to him and to our remarkable daughter, Molly Yeselson, a computer genius who stepped in and helped organize the notes for this book. Molly recently read *The Great Gatsby* for the first time in high school and reported that she "liked it." Words to gladden a mother's (and a critic's) heart.

Notes

Introduction

1 F. Scott Fitzgerald, *The Great Gatsby* (New York: Charles Scribner's Sons, 1925; New York: Scribner's, 1995), 189. All citations refer to the 1995 edition unless otherwise noted.

2 Ibid., 116.

3 Deirdre Donahue, "'The Great Gatsby' by the Numbers," *USA Today*, May 7, 2013, http://www.usatoday.com/story/life/books/2013/05/07/the-great-gatsby-is-a-bestseller-this-week/2133269/.

4 Fitzgerald, *The Great Gatsby*, 137.

5 Ibid., 24.

6 Ibid., 5.

7 F. Scott Fitzgerald, *The Crack-Up*, ed. Edmund Wilson (1945; New York: New Directions, 1993), 25.

8 Fitzgerald, *The Great Gatsby*, 27–28.

9 Ibid., 167.

10 Ibid., 153.

11 Ibid., 189.

Chapter One: Water, Water, Everywhere

1 Arthur Mizener, *The Far Side of Paradise* (London: Eyre and Spottiswoode, 1951), 257.

2 F. Scott Fitzgerald, *The Notebooks of F. Scott Fitzgerald*, ed. Matthew J. Bruccoli (New York: Harcourt Brace Jovanovich, 1978), 405.

3 *Emotional bankruptcy* was a phrase Fitzgerald used frequently in his letters and other writings, and it was also the title of a Josephine story written in 1930.

4 F. Scott Fitzgerald to John Biggs, 1937, Matthew J. and Arlyn Bruccoli Collection, Irvin Department of Rare Books and Special Collections,

Ernest F. Hollings Special Collections Library, University of South Carolina, Columbia.

5 Patricia Hampl, "F. Scott Fitzgerald's Essays from the Edge," *American Scholar* (Spring 2012), http://theamericanscholar.org/f-scott-fitzgeralds -essays-from-the-edge/#.Uh9y2BZGLbA.

6 Matthew J. Bruccoli, *Some Sort of Epic Grandeur: The Life of F. Scott Fitzgerald* (New York: Harcourt Brace Jovanovich, 1981), 406.

7 Bruccoli's version doesn't mention Zelda; Nancy Milford says Fitzgerald broke his shoulder while trying to impress a young girl at the pool. Sally Cline, who, like Milford, is a Zelda partisan, says that Scott was intending to take Zelda out to a lake to swim when he injured his shoulder the day before and disappointed her. Whether Zelda was present or not, the pool, Fitzgerald, and the wrecked shoulder are beyond dispute.

8 Nancy Milford, *Zelda* (1970; New York: Avon Books, 1971), 34.

9 Ibid., 159.

10 F. Scott Fitzgerald to Beatrice Dance, September 15, 1936, in F. Scott Fitzgerald Papers, 1897–1944, Manuscripts Division, Department of Rare Books and Special Collections, Princeton University Library.

11 Mizener, *The Far Side of Paradise*, 264.

12 F. Scott Fitzgerald, *The Great Gatsby* (New York: Charles Scribner's Sons, 1925; New York: Scribner's, 1995), 25. All citations refer to the 1995 edition unless otherwise noted.

13 F. Scott Fitzgerald to Dr. Robert S. Carroll, April 19, 1938, in F. Scott Fitzgerald Papers, Princeton.

14 Fitzgerald, *The Notebooks of F. Scott Fitzgerald*, 373.

15 Eleanor Lanahan, *Scottie: The Daughter of... The Life of Frances Scott Fitzgerald Lanahan Smith* (New York: HarperCollins, 1995), 132.

16 Jay McInerney in *American Masters*, "F. Scott Fitzgerald: Winter Dreams," directed by DeWitt Sage (PBS, 2001).

17 William Blazek and Laura Rattray, eds., *Twenty-First-Century Readings of "Tender Is the Night"* (Liverpool: Liverpool University Press, 2007), 6.

18 Fitzgerald, *The Great Gatsby*, 45, 44, 96, 97–98.

19 F. Scott Fitzgerald, "The Crack-Up," *Esquire*, February 1936.

20 Ibid., 21.

21 Andrew Turnbull, ed., *The Letters of F. Scott Fitzgerald* (New York: Charles Scribner's Sons, 1963), 70.

22 Ibid., 102.

23 Ibid., 37.

24 Ibid., 102.

25 Ibid., 79.

26 F. Scott Fitzgerald, "The Rich Boy," in *The Short Stories of F. Scott Fitzgerald: A New Collection,* ed. Matthew J. Bruccoli (New York: Charles Scribner's Sons, 1995), 317.

27 F. Scott Fitzgerald, "The Swimmers," in *The Short Stories of F. Scott Fitzgerald: A New Collection,* ed. Matthew J. Bruccoli (New York: Charles Scribner's Sons, 1995), 512.

28 Fitzgerald, *The Great Gatsby,* 13.

29 Ibid.

30 Ibid., 127.

31 Ibid., 9.

32 Ibid., 91.

33 Ibid., 170.

34 Ibid., 189.

35 Michel Mok, "The Other Side of Paradise: Scott Fitzgerald, 40, Engulfed in Despair," *New York Post,* September 25, 1936.

36 Fitzgerald, *The Great Gatsby,* 9.

37 Bruccoli, *Some Sort of Epic Grandeur,* 25.

38 Two daughters were born to the Fitzgeralds before Scott, but they died at the ages of one and three. Another daughter, born in 1900, lived only an hour.

39 Mok, "The Other Side of Paradise."

40 Fitzgerald, *The Great Gatsby,* 40.

41 Mizener, *The Far Side of Paradise,* 132–33.

42 Fitzgerald, *The Notebooks of F. Scott Fitzgerald,* 318.

43 Bruccoli, *Some Sort of Epic Grandeur,* 20.

44 Mizener, *The Far Side of Paradise,* 16.

45 Franklin, by the way, says in his *Autobiography* that he wanted to found a "swimming school" in America, and his book is studded with images of other, lesser men tumbling into rivers and succumbing to the evils of drink while he, Ben Franklin, rises up on Fortune's tide.

46 Matthew J. Bruccoli, ed., *A Life in Letters* (New York: Charles Scribner's Sons, 1994), 18.

47 Bruccoli, *Some Sort of Epic Grandeur,* 32.

48 Ibid., 34.

49 Sheilah Graham, *College of One* (1966; Brooklyn: Melville House, 2013), 15.

50 Bruccoli, *A Life in Letters,* 369.

51 F. Scott Fitzgerald, letter to Anne Ober, March 4, 1938, in ibid., 351–52.

52 Mizener, *The Far Side of Paradise,* 26.

53 Fitzgerald, *The Great Gatsby,* 61.

54 James L. W. West III, *The Perfect Hour: The Romance of F. Scott Fitzgerald and Ginevra King, His First Love* (New York: Random House, 2006), 89.

55 F. Scott Fitzgerald, letter to Frances Fitzgerald Lanahan, November 4, 1937, in Mizener, *The Far Side of Paradise*, 274.

56 West, *The Perfect Hour*, 85.

57 Turnbull, *The Letters of F. Scott Fitzgerald*, 164.

58 F. Scott Fitzgerald, "Afternoon of an Author," *Esquire*, August 1936.

59 Bruccoli, *A Life in Letters*, 368.

60 West, *The Perfect Hour*.

61 Ibid., 59.

62 F. Scott Fitzgerald, *F. Scott Fitzgerald's Ledger*, February 1915, in the Matthew J. and Arlyn Bruccoli Collection of F. Scott Fitzgerald, Irvin Department of Rare Books and Special Collections, Ernest F. Hollings Special Collections Library, the University of South Carolina.

63 Fitzgerald, *The Great Gatsby*, 175.

64 Ibid., 182.

65 Ibid., 104.

66 Ibid., 108.

67 Ibid., 109.

68 Mizener, *The Far Side of Paradise*, 67.

69 Ibid., 73.

70 Bruccoli, *Some Sort of Epic Grandeur*, 300.

71 Sheilah Graham and Gerold Frank, *Beloved Infidel* (New York: Henry Holt, 1958), 240.

72 Milford's *Zelda* first shone the spotlight on Zelda's talent and frustrations and reframed Zelda's story as one of victimhood at the hands of her domineering artist husband; Milford drew heavily from the viewpoint of Zelda's older sister, Rosalind, who held Scott responsible for his wife's mental collapse. Like Milford only more so, Sally Cline, in her 2002 biography *Zelda*, sees Zelda as Scott's victim. The subtitle of Cline's book gives a taste of her extreme take on Zelda: *The Tragic, Meticulously Researched Biography of the Jazz Age's High Priestess*. Even the recent biography by Sheila Schwartz, *Fitzgerald*, in the Modern Library of Biography series paints Fitzgerald as a bullying personality responsible for the fact that Zelda was "completely unfulfilled."

73 Fitzgerald, *The Great Gatsby*, 21.

74 Bruccoli, *Some Sort of Epic Grandeur*, 71.

75 F. Scott Fitzgerald, "The Crack-Up," in *The Crack-Up*, ed. Edmund Wilson (1945; New York: New Directions, 1993), 304.

Chapter Two: *"In the Land of Ambition and Success"*

1 F. Scott Fitzgerald, "My Lost City," in *The Crack-Up*, ed. Edmund Wilson (1945; New York: New Directions, 1993), 25.

2 Ann Douglas, *Terrible Honesty: Mongrel Manhattan in the 1920s* (New York: Farrar, Straus and Giroux, 1995), 17.

3 Andrew T. Crosland, *A Concordance to F. Scott Fitzgerald's "The Great Gatsby"* (Detroit: Gale Research, 1975), 350–52.

4 Lauraleigh O'Meara, *Lost City: Fitzgerald's New York* (New York: Routledge, 2002), 4.

5 F. Scott Fitzgerald, *The Great Gatsby* (New York: Charles Scribner's Sons, 1925; New York: Scribner's, 1995), 188. All citations refer to the 1995 edition unless otherwise noted.

6 Douglas, *Terrible Honesty*, 434.

7 Alexandra Hilton, visitor center coordinator, New York City Municipal Archives, interview with the author, May 30, 2013.

8 E. B. White, *Here Is New York* (New York: Little Bookroom, 2000), 47.

9 E. L. Doctorow, *The Book of Daniel* (New York: Random House, 2007), 93.

10 Arthur Mizener, *The Far Side of Paradise* (London: Eyre and Spottiswoode, 1951), 80, and Matthew J. Bruccoli, *Some Sort of Epic Grandeur: The Life of F. Scott Fitzgerald* (New York: Harcourt Brace Jovanovich, 1981), 97.

11 Mizener, *The Far Side of Paradise*, 80.

12 Fitzgerald, *The Great Gatsby*, 27.

13 Mizener, *The Far Side of Paradise*, 80.

14 Photograph, New York City Municipal Archives Online Gallery, NYC Department of Records, New York City.

15 Sally Cline in *Zelda*, her fiercely partisan biography of Zelda Fitzgerald, claims that Fitzgerald wasn't all that lonely during these first months in New York because he was busy having affairs with three different women. If so, I'd guess that the affairs, like his drinking, were sloppy attempts to allay his anxieties about his career and his relationship with Zelda.

16 Fitzgerald, "My Lost City," 25.

17 Andrew Turnbull, *Scott Fitzgerald* (New York: Charles Scribner's Sons, 1962), 93–94.

18 Fitzgerald, *The Great Gatsby*, 184.

19 Ibid., 125.

20 Ibid., 140.

21 White, *Here Is New York*, 19.

22 Fitzgerald, *The Great Gatsby*, 7.

23 Ibid., 64.

24 Ibid., 189.

25 Ibid., 61–62.

26 Ibid., 73.

27 Ibid., 75.

28 Ibid., 73.

29 Kenneth Jackson, ed., *The Encyclopedia of New York City* (New Haven, CT: Yale University Press), 583.

30 Fitzgerald, *The Great Gatsby*, 73.

31 On page 212 of his Explanatory Notes to the authorized text of *The Great Gatsby*, Matthew J. Bruccoli cites a 1924 letter Fitzgerald wrote to his Great Neck friend Robert Kerr: "The part of what you told me which I am including in my novel is the ship, yatch [*sic*] I mean, + the mysterious yatchsman [*sic*] whose mistress was Nellie Bly."

32 Fitzgerald, "The Swimmers," 9.

33 Bruccoli, Explanatory Notes to *The Great Gatsby*, 211.

34 Bruccoli, *Some Sort of Epic Grandeur*, 183.

35 Fitzgerald, *The Great Gatsby*, 73–74.

36 Frances Kroll Ring, *Against the Current: As I Remember F. Scott Fitzgerald* (Los Angeles: Figueroa Press, 2005), 46–47.

37 Ibid., 75.

38 Vincent Canby, review of the movie *The Great Gatsby*, *New York Times*, March 28, 1974.

39 Fitzgerald, *The Great Gatsby*, 11.

40 Matthew J. Bruccoli, ed., *A Life in Letters* (New York: Charles Scribner's Sons, 1994), 86.

41 Ibid., 87.

42 Ibid., 91.

43 Fitzgerald, *The Great Gatsby*, 13.

44 Ibid., 17.

45 Ibid., 18.

46 Ibid., 73.

47 Ibid., 131.

48 Bruccoli, *A Life in Letters*, 34.

49 Bruccoli, *Some Sort of Epic Grandeur*, 144. For rates of the New York City hotels that Scott and Zelda stayed in during their early months in Manhattan, I consulted the convention pamphlet "New York Welcomes You" (circa 1920) in the Municipal Archives of the New York City Department of Records. It's comical that that pamphlet's list of hotels and fees ends with the assurance that "New York Hotels never raise their rates."

50 Letter to Perkins, mid-July 1922, in F. Scott Fitzgerald, *The Correspondence of F. Scott Fitzgerald*, eds. Matthew J. Bruccoli and Margaret Duggan (New York: Random House, 1980), 113.

51 Jimmy Stamp, "When F. Scott Fitzgerald Judged 'Gatsby' by Its Cover," *Smithsonian* blog, May 14, 2013, http://blogs.smithsonianmag.com/design/2013/05/when-f-scott-fitzgerald-judged-gatsby-by-its-cover/.

52 Bruccoli, *A Life in Letters*, 79.

53 Fitzgerald, *The Great Gatsby*, 85.

54 Richard Maibaum, "The Question They Faced with 'Gatsby': Would Scott Approve?," *Daily Compass*, July 8, 1949.

55 Ernest Hemingway, *A Moveable Feast* (New York: Charles Scribner's Sons, 1964), 176.

56 Charles Scribner III, "*Celestial Eyes:* From Metamorphosis to Masterpiece," *Princeton University Library Chronicle* 53, no. 2 (Winter 1992): 141–55.

57 Mizener, *The Far Side of Paradise*, 144.

58 Bruccoli, *Some Sort of Epic Grandeur*, 175.

59 F. Scott Fitzgerald, letter to Xandra Kalman, fall 1922, cited in ibid., 176.

60 Mizener, *The Far Side of Paradise*, 143.

61 F. Scott Fitzgerald, "How to Live on $36,000 a Year," *Saturday Evening Post*, April 5, 1924.

62 Fitzgerald, *The Great Gatsby*, 4.

63 Bruccoli, *Some Sort of Epic Grandeur*, 184.
   Bruccoli cracks the code of some of the more cryptic references: *Rumsey* was Charles Cary Rumsey, a polo player and sculptor married to the heiress Mary Harriman: their estate was in Westbury, Long Island. *Goddard* may have been Charles William Goddard, who was a screenwriter and playwright. Allan Dwan was a movie director. Bruccoli says that Robert (Bob) Kerr was a friend of Fitzgerald's in Great Neck who provided inspiration for young James Gatz's meeting with Dan Cody. As a fourteen-year-old, Kerr had warned Major Edwin R. Gilman that his yacht would break up when the tide ran out in Sheepshead Bay in Brooklyn.

64 Ibid., 178.

65 Matthew J. and Arlyn Bruccoli Collection, Irvin Department of Rare Books and Special Collections, Ernest F. Hollings Special Collections Library, the University of South Carolina, Columbia; https://www.sc.edu/fitzgerald/facts//html.

66 Bruccoli, *Some Sort of Epic Grandeur*, 187.

67 Bruccoli, *A Life in Letters*, 65.

68 Ibid., 65–67.

69 Ring Lardner Jr., *The Lardners* (New York: Harper and Row, 1976), 163.

70 Hilton, interview with the author.

71 Ruth Prigozy, interview by Kurt Andersen, on *Studio 360: American Icons*, "The Great Gatsby," WNYC New York and Public Radio International, first broadcast July 4, 2009, https://mobile.audible.com/productDetail.htm?asin=B002VBEYQM&s=s.

72 F. Scott Fitzgerald to Maxwell Perkins, April 10, 1925, in Bruccoli, *A Life in Letters,* 106.

Chapter Three: Rhapsody in Noir

1 Alfred Kazin, *F. Scott Fitzgerald: The Man and His Work* (New York: Collier Books, 1951), 17.

2 F. Scott Fitzgerald, *The Great Gatsby* (New York: Charles Scribner's Sons, 1925; New York: Scribner's, 1995), 7. All citations refer to the 1995 edition unless otherwise noted.

3 Ibid., 186.

4 Fanny Butcher, "New Fitzgerald Book Proves He's Really a Writer," in Jackson R. Bryer, ed., *F. Scott Fitzgerald: The Critical Reception* (New York: Burt Franklin, 1978), 197.

5 Ibid.

6 Scribner's, *The Great Gatsby* announcement, *Publishers' Weekly,* April 4, 1925.

7 Linda C. Stanley, *The Foreign Critical Reputation of F. Scott Fitzgerald* (Westport, CT: Praeger, 2004), 94.

8 Ibid., 96.

9 Ibid., 90.

10 Ibid., 96.

11 Fitzgerald, *The Great Gatsby,* 179.

12 Arthur Mizener, *The Far Side of Paradise* (London: Eyre and Spottiswoode, 1951), 19, and Matthew J. Bruccoli, Scottie Fitzgerald Smith, and Joan P. Kerr, eds., *The Romantic Egoists: A Pictorial Autobiography from the Scrapbooks and Albums of F. Scott and Zelda Fitzgerald* (Columbia: University of South Carolina Press, 2003), 21.

13 F. Scott Fitzgerald, "The Dance," in F. Scott Fitzgerald, *The Fantasy and Mystery Stories of F. Scott Fitzgerald,* ed. Peter Haining (London: Robert Hale, 1991), 140.

14 Lillian Hellman, *An Unfinished Woman* (Boston: Little, Brown, 1969), 71.

15 Ibid., 2.

16 Raymond Chandler to Dale Warren, November 12, 1950, in https://www.sc.edu/fitzgerald/quotes/quotes6/html.

17 Ann Douglas, *Terrible Honesty: Mongrel Manhattan in the 1920s* (New York: Farrar, Straus and Giroux, 1995), 187.

18 Fitzgerald, *The Great Gatsby,* 208.

19 Ibid., 144.

20 Ibid.

21 Matthew J. Bruccoli, ed., *A Life in Letters* (New York: Charles Scribner's Sons, 1994), 94.

22 Fitzgerald, *The Great Gatsby*, 9.
23 Ibid., 12.
24 Ibid., 44–45.
25 Ibid., 24.
26 Bruccoli, *A Life in Letters*, 480.
27 Ibid., 106–7.
28 Fitzgerald, *The Great Gatsby*, 179.
29 Ibid., 179–80.
30 Ibid.
31 Ibid., 189.
32 Morris Dickstein, ed., *Critical Insights: "The Great Gatsby" by F. Scott Fitzgerald* (Pasadena, CA: Salem Press, 2010), 6.
33 Fitzgerald, *The Great Gatsby*, 189.
34 Ibid., 186.
35 Ibid., 188.
36 Christopher Hitchens, "The Road to West Egg," *Vanity Fair*, May 2000.
37 William Ernest Henley, "Invictus."
38 Bruccoli, *A Life in Letters*, 129.
39 Sheilah Graham and Gerold Frank, *Beloved Infidel* (New York: Henry Holt, 1958), 171, and F. Scott Fitzgerald to F. Scott Fitzgerald, n.d., F. Scott Fitzgerald Papers, 1897–1944, Manuscripts Division, Department of Rare Books and Special Collections, Princeton University Library.
40 Fitzgerald, *The Great Gatsby*, 104.
41 Sheilah Graham, *The Real F. Scott Fitzgerald: Thirty-Five Years Later* (New York: Grosset and Dunlap, 1976), 26.
42 Sheilah Graham note, 1939, in F. Scott Fitzgerald Papers, Princeton.
43 Graham and Frank, *Beloved Infidel*, 234.
44 Ibid., 231.

Chapter Four: A Second-Rate Midwest Hack and the Masterpiece He Wrote

1 F. Scott Fitzgerald, *The Great Gatsby* (New York: Charles Scribner's Sons, 1925; New York: Scribner's, 1995), 90. All citations refer to the 1995 edition unless otherwise noted.
2 Ibid., 91.
3 Ibid., 94.
4 Ibid., 101.
5 Ibid.
6 Ibid., 102.
7 Ibid., 107.

8 F. Scott Fitzgerald, *The Great Gatsby: A Facsimile of the Manuscript,* ed. Matthew J. Bruccoli (Washington, DC: Microcard Editions, 1973), ix.
9 Andrew Turnbull, *Scott Fitzgerald* (New York: Charles Scribner's Sons, 1962), 141.
10 F. Scott Fitzgerald, *Correspondence of F. Scott Fitzgerald,* eds. Matthew J. Bruccoli and Margaret M. Duggan (New York: Random House, 1980), 138.
11 Ibid.
12 Turnbull, *Scott Fitzgerald,* 135.
13 Ibid., 139. Fitzgerald himself tells the anecdote in "My Lost City."
14 Fitzgerald, *The Great Gatsby,* 107.
15 Matthew J. Bruccoli, ed., *A Life in Letters* (New York: Charles Scribner's Sons, 1994), 109.
16 Ibid., 110.
17 H. L. Mencken, "As H.L.M. Sees It," *Baltimore Evening Sun,* May 2, 1925; *Chicago Tribune,* May 24, 1925.
18 Fitzgerald, *Correspondence of F. Scott Fitzgerald,* 144.
19 Fitzgerald, *The Great Gatsby,* 125.
20 Ibid.
21 Ibid., 129–30.
22 Ibid., 139–40.
23 Matthew J. Bruccoli, *Some Sort of Epic Grandeur: The Life of F. Scott Fitzgerald* (New York: Harcourt Brace Jovanovich, 1981), 298.
24 A. Scott Berg, *Max Perkins: Editor of Genius* (1978; New York: Berkeley Books, 2008), 66.
25 Andrew Turnbull, ed., *The Letters of F. Scott Fitzgerald* (New York: Charles Scribner's Sons, 1963), 173.
26 Fitzgerald, *The Great Gatsby,* 52.
27 F. Scott Fitzgerald, *The Crack-Up,* ed. Edmund Wilson (1945; New York: New Directions, 1993), 309.
28 Fitzgerald, *The Great Gatsby,* 189.
29 Jonathan Yardley, "'Gatsby': The Greatest of Them All," *Washington Post,* January 2, 2007, http://www.washingtonpost.com/wp-dyn/content/article/2007/01/01/AR2007010100958.html.
30 Burton Rascoe, "A Bookman's Day Book," *New York Tribune,* May 6, 1923.
31 Eleanor Lanahan, e-mail to the author, June 17, 2013.
32 Fitzgerald, *The Great Gatsby,* vii.
33 Ibid., 188.
34 Ibid., 115.
35 Ibid., 31.

36 Ibid.

37 Ibid., 41.

38 Ibid.

39 Robert Long, *The Achieving of "The Great Gatsby"* (Cranbury, NJ: Associated University Presses, 1979), 124.

40 Fitzgerald, *The Great Gatsby*, 170.

41 Jeffrey Meyers, *Scott Fitzgerald: A Biography* (New York: HarperCollins, 1994), 334.

42 Turnbull, *Scott Fitzgerald*, 321.

43 Scottie Fitzgerald Lanahan, conversation with Matthew J. Bruccoli, recorded in 1977 for *Some Sort of Epic Grandeur*. CD included in exhibition booklet from *Scottie Fitzgerald: The Stewardship of Literary Memory*, October–December 2007, University of South Carolina Libraries, Columbia.

44 Fitzgerald, *The Great Gatsby*, 6.

45 F. Scott Fitzgerald letter to Maxwell Perkins, September 10, 1924, in *Correspondence of F. Scott Fitzgerald*, 146.

46 Letter to Frances Turnbull, November 9, 1938, in Bruccoli, *A Life in Letters*, 368.

47 Eleanor Lanahan, *Scottie the Daughter Of...: The Life of Frances Scott Fitzgerald Lanahan Smith* (New York: HarperCollins, 1995), 141.

48 Ibid., 198.

49 Don C. Skemer, e-mail to the author, December 13, 2013.

50 F. Scott Fitzgerald, *Trimalchio: An Early Version of "The Great Gatsby,"* ed. James L. W. West III (Cambridge: Cambridge University Press, 2002), xiii.

51 Fitzgerald letter to Maxwell Perkins, January 24, 1925, in Bruccoli, *A Life in Letters*, 94.

52 Susan Bell, *The Artful Edit* (New York: W. W. Norton, 2007), 43.

53 Bruccoli, *Some Sort of Epic Grandeur*, 219.

54 Ibid., 211.

55 Jackson R. Bryer, ed., *F. Scott Fitzgerald: The Critical Reception* (New York: Burt Franklin, 1978), 195–249.

56 Fitzgerald, *Correspondence of F. Scott Fitzgerald*, 164.

57 Fitzgerald, *The Crack-Up*, 310.

58 Bryer, *Critical Reception*, 239–40.

59 Fitzgerald, *Correspondence of F. Scott Fitzgerald*, 167–75.

60 Ibid., 161.

61 Ibid.

62 Bruccoli, *Some Sort of Epic Grandeur*, 221.

63 Bruccoli, *A Life in Letters*, 112–13.

64 Matthew J. Bruccoli, *Dictionary of Literary Biography: F. Scott Fitzgerald's "The Great Gatsby"* (Toronto: Gale, 1999), 219.

65 Ibid., 220.

66 Ibid., 224.

67 Turnbull, *The Letters of F. Scott Fitzgerald*, 301.

68 Ibid.

69 F. Scott Fitzgerald list of "Possibly Valuable Books" in F. Scott Fitzgerald Papers, 1897–1944, Manuscripts Division, Department of Rare Books and Special Collections, Princeton University Library.

70 Frances Kroll Ring, *Against the Current: As I Remember F. Scott Fitzgerald* (Los Angeles: Figueroa Press, 2005), 66.

71 Bruccoli, *A Life in Letters*, 445.

Chapter Five: "Here Lies One Whose Name Was Writ in Water"

1 "Scott Fitzgerald, Author, Dies at 44," *New York Times*, December 23, 1940.

2 Arnold Gingrich letter to Sheilah Graham, December 27, 1940, F. Scott Fitzgerald Papers, 1897–1944, Manuscripts Division, Department of Rare Books and Special Collections, Princeton University Library.

3 Westbrook Pegler, "Fair Enough," December 26, 1940; reprinted in the *Los Angeles Times*, March 4, 2010.

4 Alfred Kazin, *F. Scott Fitzgerald: The Man and His Work* (New York: World Publishing, 1951), 198.

5 Letter to F. Scott Fitzgerald, "Fan Letter Folder," n.d., in F. Scott Fitzgerald Papers, Princeton.

6 Ruth Prigozy, *The Cambridge Companion to F. Scott Fitzgerald* (Cambridge: Cambridge University Press, 2002), 18.

7 Frances Kroll Ring, *Against the Current: As I Remember F. Scott Fitzgerald* (Los Angeles: Figueroa Press, 2005), 151.

8 *Adventures in American Literature* (New York: Harcourt Brace, 1941), 1207.

9 Charles Lee, ed., *North, East, South, West: A Regional Anthology of American Writing* (New York: Howell, Soskin, 1945).

10 *Adventures in American Literature* (New York: Harcourt Brace, 1958), 136.

11 Clarence A. Brown and John T. Flanagan, *American Literature: A College Survey* (Spokane, WA: Marquette, 1961), 715.

12 Andrew J. Porter, Henry L. Terrie, and Robert A. Bennett, eds., *American Literature* (Oxford: Ginn, 1964), 564.

13 Perry Miller, ed., *Major Writers of America* (n.p.: Major Writers of America, 1962), 678.

14 *Adventures in American Literature* (New York: Harcourt, Brace, 1968), 551.

15 Jennifer Govan, e-mail message to Katie Collins, October 24, 2012.

16 Sheilah Graham and Gerold Frank, *Beloved Infidel* (New York: Henry Holt, 1958), 338.

17 Sheilah Graham, *College of One* (1966; Brooklyn: Melville House, 2013), 275–76.

18 Paul McPharlin, "Soldiers Who Read," *Publishers' Weekly* (September 11, 1943).

19 John Y. Cole, ed., *Books in Action: The Armed Services Edition* (Washington, DC: Library of Congress, 1984), viii, and James M. Dourgarian, "Armed Services Edition," *Firsts: The Book Collector's Magazine* (November 2001): 24–35.

20 Cole, *Books in Action*, 9.

21 Dourgarian, "Armed Services Edition," 30.

22 F. Scott Fitzgerald, *The Great Gatsby*, Armed Services ed. (New York: Council on Books in Wartime, 1945).

23 Council on Books in Wartime, "Ideas for Americans at War Spread by Council on Books," *Publishers' Weekly* (December 25, 1943): 2300–13. Other sources include Dourgarian, "Armed Services Editions"; Cole, *Books in Action*; and Daniel J. Miller, *Books Go to War* (Charlottesville, VA: Book Arts Press, 1996).

24 A. Scott Berg, *Max Perkins: Editor of Genius* (1978; New York: Berkeley Books, 2008), 427.

25 Melanie McGee Bianchi, "Living Incidentally," *Verve: Asheville's Magazine for Women*, August 30, 2012.

26 Letter from Zelda Fitzgerald to Noel Parrish, February 1, 1943, in Noel Francis Parrish Papers (1894–1987), Box 7, Manuscript Division, Library of Congress, Washington, DC.

27 Matthew J. Bruccoli, ed., *F. Scott Fitzgerald: A Life in Letters* (New York: Charles Scribner's Sons, 1994), 475.

28 Stephen E. Ambrose, *D-Day: June 6, 1944: The Climactic Battle of World War II* (New York: Simon and Schuster, 1995), 155.

29 F. Scott Fitzgerald, *The Great Gatsby*, Bantam ed. (New York: Bantam Books, 1951), 1.

30 Charles Scribner's Sons to Scottie Fitzgerald Lanahan, royalty report of February 1, 1952, in the Matthew J. and Arlyn Bruccoli Collection of F. Scott Fitzgerald, Irvin Department of Rare Books and Special Collections, Ernest F. Hollings Special Collections Library, University of South Carolina.

31 Catherine Lewis, "Second Act," in *F. Scott Fitzgerald Centenary Exhibition, September 24, 1896–September 24, 1996,* ed. Matthew J. Bruccoli (Columbia: University of South Carolina Press), 86.

32 Blake Bailey, *Farther and Wilder: The Lost Weekends and Literary Dreams of Charles Jackson* (New York: Alfred A. Knopf, 2013), 81.

33 Ibid., 82.

34 John K. Hutchens, "People Who Read and Write," *New York Times,* September 15, 1946.

35 Leslie Fiedler, "Some Notes on F. Scott Fitzgerald," fitzgerald.narod .ru/critics-eng/fiedler-somenotes.html.

36 Eleanor Lanahan, *Scottie the Daughter Of…: The Life of Frances Scott Fitzgerald Lanahan Smith* (New York: HarperCollins, 1995), 14.

37 Matthew J. Bruccoli, preface to *The Great Gatsby,* by F. Scott Fitzgerald (New York: Scribner's, 1995), vii–viii.

38 For the basic Bruccoli story, see Chris Horn, "Collecting Fitzgerald: A Passion as Big as the Ritz," University of South Carolina, last modified July 22, 1996, http://www.sc.edu/fitzgerald/collection/horn.html.

39 "Bruccoli the Bulldog," *Columbia State,* July 25, 2004.

40 F. Scott Fitzgerald, *F. Scott Fitzgerald: Inscriptions,* ed. Matthew J. Bruccoli (Columbia, SC: Bruccoli, Clark, Layman, 1988).

41 Francis Ford Coppola, "Gatsby and Me," *Town and Country,* May 2013.

42 Ibid.

43 Lanahan, *Scottie,* 427–28.

44 Ibid., 364.

45 Edmund Wilson note to Howard Allen, October 22, 1971, Matthew J. and Arlyn Bruccoli Collection of F. Scott Fitzgerald, Irvin Department of Rare Books and Special Collections, Ernest F. Hollings Special Collections Library, University of South Carolina.

46 Tributes from these writers and others were collected in a limited-edition commemorative booklet printed in conjunction with the *F. Scott Fitzgerald Centenary Celebration.*

47 J. D. Salinger, *The Catcher in the Rye* (Boston: Little, Brown, 1951), 183.

Chapter Six: "I Didn't Get It the First Time"

1 F. Scott Fitzgerald, *The Great Gatsby* (New York: Charles Scribner's Sons, 1925; New York: Scribner's, 1995), 65. All citations refer to the 1995 edition unless otherwise noted.

2 Ibid., 121.

3 Azar Nafisi, *Reading "Lolita" in Tehran: A Memoir in Books* (New York: Random House, 2003), 142.

4 Evan Osnos, "Reading 'Gatsby' in Beijing," *New Yorker* blog, May 2, 2013, http://www.newyorker.com/online/blogs/comment/evan-osnos.

5 Peter Conn, e-mail to the author, August 15, 2013.

6 Sara Rimer, "Gatsby's Green Light Beckons to a New Set of Strivers," *New York Times,* February 17, 2008.

7 Fitzgerald, *The Great Gatsby,* 99.

8 Ibid., 104.

9 I'm indebted to Scott Shepherd for this insight; Shepherd, e-mail to the author, December 13, 2013.

10 Fitzgerald, *The Great Gatsby,* 189.

11 Ibid., 101.

12 Edmund Wilson, *Edmund Wilson: Literary Essays and Reviews of the 1920s and 1930s* (New York: Library of America, 2007), 30.

13 Fitzgerald, *The Great Gatsby,* 162.

14 Ibid.

15 Ruth Prigozy, interview by Kurt Andersen, *"The Great Gatsby," Studio 360: American Icons,* WNYC New York and Public Radio International, July 4, 2009, https://mobile.audible.com/productDetail.htm ?asin=B002VBEYQM&s=s.

16 Fitzgerald, *The Great Gatsby,* 117.

17 Scott Shepherd, telephone interview with the author, August 17, 2013.

18 Fitzgerald, *The Great Gatsby,* 186.

19 Jonathan Yardley, "'Gatsby': The Greatest of Them All," *Washington Post,* January 2, 2007, http://www.washingtonpost.com/wp-dyn/content/article/2007/01/01/AR2007010100958.html.

Bibliographical Notes

The Fitzgerald Revival that began in the late 1940s has never really ended. Every year adds to the Diamond-as-Big-as-the-Ritz-sized mountain of Fitzgeraldiana. The bibliographical notes that follow highlight the primary sources, as well as the critical books and articles I found essential to researching and writing *So We Read On*.

Fitzgerald's Life

F. Scott Fitzgerald was a scrupulous chronicler of his own life. His *Letters* not only provide an intimate glimpse into his mind and heart, but—as should be evident from the many quotations in my book—they contain some of his finest writing. I relied on several editions: *F. Scott Fitzgerald: A Life in Letters*, edited by Matthew J. Bruccoli (Charles Scribner's Sons, 1994); *The Letters of F. Scott Fitzgerald*, edited by Andrew Turnbull (Charles Scribner's Sons, 1963); *Correspondence of F. Scott Fitzgerald*, edited by Matthew J. Bruccoli and Margaret M. Duggan (Random House, 1980); *Dear Scott, Dearest Zelda*, edited by Jackson R. Bryer and Cathy W. Barks (St. Martin's

Press, 2002); and *As Ever, Scott Fitz—*, edited by Matthew J. Bruccoli (J. B. Lippincott, 1972).

F. Scott Fitzgerald's Ledger (1919–1938) has been digitized and is available online thanks to the Irvin Department of Rare Books and Special Collections, University of South Carolina. Begun shortly after he moved to New York City in 1919, the ledger provides rich details—including earnings and publication history—about the erratic life of a professional writer, even one as successful as Fitzgerald. *The Notebooks of F. Scott Fitzgerald*, edited by Matthew J. Bruccoli (Harcourt Brace Jovanovich, 1978), date from 1932 to his death. They include reflections on the art of fiction and unvarnished commentary about his friends and his own state of mind. *The Crack-Up*, edited by Edmund Wilson (New Directions, 1945), features selections from Fitzgerald's notebooks and classic personal essays such as "My Lost City," "Echoes of the Jazz Age," and "The Crack-Up." *The Romantic Egoists* (University of South Carolina Press, 2003), edited by Matthew J. Bruccoli, Scottie Fitzgerald Smith, and Joan Kerr, is a poignant collection of family photos and clippings from the Fitzgeralds' own scrapbooks.

If I were forced to choose one biography of F. Scott Fitzgerald out of the trio that vie for the honor of being the best life of Fitzgerald, I would reach for Matthew J. Bruccoli's *Some Sort of Epic Grandeur* (Harcourt Brace Jovanovich, 1981) because of its exhaustive detail and unapologetic love for its subject (which some critics see as a flaw). Arthur Mizener's *The Far Side of Paradise* (Houghton Mifflin, 1951) has the advantage of being the first biography of Fitzgerald, written when many of his friends were still alive, but because of that fact it strikes this contemporary reader as being overly discreet. When he was a young boy, Andrew Turnbull came to know the Fitzgeralds after they moved to a house (La Paix) outside Baltimore owned by his mother. His biography, *Scott Fitzgerald* (Charles Scribner's Sons, 1965) is gracefully written and informed.

Out of the many other Fitzgerald biographies, Scott Donaldson's *Fool for Love* (St. Martin's Press, 1985), is intriguing for its psychological readings of Fitzgerald and, particularly, his mother. Jeffrey Meyers's *Scott Fitzgerald* (1994; Harper Perennial reprint, 2014) also embraces a psychological—and less sympathetic—approach to Scott and Zelda. Ruth Prigozy's *F. Scott Fitzgerald* (Overlook Press, 2004) is a good short introduction to Fitzgerald's life, enhanced by many photographs. The source to go to for biographical information about Fitzgerald's early romance with Ginevra King is *The Perfect Hour* by James L. W. West III (Random House, 2006). *Against the Current* (Figueroa Press, 2005), Frances Kroll Ring's account of her time working as Fitzgerald's secretary in Hollywood (1939–40) is a small treasure of a memoir that brings its chief subject and the Golden Age of Hollywood to life. *Crazy Sundays* by Aaron Latham (Viking, 1970) chronicles Fitzgerald's unhappy career as a screenwriter in Hollywood. Sheilah Graham wrote several memoirs of her relationship with Fitzgerald during that same Hollywood period. The best known are *Beloved Infidel* (Henry Holt, 1958) and *College of One* (1966; Neversink Library reprint, 2013) and they both hold up as illuminating (if somewhat selective) accounts of her life with Fitzgerald.

Despite more recent challengers, *Zelda* by Nancy Milford (Harper and Row, 1970) remains the best—and most balanced—biography of Zelda Fitzgerald. *Scottie: The Daughter of...* by Eleanor Lanahan (HarperCollins, 1995) is a sensitive and revealing portrait of one of literature's most caring daughters, Scottie Fitzgerald, written by one of her own daughters. I was given a brief but vivid entry into Scottie Fitzgerald's memories by listening to a recording of a conversation she had with Matthew J. Bruccoli in Montgomery, Alabama, in 1981. The CD of that conversation is contained with the exhibition booklet of *Scottie Fitzgerald: The Stewardship of Literary Memory*, put together by the Matthew J. and Arlyn Bruccoli Collection of F. Scott Fitzgerald, Thomas Cooper Library, University of South Carolina, 2007.

The Novel and Some of Its Best Critics

The edition of *The Great Gatsby* that I relied on while writing this book is the 1995 Scribner paperback edition with notes and a preface by Matthew J. Bruccoli. Anyone interested in *Gatsby*'s gestation should read *Trimalchio*, edited by James L. W. West III (Cambridge University Press, 2000). The "autograph manuscript" of *The Great Gatsby* resides in a vault within Princeton University's Library, but is accessible online for everyone to view thanks to the Princeton University Digital Library at http://pudl.princeton.edu/results.php?f1=kw&v1=gatsby.

I've said that Fitzgerald brings out the best critical writing in his admirers, and I think that continues to be the case. *F. Scott Fitzgerald: The Man and His Work* (Collier Books, 1962), the landmark 1951 essay collection edited by Alfred Kazin that I talk about in chapter five, is a must-read for anyone interested in what mid-twentieth-century public intellectuals like

Edmund Wilson, H. L. Mencken, Lionel Trilling, and Kazin himself had to say about Fitzgerald. These essays are models of erudition and stylistic ease. Other essay collections about Fitzgerald and *The Great Gatsby* that I found well worth reading, particularly for their discussions of race and gender in *Gatsby*, are: *Critical Insights: The Great Gatsby*, edited by Morris Dickstein (Salem Press, 2010); *The Cambridge Companion to F. Scott Fitzgerald*, edited by Ruth Prigozy (Cambridge University Press, 2002); and *F. Scott Fitzgerald in the Twenty-first Century*, edited by Jackson R. Bryer, Ruth Prigozy, and Milton Stern (University of Alabama Press, 2003).

Among the many other books devoted to Fitzgerald's writing and *Gatsby* in particular, I found the following to be among the most useful. *Dictionary of Literary Biography: F. Scott Fitzgerald's The Great Gatsby,* edited by Matthew J. Bruccoli (Gale, 2000) is a sweeping critical and pictorial history of *Gatsby*'s origins and reception. Jackson R. Bryer's *F. Scott Fitzgerald: The Critical Reception* (Burt Franklin, 1978) comprehensively gathers together the reviews of *The Great Gatsby*, as well as Fitzgerald's other novels, short stories, and ill-fated play, *The Vegetable. The Foreign Reputation of F. Scott Fitzgerald* by Linda C. Stanley (Praeger, 2004) does much the same for reviews, translations, criticism, and film treatments of Fitzgerald's work outside of the United States. The *Winding Road to West Egg* by Robert Roulston and Helen H. Roulston (Bucknell University Press, 1995) is a solid account of Fitzgerald's artistic development and the early hints of *Gatsby* that appeared in his short stories, as well as the *Trimalchio* draft. Ronald Berman's *The Great Gatsby and Fitzgerald's World of Ideas* (University of Alabama, 1997) offers some excellent close readings of *Gatsby*, as well as discussions of some of the ideas about race and religion that animate its pages. *The Achieving of The Great Gatsby* by Robert Long (Associated University Presses, 1979) is a revelatory close reading of *Gatsby*'s universe of symbols. *American Icon* by Robert Beuka (Camden House, 2011) surveys *Gatsby*'s initial reception and ongoing afterlife.

Gatsby's World

For an understanding of the New York City Fitzgerald knew during the 1920s, I relied on Ann Douglas's superb cultural history, *Terrible Honesty* (Farrar, Straus and Giroux, 1995). *Capital of the World* by David Wallace (Lyons Press, 2011) provided additional information on the nightclubs, dances, and newspaper columnists of Jazz Age New York. *The Great Gatsby and Modern Times* by Ronald Berman (University of Illinois Press, 1994) is an extraordinarily comprehensive survey of how the world of the 1920s—its prejudices, entertainments, and language—influenced *The Great Gatsby*. I also gleaned information about the specific debt *The Great Gatsby* owes to New York City from Lauraleigh O'Meara's *Lost City* (Routledge, 2002). Frederick Lewis Allen's *Only Yesterday* (1931; Harper Perennial Modern Classics reprint, 2010) is a marvelous nonfiction work of literary time travel back into the 1920s. Sarah Churchwell's *Careless People* (Penguin, 2013) offers a lively look at New York City in the 1920s and makes a provocative argument for the importance of the Hall-Mills murder case to Fitzgerald's novel.

The Lardners by Ring Lardner Jr. (Harper and Row, 1976) serves up tantalizing glimpses of the Fitzgeralds and their friends during the heady years they spent in Gatsby's territory of Great Neck, Long Island. *Max Perkins* by A. Scott Berg (Penguin, 1978) still provides the most sweeping view of the New York City literary and publishing world of the 1920s and 1930s, as well as an affecting portrait of one of F. Scott Fitzgerald's greatest and most steadfast champions. Lewis M. Dabney's biography *Edmund Wilson* (Johns Hopkins University Press, 2007) offers a discerning look at the long friendship between Wilson and Fitzgerald; Dabney also examines Wilson's important influence on Fitzgerald's development as a writer and his crucial role in the Fitzgerald revival. *Everybody Was So Young* by Amanda Vaill (Houghton Mifflin, 1998) evokes the fleeting glamour of Paris and the Riviera as the Fitzgeralds and their circle of friends experienced it. I took Morley Callaghan's 1963 memoir, *That Summer in Paris,* with the proverbial grain of salt but appreciated its vignettes of Fitzgerald and Hemingway in that city in the period following the publication of *The Great Gatsby.* Ernest Hemingway's *A Moveable Feast* (Scribner, 1964) is a classic memoir of the score-settling type, but it's also a luminous and indispensable personal record of Paris in the 1920s; I've reread it many times with admiration.

Gatsby and World War II

To learn more about the Armed Services Editions, which were crucial to *The Great Gatsby*'s revival during and after World War II, I recommend *Books in Action*, edited by John Y. Cole (Library of Congress, 1984) and *Books Go to War* by Daniel J. Miller (Book Arts Press, 1996).

Index

Page numbers in *italic* refer to illustrations.

Index

Fitzgerald, Edward (father), 46–48, 51, 62–63, 82–83

Fitzgerald, F. Scott, 9, 12; advertising job held by, 85, 87; alcoholism and heavy drinking of, 13, 27, 34–35, 53, 55, 73, 113, 124, 159, 165, 187, 188, 220, 242; birth, childhood, and schooling of, 19, 46–49, 51–55; Catholicism of, 54–55; craftsmanship of, 189–92; death, funeral, and burials of, 25, 34, 35, 50, 65, 73, 161, 183–85, 196, 217–18, 273; depression suffered by, 28–30, 45, 70, 219; diving accident of, 30–31, 35, 53, 160, 312n.7; enlistment and military service of, 65–68, 74–75, 83; European sojourns of, 28, 31, *32*, 63, 69, 105–6, 124, 156–57, *161*, 166–67, 171, 189, 202–3, 258; first work published by, 74–75; in Hollywood, 34, 57, 73, 157–61, 213, 255; insider-outsider status of, 48, 49–51, 56; as letter writer, 188–89; money problems of, 27–28, 73, 164, 165–66; obituaries for, 217–18; physical appearance of, 51–52, 55; play written by (*The Vegetable*), 115–16, 175, 180; political views of, 37–38; at Princeton, 50, 53, 54, 55–56, 61–62, 63, 82–83, 85, 193, 194; reconsiderations of, after his death, 215–65 (*see also* Fitzgerald Revival); recordings of voice of, 207–8; rock-bottom year of (1936), 27–31, 45; romances of, 56–61, 68–75, 158–60, 284 (*see also* Fitzgerald, Zelda; Graham, Sheilah; King, Ginevra); self-deprecating behavior of, 50–51; self-doubts of, 115, 116–17; self-improvement as concern of, 52–53; suicide attempt of, 34

Fitzgerald, F. Scott, essays by, 37; "Afternoon of an Author," 60; *The Crack-Up*, 29, 188, 219, 263; "The Death of My Father," 62; "Echoes of the Jazz Age," 37, 226, 328; "The High Cost of Macaroni," 202; "How I Would Grade My Knowledge at 40," 55; "How to Live on $36,000 a Year," 165–66; "My Lost City," 17, 70, 77, 87

Fitzgerald, F. Scott, novels by: *The Beautiful and Damned*, 72, 106, 131, 187–88, 225; "The Boy Who Killed His Mother" (working title), 142; *The Love of the Last Tycoon* (edited and published as *The Last Tycoon*), 34, 96, 158, 188, 241, 263; *Philippe, Count of Darkness*, 115; relative quality of works, 185–89; "The Romantic Egoist" manuscript, 74, 83; *Tender Is the Night*, 28, 31, 34, 36, 72, 115, 169, 185–87, 210, 212, 225; *This Side of Paradise*, 27, 35, 48, 54, 59, 60, 74–75, 79, 80–81, 102–3, 115, 131, 167, 187, 190. *See also Great Gatsby, The*

Fitzgerald, F. Scott, short stories by, 28, 69, 86, 103, 105, 113, 131, 164, 188; "Absolution," 54, 106, 107, 112, 192; in American literature anthologies, 225; in ASEs, 234, 238; "Babes in the Woods," 86; "Babylon Revisited," 241; Cowley's collection of, 220; "The Curious Case of Benjamin Button," 246; "The Dance," 142; "The Diamond as Big as the Ritz," 213, 234, 238, 249; "Echoes of the Jazz Age," 226; *Gatsby* cluster, 106–7, 113–14, 188; "The Mystery of the Raymond Mortgage," 141–42; "The Rich Boy," 39, 40, 60, 107, 202, 225, 226, 241; "Ring," 226; "The Sensible Thing," 107, 113–14; "The Swimmers," 40, 94, 301–2, *303*; *Tales of the Jazz Age*, 132, 257; television adaptations of, 241; "Winter Dreams," 59–60, 107, 225

Fitzgerald, Mollie McQuillan (mother), 46–48, 52, 62, 63, 83–84

Fitzgerald, Scottie (daughter; Frances Scott Fitzgerald), 13, 14, 25, 28, 29, 34, 52, 69, 71, 72, 73, 75, 111, 157, 160, *161*, 185, 186, 187, 188, 212, 241, 247, 248, 261; birth of, 106; Bruccoli's relationship with, 248, 250, 251; father's letters to, 38–39, 55, 59, 189, 240, 246; father's papers and, 192–93, 194–95, 245–46; father's posthumous reputation and, 245–46; typewriter eraser given to father by, *197*, 255

337

Index

Index

About the Author

Maureen Corrigan is the book critic for NPR's *Fresh Air* and the critic in residence at Georgetown University. Her literary memoir, *Leave Me Alone, I'm Reading,* was published in 2005. Corrigan is a regular reviewer for the *Washington Post,* serves on the advisory panel of *The American Heritage Dictionary,* and was a juror for the 2012 Pulitzer Prize in Fiction. In 1999, she won the Edgar Award for Criticism presented by the Mystery Writers of America. She lives in Washington, DC, with her husband and daughter.